THE FOUR PRIORITIES

Dr. John Tolson and Larry Kreider

The Gathering/USA, Inc.
Orlando, Florida

The Four Priorities, 2nd Edition
Copyright © 2007 by The Gathering/USA, Inc.
All rights reserved.

Produced with the assistance of The Livingstone Corporation (www.LivingstoneCorp.com). Project staff includes David R. Veerman, Kirk Luttrell, Joel Bartlett, Jake Barton, and Will Reaves.

Contributing writer: Greg Asimakoupoulos

Words to "My Lord Has Gone" by Johnny Cash on page 129 are taken from Cash: An American Man © 2004 by Bill Miller. Published by Pocket Books.

Unless otherwise noted, all Scriptures are taken from the Holy Bible, New International Version. Copyright © 1973, 1978, 1984 by International Bible Society. All rights reserved. Use by permission of Zondervan Publishing House.

Scripture quotations marked (HCSB) are taken from the *Holman Christian Standard Bible*®. Copyright © 1999, 2000, 2002, 2003 by Holman Bible Publishers. Used by permission.

Scripture quotations marked (KJV) are taken from *The Holy Bible,* King James Version.

Scripture quotations marked (NKJV) are taken from The Holy Bible, New King James Version. Copyright ©1979, 1980, 1982 by Thomas Nelson, Inc. Used by permission. All rights reserved.

Scripture quotations marked (PHILLIPS) are taken from the *New Testament in Modern English* translated by J. B. Phillips. Copyright © 1958, 1959, 1960, 1972 by J. B. Phillips.

Scripture quotations marked (THE MESSAGE) are taken from the *THE MESSAGE.* Copyright © 1993, 1994, 1995, 1996, 2000, 2001, 2002 by Eugene H. Peterson. Used by permission of NavPress Publishing Group.

Scripture quotations marked (TLB) are taken from *The Living Bible,* copyright © 1971. Used by permission of Tyndale House Publishers, Inc. P.O. Box 80, Wheaton, Illinois 60189.

ISBN 0-9773388-0-0

Printed in the United States of America

09 10 — 10 9 8 7 6 5 4 3

CONTENTS

Priority Three: A Personal, Progressive Commitment to Relationships

Priority Four: A Personal, Progressive Commitment to the World

Acknowledgments

Life is made up of the sum of the events and people who come and go and leave a marker by which you evaluate the past and chart the course for the future.

There are many people who helped craft, contribute, encourage, and strengthen the development of *The Four Priorities*. This book would not have happened without the financial contribution from Braxton Green and Bob Stine. We will be forever grateful. The oversight of Dave Veerman and The Livingstone Corporation was invaluable. The contributing writings from Greg Asimakoupoulos were essential. Dr. Finn Amble provided both the insight and words for chapters 11 and 12. JoAnne Reilly generously and tirelessly transcribed John Tolson's Sunday school lectures and Kathy Pierson joyfully word processed every page of this book. The basic concepts for three of the four priorities were introduced to John Tolson in 1970 by Chuck Miller and became the guiding paradigm for the Christian life.

Making the Four Priorities the number one priority and focus of ministry came from Craig Mateer, who relentlessly said, "Find that one thing that defines you and give your life to it."

Last, but certainly not least, is the ongoing encouragement of those people who heard the lessons (at the BASICS Class at First Presbyterian Church in Orlando and the Tuesday Gathering lunch studies) and family members who knew how important this message was and who lived it out as an example of its effectiveness. John's first wife, Ruth Anne, championed the project. After she went to be with the Lord, John's wife, Punky, has continued the role as encourager.

The Four Priorities book has been translated into Spanish and Portuguese thanks in no small part to the generous gift from Tandy and Lee Roy Mitchell and the Mitchell Foundation. It is a testimony to the impact Christ has made in their lives and the impact they want to make in the lives of others for Christ's sake.

John and Larry can teach this material with confidence because their families attest by their lives that it is true. John's wife, Punky, and their children, Christin and Luke; Larry's wife, Susan, and two children, Brett and Erica, have formed a team of encouragement without which this project would not have been possible. They make Priority Three shine!

How to Make a Difference for Christ Using This Book

Since *The Four Priorities* was originally published in 2005, we, John and Larry, have gained a great deal of experience in the effective use of this book to make a difference for Christ in the world. *The Four Priorities* book has been used in ways by churches and individuals that we did not originally anticipate. We have led many small groups of people through the book as well as observed and/or heard from others about their experience in using *The Four Priorities* to reproduce disciples of Jesus Christ. We now have individuals working with the 3rd generation of discipleship teams, i.e., members of an original small group, who started their own groups whose members are now working with their new groups – three generations! With the publication of this new edition, we will also be releasing a Spanish and a Portuguese version for distribution not only in the United States, but also in Latin and South America.

We wanted to share with you what we have learned since 2005 to aid you in being as impactful with this book as the Lord wants you to be. As with many human endeavors, there is no one "right" way to use this book. We will share with you some ideas of what has worked for us and others. If you find new ways to make a difference using this book, we would enjoy hearing from you about your experience. Please e-mail us directly or go to our user forum on our Four Priorities web site – www.the4priorities.com

We have organized our learnings around a few questions we are asked most often by others:

- What qualifications does a study leader/facilitator need?
- How do I find participants and what should I be looking for?
- Is the only alternative to study this book in a small group?
- Are we talking about forty chapters in forty weeks? Seems like a big commitment of time.
- Do you have a recommended agenda for each weekly meeting?
- What other suggestions do you have for group leaders?

What qualifications does a study leader/facilitator need?

Whatever your situation, leaders of 4P groups should be men and women who:

- Are committed to Jesus Christ. They are Christ-followers who want to live as He wants in every area of life.
- See the validity of the Four Priorities. They understand that making and living these commitments can be life changing and life directing.
- Are willing to live out the 4Ps, not just see them as mere information.
- Desire to relate the 4Ps to others. They have an outreach mentality.
- Will lead with the intent to reproduce reproducers, developing other group leaders.

Group leaders don't have to be "super Christians" or be dynamic and charismatic communicators. They just need to be men and women who love Jesus and who want to live for Him and help others do the same—someone like you.

How do I find participants and what should I be looking for?

Who should be in a 4P group? The answer to this question depends on the leader's goal. If, for example, the leader's aim is to train trainers or reproducers, then the group should consist of men and women with that potential. In fact, those joining such a group should understand, at the front end, the expectation that they will "reproduce" by forming their own groups and, thus, continue the process.

Successful groups can have a mix of those who want to reproduce and those not willing to make that commitment, but those groups still should have at least one or two who are willing to lead. As you select people to be in your group, have at least one person you have personally challenged on the front end who has agreed to start to reproduce.

If you already have a Bible study group that meets regularly, you could introduce the book as your next course of study. Or you could start a new group with the express purpose of working through the book.

God will lead you to the right people *He* has for you. Make this a matter of prayer.

In a small group, make sure to select people who are compatible. There are no guarantees, of course, but you probably have a pretty good idea of a group's chemistry, of who will mix well with whom according to their personalities and temperaments. This is the best way to select participants. A group may take weeks to gel and feel comfortable if they are all are strangers in the beginning.

These groups will work best if they consist of all men, all women, or all married couples.

Some comments that others have shared with us that may be helpful as you discuss this course of study with potential participants are:

> "I have completed other group studies using other discipleship curriculum. The unique aspects of *The Four Priorities* is its clarity, ease of understanding and its directness. However, the truly revolutionary nature of the material is the inclusion of Priority Two. When Christ said to love each other as we love ourselves, He meant we first have to address our relationship with ourselves before we can love others effectively. The other discipleship courses I have taken just skipped over most of the material in Priority Two."

> "Priority One has some pretty safe, but important subjects. Priority One allowed us as a group to get to know one another. Our group really didn't gel until Priority Two and I think it was because we started with Priority One before having to get truly vulnerable with one another, because of the personal nature of the topics within Priority Two. If you can get your group through Priority One and started into Priority Two, you will have hooked all your participants. Getting them to show up each week will no longer be an issue."

> "Resist the temptation to shortcut Priority Two. Once our group as we were completing Priority One thought we could do two chapters a week in Priority Two to kind of pick up the pace. We were all guys who thought that we didn't need to spend a lot of time on that personal stuff. We changed our plan after our first week on Priority Two. The reason we didn't think we needed to spend as much time on it was that we never had. Once we had a curriculum that set up the topics for us, the floodgates opened. It was a powerful experience for each of us. Let me repeat, 'Don't shortcut Priority Two!'"

Is the only alternative to study this book in a small group?

This book and the study can also be effectively used one-to-one. It would work well, for example, in a personal discipling or mentoring relationship. Hopefully, the mentor in each case will get a commitment from the mentee on the front end to be a reproducer.

Are we talking about forty chapters in forty weeks? Seems like a big commitment of time.

Yes, we wrote the book with the intent of having a group study one chapter a week. Obtaining such a significant commitment of time from your study participants at the outset can be an obstacle at first. We will show you two additional approaches in addition to our original study plan.

Plan 1—a 40 week experience

This means that the group commits to read each chapter, underline statements or passages that hit a nerve or at least create interest, and then attend as many of the 40 week sessions as possible.

You can do two chapters a week, but that would only work in the one-to-one setting; it would be too much to cover in a group meeting.

Because of holiday breaks, summer vacations, and other special events, a 40 week commitment may, in reality, take around 52 weeks. Having two facilitators per group seems to work best. That way one can fill in when the other is absent. Each facilitator should have an e-mail list of the group members in order to encourage them along the way or to inform them of schedule changes and prayer requests.

The discussion questions at the end of each chapter are intended to help each reader/participant process the information throughout each week. *The intent is not to get everyone in the group to respond to each question during a meeting mechanically until all the questions are answered.* That would be boring and long and would kill the group.

Plan 2—four, 10 week sessions

This is the same as a continual 40 week session but with intentional breaks between each Priority. For potential participants that are hesitant to make the full 40 week commitment until they try out the experience, you may request to start with a 10 week commitment.

With this strategy, some may drop out after the conclusion of one of the Priorities due to time conflicts or an altered schedule.

The length of the break should not be longer than 4 or 5 weeks, with the exception of a longer summer break to allow for vacations.

Plan 3—a four week "overview" study

This approach provides an overview of each Priority with the possibility of a longer study thereafter. This is a time to kick the tires and see if participants want to go deeper.

Included at the end of this section is a list of questions for leaders to ask themselves and their group members as a part of a four week overview study.

Do you have a recommended agenda for each weekly meeting?

We both recommend that the group members plan on meeting for about 75 minutes each week (1 ¼ hours).

John recommends the following agenda for each weekly meeting:

✖ Share in a brief prayer to open the meeting.

✖ Share observations and commments from *The Four Priorities* chapter being studied.

✖ Challenge people to find one application they will live out from each study.

✖ Share briefly your schedules (key events) for the week.

✖ Share briefly your relationships.

✖ Share briefly where you are now (stress points, good points, etc.).

✖ Close in prayer. Have one person pray or open it for all to pray (if people are ready). Pray about those matters that people shared in the time you have been together.

Larry has used the following agenda for his weekly meetings:

✖ Warm up with small talk about sports/news/or personal matters over a cup of coffee—15 minutes.

✖ Open in prayer and review the chapter theme for the day—5 minutes.

✖ Go over statements in the chapter that created interest. Let the group chase a few rabbits (tangential subjects) but rein in the discussion fairly quickly each time. Read appropriate passages from Scripture and explain how they apply. In one group, a man would bring news articles or quotes from other sources to add to the discussion—30 minutes.

✖ Select two or three discussion questions for everyone to process and share their thoughts. If it is obvious participants have not been answering the questions throughout the week, they need to be challenged to get in the game, to make the experience worthwhile—15 minutes.

✖ Ask for prayer requests. Then pray and wrap up—10 minutes.

What other suggestions do you have for group leaders?

Here are some lessons gleaned from the experience of many groups and group leaders.

1. If the men or women know up front that they are expected to start their own groups at some point, they will be far more attentive, take copious notes, and engage more enthusiastically in the discussion.

2. If you get questions you can't answer, say that you'll have a response at your next meeting.

3. As the Boy Scouts say, "Be prepared!" Be sure to study the chapter well in advance of the meeting, selecting the questions to highlight and arming yourself with other appropriate Scriptures for the lesson.

4. You are developing friendships—so be a friend!

5. Almost all of the participants feel inadequate to lead a group. This is one more reason for having a co-leader to help boost the discussion. Give your leaders resources to help them lead and answer questions. For example, the Holman Personal Evangelism New Testament or *Share Jesus Without Fear* includes 36 answers for the most common objections to receiving Christ and can help build confidence that the facilitators can anticipate in advance the answers to tough questions.

6. Add personal stories to the discussion or other sources of information regarding the subject matter. Also, write in the margins of your book the comments that will be worth remembering and sharing in future group studies.

7. Plan social events where the group can get together outside of the study. You could go out to dinner, go to a ball game, play golf,

or something similar. The purpose of the Four Priorities group is not just to process information but to become a living, vital experience of what is being taught in the material. As you get into Priority Four, the group should be discussing how each individual is going to live out that priority. How will they be involved in evangelism, caring for those who hurt, living out their calling, and caring for the earth?

8. Some of the chapters will hit close to home and may make certain individuals feel uncomfortable. The topic might be bitterness, depression, marriage, parenting, stewardship, or something else. The facilitator needs to explain that no one escapes the feeling of being in the bull's-eye and to listen to the conversation without feeling everyone is looking at him or her. At this point, remind the group that everyone has "enemy held territory" that is a part of their journey.

9. This study will uncover a wide divergence in political and theological opinions. So encourage expression without being judgmental. Maturity will come in time if everyone is kind to one another and no one is put down for holding a contrary view.

10. The ambiance of the room is important. The meeting location should be easily accessible, have a feeling of warmth, be comfortable (with comfortable chairs), have coffee available and a restroom nearby, etc. In some cases, participants may want to photocopy a chapter to send to a friend, so consider what equipment is available as well.

Remember!

The original intent of The Four Priorities is that it be a tool to use in discipling people to disciple others who will disciple others. (2 Timothy 2:2)

The goal is for individuals to *know the 4Ps and live them out.* They may forget some of the content of the book, but it is critical that they remember the 4Ps!

The 4Ps should become the filter through which we plan our calendars and then live our lives.

Overview Questions for Leaders and Group Members as They Grow in The Four Priorities

Priority #1: *A Personal, Progressive Commitment to Jesus Christ*

"Seek God First" . . . . Matthew 6:33, 22:37-38

1   Describe your time alone with the Lord.

2   What have you been reading in the Word?

3   What are you learning and living in the Word?

4   Describe the quality of your prayer life. How can you improve it?

5   Describe your public worship time.

   a. Are you worshipping regularly?

   b. Are you on time?

   c. How is your concept of God expanding through public worship?

6   How are you being faithful to tithe?

Priority #2: *A Personal , Progressive Commitment to Yourself*

"Love Your Neighbor as Yourself" . . . . .Matthew 22:39

1   How are you developing mentally?

   a. What are you reading?

   b. What are you watching?

   c. To what are you listening?

2   How are you developing physically?

    a. Are you getting proper and balanced nutrition?

    b. Are you exercising regularly?

    c. Are you getting enough sleep?

    d. Are you getting an annual medical check-up?

3   How are you developing socially?

    a. How are you using your relationships for the Lord?

    b. What could you do to use your social contacts to share the love of Jesus?

4   How are you developing emotionally?

Priority #3: *A Personal, Progressive Commitment to Relationships*

. . . . John 17; Philippians 2:25

1   What are you doing to make your marriage the best it can be?

2   What are you doing to be an effective parent or grandparent?

3   Describe the health of your support team.

4   Who in the Body of Christ can you serve this week?

    a. What will you do?

    b. When will you do it?

Priority #4: A Personal, Progressive Commitment
to the World

. . . . .Acts 1:8; Matthew 10:42

1   How are your relationships with non-believers developing?

2   Maintain a list of non-believers you pray for and build a
    relationship with. How is that going?

3   How could you reach out in an "act of compassion" and meet
    the need of someone who is not a follower of Jesus?

INTRODUCTION

*Time is the scarcest resource and unless it is
managed nothing else can be managed.*

Peter F. Drucker

Life is too short to get it wrong!

Take a walk through your local cemetery. Study the inscriptions on the grave markers. On a smooth piece of granite or marble, you'll see the name of the person who lies six feet beneath. You'll also see the year of birth and the year of death. And there's more. You will see a brief dash in between. It's a dash that represents the life that was lived from their first day in the hospital nursery to their last day in a nursing home. In every case, the dash is a short one.

Life is far too short to get it wrong. And yet many people do. They live and die with sincere intentions of making the most of the time God gives them, but for far too many they get it sincerely wrong.

Robert is in his early seventies, and by all external means of measurement, he got it right. He spent a lifetime developing a multi-million dollar publishing company, but neglected his family and health. He would proudly take you on a tour of his ranch in Montana or his beautiful home in Palm Springs, California, all purchased after selling his business and freeing up his time to enjoy the good life.

He has an insatiable appetite for buying stuff, mostly useless stuff, and the stuff sits in unopened boxes and continues to multiply like an amoeba splitting and then splitting again to fill whatever space is available.

Robert has a beautiful million-dollar motor home and is constantly on the move both geographically and from wife to wife, or one live-in girlfriend to another. He battles alcohol addiction, hardly knows his children, and will cut your throat in business, whether you are a casual acquaintance, a long time friend, or even a family member. As one close observer said, "His life is a mess."

> Life is far too short to get it wrong. And yet many people do.

Life is running out on Robert. He has few tomorrows left. More than likely he will not get it right and will leave a trail of broken promises, relationships, and dreams in the dust.

Kay didn't get it right either. She grew up in West Texas in the 1950s. From the time she was a little girl, she was expected to pitch in and help out on the family ranch. Kay assisted her six older brothers after school and on weekends. Although the neighboring ranchers made time for church on Sundays, Kay's dad resisted the cultural squeeze of the Bible Belt. "Dressing up and driving to town for an hour service kills half a day of work," he would say. So attending a local church and exposure to the Scriptures were never part of Kay's upbringing. Although she never learned the foundations of Christianity, she did learn how to work hard.

By the time Kay was in high school, she had taken over her father's accounting books. He could tell she had an eye for numbers. So it didn't surprise him when she got an academic scholarship to college and majored in economics. Following graduation she went on to get her MBA and then landed an enviable position in a Fortune 500 company. Because Kay had grown up in a large family, she knew the secret of getting along with people. That served her well as she continued to climb the corporate ladder. She was well liked, and she liked those with whom she worked.

By the age of forty-five, Kay was the pride of her aging parents. Not only was she pulling down a six-figure income, driving three luxury cars, and living in a 4,800-square-foot Dallas penthouse, she was also vice president of her firm. Still Kay spent weekends alone at home. By most standards she was a success. But she didn't feel like one. Her inner life was empty. She had proved her worth in the business world, but not in the world that really counted in the long run. As far as her brothers and parents were concerned, Kay had gotten life right. So why was it she felt so wrong?

Meet someone who did get it right. His name is Braxton.

Braxton's wake up call came at around age forty-three. A highly driven man who poured his life into both his business and his family, Braxton reached his financial goals at a rather early stage in life due to the booming housing market in Central Florida. His construction company was at the top of the game, but his personal habits were not in check.

Having met his financial goals, Braxton found that he had lost his drive to make more money just for the sake of making money. He started attending the BASICS Sunday school class taught by John Tolson where he was introduced to a whole new perspective on life. Being concerned about the future of his three teenage sons, Braxton set up a counseling appointment with John.

He told John that his highest agenda item for discussion was to find some good college options for his sons and how to help them avoid some of the mistakes he had made at their age. John turned the discussion around to focus on Braxton when he said, "The best thing you can do for your kids is to make sure your own life is on

Meet some-
one who did get it
right. His name is
Braxton.

track." John gave Braxton a copy of *Moving Beyond Belief*, the first workbook on the Four Priorities produced by The Gathering/USA. Braxton jumped in with both feet. When he got to Dave Veerman's chapter on the Holy Spirit, he realized he had tried to live life without plugging into the power source. It was the beginning of a genuine conversion for Braxton.

Braxton then began to read the Bible every morning at 5:30 and to read other books that would stimulate his faith. In 2003 he read thirty-two books, whereas before he usually read three books a year, mostly about real estate. One of the books, *On My Own*, a handbook by Bob Biehl, led to another turning point for Braxton. He told his three sons that he was going to hire them for a summer job. Their responsibility was a 10-week assignment to read for 45 minutes each day the principles contained in Biehl's book. They also had to memorize these principles. The boys did it, and each was paid $400 for completing their task.

Did you ever stop long enough to consider whether God had any role in your life?

Braxton continues to read, sign up for Christian leadership conferences and courses, and to make a huge difference with his employees and the members of his family. He is getting it right. He is committed to the value of *The Four Priorities*.

Regardless of your age or stage of life, you too have to deal with what it means to get it right. No matter how long or short the dash on your grave marker, what matters is if that dash represents the fact that you got it right. The bottom line is not the total worth of your investment portfolio or the status you achieved. Rather, "getting it right" at the end of your life is measured by asking four introspective questions:

- Did you ever stop long enough to consider whether God had any role in your life?
- Did you continue to grow and develop in every dimension of your life, resisting the temptation to coast and grow stale?
- Did you succeed at developing and maintaining meaningful relationships with others?
- As you reflect on the footsteps you left in this world, did you leave a lasting imprint on the lives of people and your community?

Believe it or not, all that Jesus talked about in the Bible falls into one of those four categories. Those four categories are foundational to all of life. These categories provide the standard of "accuracy" when it comes to getting life right. Quite simply, they define what it means to live God's way.

These four categories comprise *The Four Priorities* about which this interactive workbook is concerned. These are not just four statements; they are priorities that, if implemented, will revolutionize your life:

> **1. A personal, progressive commitment to Jesus Christ**
>
> **2. A personal, progressive commitment to yourself**
>
> **3. A personal, progressive commitment to relationships**
>
> **4. A personal, progressive commitment to the world**

As you might guess, these Four Priorities are what characterize those who are known as Christ's disciples. And based on the wording of each of the Priorities, you might also guess that the life of one who claims to be a follower of Jesus is active and alive. They are personally involved in life and committed to what really matters on this planet. Let us be perfectly clear what we mean by this. The word *Christian* is mentioned three times in the New Testament and the word *disciple* is mentioned at least 244 times. The weight of the New Testament is on what it means to be a disciple! If people ever grasp this, it will profoundly change them and their world. Allow me to illustrate.

Do you know what the best selling chair in America is? You're right. The La-Z-Boy® recliner. And the reason is easy to see. Ours is a society where an increasing number of people are content to be "couch potatoes" at home or "pew potatoes" in the church.

As John Ortberg says, Jesus' disciple Peter could hardly have been called a "lazy boy." In Matthew 14, Peter and the others are pictured in a boat. As Jesus walked toward them on the water, He called out to Peter and invited him to walk to Him on the waves. Although often criticized for his impetuous nature, Peter nonetheless had the guts to get out of the boat and go to Jesus. He had the courage and the commitment to try his hand (or more literally, his feet) at walking on water.

The impetuous disciple was willing to take a risk that his colleagues (and many of ours) weren't (and aren't) willing to take in their lives or in their faith. Perhaps you're one who is content to play it safe in your business life as well as in your faith. Only a few say, "Okay, Lord, if You are for real and You have a plan for my life, I want to sign up to do it." As a result, only a few know the thrill and adventure of "walking on water with Jesus."

Eileen Guder's description of such cautious people is right on. "You can live on bland food so as to avoid an ulcer, drink no tea, coffee, or

> . . . only a few know the thrill and adventure of "walking on water with Jesus."

other stimulants in the name of health, go to bed early and stay away from the night life. Avoid all controversial subjects so as to never give offense, mind your own business, avoid involvement in other people's problems, spend money only on necessities and save all you can. You can still break your neck in the bathtub and it will serve you right."

In 1859 a famous tightrope walker by the name of Jean Francois Blondin had stretched a cable across Niagara Falls. His stunt was to walk from the Canadian side to the American side, little by little. One day five thousand people on the American side stood waiting and cheering for him to go across on the tightrope. They called, "Blondin! Blondin! Blondin!" as he inched his way over the falls. When he finally got to the other side the people went wild with excitement.

Blondin looked at the gathered crowd and asked, "Do you believe in Blondin?" In one voice they responded in a sort of chant. "We believe! We believe! We believe!" Finally he quieted them down and said, "I'm going to go back to the other side. But this time as I return over the falls, I'm going to take one of you over, strapped to my back. Do you believe I can do that?"

Again the crowded shouted enthusiastically "We believe! We believe! We believe!" Hearing them, the showman loudly asked, "Who of you will be willing to get on my back?" There was total silence. No one volunteered. Finally one brave soul stepped forward and proceeded to climb onto Blondin's back. Together they inched across the cable over the falls to the Canadian side.

Think of it. Five thousand people said they believed, but one out of five thousand had the courage to come forward and make a commitment. Sadly, this is a picture of the easy believe-ism observable in North American Christianity. There's a lot of professed belief, but not nearly enough acting on what we say we believe. Christians are plentiful, but disciples are few.

What does it mean to be a disciple? Howard Hendricks put it this way: "The greatest threat to Christianity is not materialism or atheism. The greatest threat to Christianity is Christians trying to sneak into heaven incognito without ever sharing their faith." Too many followers of Christ never become involved in the most significant work on earth. And what work is that? It's the dynamic of impacting the lives of other people for Jesus' sake. It's the impact of making disciples.

As a result, churches are filled with undisciplined "lazy boy" believers. No wonder our culture doesn't have much respect for the local church. Most people's perception of the local church is that it is a collection of losers: men and women who can't get along in real life so they rely on a crutch. People who don't go to a local church often view it that way. Unfortunately, many who call themselves Christians

> Christians are plentiful, but disciples are few.

and regularly go to church are pretty boring people. They lack focus in their lives and often seem to lack the ability to live out what they say they believe. But this is not how Christ intended His followers to live.

The way to reverse the "lazy boy" ineffectiveness of easy belief-ism is really quite simple. It is to experience the adventure of a personal, progressive relationship with Jesus Christ. To understand what it means to be a disciple of Jesus Christ and what is involved in making disciples. That is the calling of every Christian.

The Christian life is not a natural one. We cannot live it by deciding to, or by relying on our own energy. It is a supernatural one. Oswald Chambers wrote, "Since the Christian life is all about Jesus, you'd better stay close to the Source." His point is that Jesus' dynamic life will transform yours. **The Christian life is the life of Christ reproduced in you by the power of the Holy Spirit through an obedient response in your life to the Word of God.**

The Critical Areas

To get men and women of faith moving forward, we must address three critical areas. Picture these three components of Christian growth as three sails on a boat. As the wind of God's Spirit catches these three sails, a person's life begins to experience the spiritual adventure God intends, and he or she begins to leave a wake that will impact others (John 17:18,20). These three sails are the three elements of discipleship.

A Disciple Is a Learner

First, a disciple is a learner. Matthew 11:28–29 records Jesus saying, "Come to me, all you who are weary and burdened, and I will give you rest. Take my yoke upon you and learn from me." Disciples have that essential characteristic of "teachability." They sit on the edge of their seats in worship or in a Sunday school class with their Bibles open, ready to take notes, as they attempt (with enthusiasm) to understand the things of God. The learner never has the attitude that says, "I know it all." One college professor was asked why the light in his office was always on late at night. His answer spoke to the need to constantly be learning. He said, "I'd rather have my students drink from a running stream than from a stagnant pool."

A big part of the learning component of being a disciple is actually being discipled by another. "Every person has specific needs that must be targeted by a trusted mentor who has taken the time and put forth the effort to develop a meaningful one-to-one relationship,"

> "Come to me, all you who are weary and burdened, and I will give you rest. Take my yoke upon you and learn from me."
>
> *Matthew 11:28–29*

says Bill Hull. Much of discipleship is caught rather than taught. We all need someone or some others in our lives to help us become the persons God wants us to be so that we'll be able to do what He wants us to do. Based on the kind of regular interaction you have with these individuals, ask yourself what kind of changes are taking place in your life and how are you being pushed to increasingly resemble Jesus.

As long as you live, you learn, and as long as you learn, you live. The goal of the disciple and the disciple-maker is to perpetuate the learning process. Being a disciple is like being part of a football team. You gather in the huddle to know the play and then to go out and execute it. The huddle is never designed as a place where people just hang out. It's a place to learn, then scatter and make a difference. You see, true learning only takes place when what you learn changes how you live. And that includes passing on to others what has been life-changing in your life (Colossians 1:6). True learning, Biblically speaking, only takes place when it transforms your life. Just because one has been exposed to the truth doesn't mean they have been changed by the truth.

A Disciple Is a Follower

> "Follow my example, as I follow the example of Christ."
> *1 Corinthians 11:1*

Secondly, a disciple is a follower. He or she is one who follows and imitates the life and teachings of another person. For the Christian, that means following another who is close on Jesus' trail—obeying what He taught. When we say we are disciples, we affirm that we take our cues from the One we shadow. And beyond that, we invite others to "go and do likewise." The Apostle Paul understood that. In 1 Corinthians 11:1 he wrote, "Follow my example, as I follow the example of Christ." Wow! Imagine that kind of confidence. He was so consistent in the way he followed Jesus that he could look someone in the eye and invite that person to just do what he was doing. No wonder Paul had such a positive influence on others. He took his follower-ship of Jesus seriously.

The question we need to ask ourselves is, "What kind of impact are we having on others?" Like it or not, we influence others just by being around them. But to have the kind of impact that God desires, we need to make sure we are following Christ ourselves. Influence by example is called "modeling." It's the most effective approach. The greatest way to package the message of Jesus is by living out what He taught. Who we are is far more important than what we say. But there is also an important place for words or explanation; we need both life (modeling) and lips (words).

If you think you have to be a perfect model, think again. The Lord knows we are imperfect humans. Our job is to point to Him. He is the only perfect model we'll ever find. Jesus' actions never contradicted His words. And although we'll never achieve that, we can create the desire in others to follow who we're following. What matters is consistency in light of our tendency to fail. Remember our friend Peter who dared to walk on the water? He had his share of failure, too. Yet Jesus didn't disqualify him. The Lord said to His willing follower, "I have prayed for you, Simon, that your faith may not fail. And when you have turned back, *strengthen your brothers*" (Luke 22:32, italics added). Strengthen your brothers on the basis of your failure, your weakness, and what you learned from God's abundant mercy.

> "And when you have turned back, strengthen your brothers."
>
> *Luke 22:32*

A Disciple Is a Reproducer

Third, to be a disciple means to be a reproducer. It involves taking what the Lord has invested into our lives and depositing those truths in the lives of others. The essence of being a disciple is to be a dispenser of truth, not simply a depository of truth. But too many Christians just keep taking in information instead of letting what they learn change them and then giving it out (Ezra 7:10). When we are primarily "takers," we become easily bored. Nothing is more adventuresome in life than investing yourself in someone else for an eternal purpose. It's being responsible for another.

Although this is the key aspect of a disciple making an impact, few are doing it. One study indicates that less than 10 percent of all people in local churches have led someone else to Christ. Fewer still are discipling new believers. Another study revealed that 95 percent of those who claim to follow Jesus have never led one other person to the Lord. Isn't that shocking? It almost makes you wonder if the average Christian really believes what he or she claims to believe.

How tragic. Christ has already set in place a strategy for maximum impact. Because the Church is not a building but people (the Body of Christ), wherever His followers go, the Church goes. As such, the Church is already in position to connect where Jesus wants to make an impact. Every city in which Christ wants to make an inroad already has a cadre of men and women in every key area. But they must be willing to allow Jesus to work through them in order to make the impact He desires.

How would you describe your progress in each of these three phases: learner, follower, reproducer?

PRIORITY
ONE

OVERVIEW OF PRIORITY ONE:

A Personal, Progressive Commitment to Jesus Christ

To understand what **Priority One** is all about, take a close look at each word.

Personal

The phrase "personal relationship" is redundant. To be in relationship assumes another person is involved. There is interaction and communication. Your relationship with Jesus is between you and Him. Although other people can contribute to your understanding of what is involved in being a disciple, your relationship with Christ is paramount.

Progressive

Your relationship with Jesus is developed over a lifetime. Although He knows you already better than you know yourself, getting to know Him requires time. It's a process. When you begin the race of faith, the gun sounds. But we can't confuse the starting line with the finish line. It takes time for your relationship with the Lord to mature.

Commitment

The process of walking with Jesus involves an ongoing surrender to what you discover He desires of you. Simply put, it is a day-by-day, moment-by-moment decision to commit all that you understand of yourself to all that you understand of Christ.

Jesus Christ

The object of your faith is not a set of rules or a well-rehearsed ritual. It is a person. The living Lord, who came to earth, lived, taught, performed miracles, died, came back from the grave, and ascended into heaven encounters those who seek Him.

CHAPTER ONE

WHY JESUS?

History. Now there's a word that calls to mind frightful memories of that final you failed in high school. But there is more to that word. Look at it closely. That one word appears as if it could be the contraction of two words: "his" and "story."

When we look at the impact Jesus made on our world, that's exactly what history means. It really is *His story.* No other man has changed history like that first-century carpenter's son from Nazareth. Go ahead and examine the evidence. Or if you want, just pull out that Christmas card from last year's stack, you know the one, the card with "One Solitary Life." In this popular sentiment is an impressive summary of just how much history has been shaped by the baby in Bethlehem.

One Solitary Life

Here is a man who was born in an obscure village, the child of a peasant woman. He grew up in another village. He worked in a carpenter shop until He was thirty. Then for three years He was an itinerant preacher.

He never owned a home. He never wrote a book. He never held an office. He never had a family. He never went to college. He never put His foot inside a big city. He never traveled two hundred miles from the place He was born. He never did one of the things that usually accompany greatness. He had no credentials but Himself. . .

While still a young man, the tide of popular opinion turned against Him. His friends ran away. One of them denied Him. He was turned over to His enemies. He went through the mockery of a trial. He was nailed upon a cross between two thieves. While He was dying his executioners gambled for the only piece of property He had on earth—His coat. When He was dead, He was laid in a borrowed grave through the pity of a friend.

Nineteen long centuries have come and gone, and today He is a centerpiece of the human race and leader of the column of progress.

I am far within the mark when I say that all the armies that ever marched, all the navies that were ever built; all the parliaments that ever sat and all the kings that ever reigned, put together, have not affected the life of man upon this earth as powerfully as has that one solitary life.

> No other man has changed history like that first-century carpenter's son from Nazareth.

Master of History

But there is a reason why this solitary life changed history. Jesus was more than a carpenter's son. This Man, whose life literally divided the timeline of history from BC to AD, actually claimed to be God. While attempting to explain His identity to one of His followers named Philip, Jesus said, "Anyone who has seen me has seen the Father" (John 14:9). His voice held no hesitation. In much the same way, Jesus attested to His divine origin when scrutinized by a skeptical crowd. Looking them confidently in the eyes, Jesus drew an unmistakable correlation between Himself and the divine name for the Creator. He said, "Before Abraham was born, I am!" (John 8:58).

In addition to asserting that He was alive before history began, Jesus also announced that He would be on the scene when history reached its culmination. "They will see the Son of Man coming on the clouds of the sky, with power and great glory. And he will send his angels with a loud trumpet call, and they will gather his elect from the four winds, from one end of the heavens to the other" (Matthew 24:30–31).

But that isn't all. Jesus drew crowds wherever He went and taught truths they had never heard before. Oh yes, they were accustomed to the teachings of the Mosaic Law, laws that had been handed down from Moses and read regularly in the temple. They had benefited from the traditions taught by rabbis that were based on the Old Testament. But they had never heard anything quite like what fell from Jesus' lips. Unlike most rabbis, Jesus didn't footnote His comments or punctuate His messages with others' quotes. Rather, "The people were amazed at His teaching, because He taught them as one who had authority, not as the teachers of the law" (Mark 1:22).

Based upon such unprecedented claims, Jesus left no doubt that He was indeed the *Master of History*. But as you leaf through the pages of the New Testament, you also see that Jesus was the Master of many things. Let's look at some of them.

Master of Quality

Take the occasion of Jesus' first public miracle recorded in John chapter 2. At that celebrated wedding in Cana, Jesus miraculously transformed water into wine that tasted far better than the previous batch. And speaking of water, just two chapters later Jesus encounters a woman at a well in Samaria. He promises her living water that can't be drawn from a bucket on a rope. In fact, He claims that the water He alone can give her will be of such remarkable quality whoever drinks of it will never thirst again (John 4:7–14). What Jesus touches, He transforms. Where do you need His touch in your life?

> "Anyone who has seen me has seen the Father."
> John 14:9

> Based upon such unprecedented claims, Jesus left no doubt that he was indeed the *Master of History*.

Master of Distance

Yes, Jesus is the master of history and of quality. But He is also the *Master of Distance*. Time and space limit our ability, but Jesus was not so curtailed. His power extended beyond where His feet were planted. This remarkable characteristic is illustrated in John's gospel. The son of a royal dignitary was on his deathbed. Nothing could be done to save the boy's life. When the father learns that Jesus has been spotted near to where he lived, hope flickers in his heart. Tracking Jesus down in the town of Cana, the man begs the itinerant teacher to return with him to Capernaum. But Jesus, sensing the man's desperation, simply tells him to head home. Without going to where the boy is, Jesus heals him (John 4:43–54). You can never be too far away from the life and power of Jesus and His ability to touch your life.

Master of Time

In John 5 we see Jesus proving that He has every right to be called the *Master of Time*. When He sees an invalid sitting beside the pool near the Sheep Gate in old Jerusalem, Jesus' heart goes out to the guy. It doesn't matter that this fellow has been pushed to the margins of society for thirty-eight years. In one moment, Jesus erases the wasted years and empowers the man to take up his mat and walk (John 5:1–9). No matter how long you have been away from Jesus, He will still draw near.

> Jesus wants to take your life, whatever little you have, and multiply it.

Master of Quantity

John portrays Jesus as the *Master of Quantity* as well. In other words, He was not limited to the cause and effect laws of the natural order. When a crowd follows Jesus into the wilderness to hear Him teach, He is concerned that they may be hungry and need to be fed. He takes a young boy's lunch of five little loaves of bread and two small fish and miraculously multiplies them so that a crowd in excess of five thousand people is able to eat (John 6:5–13). Jesus wants to take your life, whatever little you have, and multiply it.

Master of Nature

In John 6 we again see Jesus as nothing less than the *Master of Nature*. Following the miraculous feeding of the crowd, the Teacher proved that He had power over the forces of nature and the laws of gravity. While the disciples battle the winds and waves of a stormy sea and strain every muscle to make forward progress, Jesus walks toward them effortlessly as if the water is pavement (John 6:16–21). He who calmed the storm wants to live with you—and in you—to bring peace in the midst of the challenges of life.

Master of Circumstances

The ninth chapter of John shows Jesus as seen as the *Master of Circumstances*. He supernaturally gives sight to a man who was born blind. When questioned by His critics as to why the blindness had occurred to begin with, Jesus doesn't blink an eye. He makes it clear the man's predicament isn't his fault or his parents. Instead, Jesus insists, it is so that the work of God might be displayed. Jesus is fully in control of the circumstances (John 9:1–5). No matter what your circumstances have been or are, He can act and work in you.

Master of Life and Death

According to what we see in John chapter 11, Jesus is also the *Master of Life and Death*. When Jesus' friend Lazarus succumbs to a life-threatening illness, Jesus weeps. He feels human emotions at their rawest. He empathizes with the indescribable sorrow felt by those who love the man. But Jesus proves He has power over the grave. After enough days had passed (so that there was no question that Lazarus was dead and not just in a coma), Jesus stands at the entrance to His friend's tomb and calls for Lazarus to come out. To the amazement of all those standing around, that is exactly what Lazarus does (John 11:17–44)! Jesus wants to give you life, too, now and for eternity.

One Unique Life

> No matter what your circumstances have been or are, He can act and work in you.

It's amazing! Throughout the Gospel of John, Jesus leaves His fingerprints in every dimension of life. Those who dust for those prints are forced to conclude that they are fingerprints of Deity. In Jesus we see One who is unique, One of a kind. Of all those about whom historians have filled parchments and pages, no one can be found just like Him.

Jesus' birth was unique. Unlike any other person in history, His mother became pregnant without ever having sexual intercourse.

His life was unique. Unlike any other person in history, He lived a morally unblemished life. What is more, His response to those who were spiritually flawed was remarkable. Consider the reflections of His mother, Mary, who had observed Him all His life—always doing that which was right. Rightly did she say to the stewards at a wedding, "Do whatever He tells you" (John 2:5).

Jesus' death was unique as well. While countless individuals throughout history have been inhumanely tortured and unjustly executed, Jesus alone suffered sacrificially, willingly taking on Himself the sins of the world (Romans 3:23–26).

Jesus' resurrection was unique. He is the only person in history to come back to life by His own power after being in a grave for three days.

Go ahead and check out the other three Gospels of Matthew, Mark, and Luke. As you read them you can't help but admit that this One, who claimed to be God, was unlike any other man who has ever lived. And it was this one-of-a-kind individual who focused His unique power toward people in need. The story of Jesus is a story of a Man with supernatural qualities who spent His years on this earth transforming human lives.

Look at the disciples. Those twelve men had no extraordinary qualities: some commercial fishermen, an IRS collection agent, a few blue-collar tradesmen—that's all, just plain folks, average Joes. But they didn't remain average Joes for long. After three years of shadowing the Savior, eleven of the twelve became leaders of a movement that would rock the Roman world. Simon Peter is a classic example. So is the woman Jesus encountered at the well in Samaria. Although burned by previous relationships and living with a man (without benefit of marriage), this spiritually thirsty woman found forgiveness and new purpose in life after a midday conversation with the One who offered her living water.

Don't forget about the woman of the night who was nearly stoned to death at high noon. When Jesus scribbled in the sand, He wrote a new chapter in her life. He did the same for a pharisaical religionist from Tarsus by the name of Saul. Because of Jesus' ability to transform his life, two thirds of the New Testament was written by this convinced follower.

Did Muhammad transform sinners into saints? No. Buddha didn't. Confucius couldn't. Sun Jung Moon's efforts were eclipsed by the Son of Righteousness. It's true! Only Jesus can leave lasting footprints on the hearts of people who have surrendered to His overtures of grace. It was true in the first century. It continues to be true today. Has He changed your life? Have you surrendered to His claim on it?

> Only Jesus can leave lasting footprints on the hearts of people who have surrendered to His overtures of grace.

Jesus, the Life Changer

Larry Snydal is a case in point. After succumbing to the numbing power of alcohol, this burly construction worker lost his marriage and kissed his relationship with his three daughters good-bye. In exchange for a constant buzz, Larry had lost it all. But not for good. When Larry learned that Jesus loved him and was willing to give him a fresh run at life, the bearded boozer raced into the arms of the Savior. He found a new purpose for living—his affections changed (2 Corinthians 5:17).

That's not all. He found a widow in her forties with five kids in need of a dad. Larry and Linda married. After being nurtured in a church, they responded to a call from God to the mission field. Today they are serving with Wycliffe Bible Translators as career missionaries. The once hot-tempered hammer-slinging sinner is known by his Christ-like temperament. Just ask his daughters, who are no longer estranged. Larry Snydal is a living testimony of the power of Jesus Christ to transform a life. He is proof positive that Jesus Christ is nothing less than the living God.

Daily Reflection Questions

Day One

1   Read through *One Solitary Life* again. What one lasting impact of Jesus' life in our world stands out in your mind as simply amazing? Why?

2   In the classic Christmas movie *It's a Wonderful Life,* George Bailey is given the opportunity to see what the world would have been like had he never been born. What do you think our world would be like if Jesus had never been born?

3   Read John 1:1–14. Based on this passage of Scripture, what role did Jesus have in the origin of life?

Day Two

1   What significance do you see in the way Jesus responded to His critics by saying, "Before Abraham was born, I am"? What Old Testament references does it remind you of?

2   C. S. Lewis said Jesus was the Son of God (as He claimed) or He was delusional or overtly deceitful. Why do you think there is no other option?

3   If Jesus has the powers of Almighty God (the Creator and Sustainer of the cosmos), what impact should that have on the seemingly impossible circumstances you are facing today?

Day Three

1   When Jesus turned the water into wine, He altered the laws of nature. The same is true of the miracle of the loaves and fish. What importance do you think miracles had in Jesus' earthly ministry?

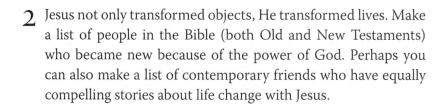

2　Jesus not only transformed objects, He transformed lives. Make a list of people in the Bible (both Old and New Testaments) who became new because of the power of God. Perhaps you can also make a list of contemporary friends who have equally compelling stories about life change with Jesus.

3　What is similar about these examples of God's transforming touch, and how did that message come to them? (Colossians 1:6)

Day Four

1　How does the account of Jesus engaging the Samaritan woman illustrate the fact that Jesus is the master of quality?

2　In John 10:10, Jesus said He came into the world that we might have life to the full. What do you hope that means for you personally?

3　Other than the fact that Jesus promised to give the woman water that exceeded anything else she'd been exposed to, what evidence do you see in John 4 that Jesus had supernatural powers?

Day Five

1 Who is someone you know who has experienced the transforming power of Jesus similar to what Larry Snydal experienced? What adjective would you use to describe their lives "before" and "after" becoming a follower of Jesus?

2 Make a "before and after" list of your own. Write down words and phrases that describe your life "before" you became a Christian. Then do the same under the word "After."

BEFORE	AFTER

3 Spend some time praying for those you care about who are still trapped in self-destructive lifestyles and need to be touched by Jesus.

CHAPTER TWO

WHY DO I NEED JESUS?

Once upon a time . . . You know how that goes, right? That's the way all stories begin. Only in the case of this particular story, it's not a fairy tale. It really happened. It's a true story as old as time itself. This story has touched my life and yours.

> Once upon a time a man and a woman vacationed in a tropical forest without a care in the world. It was a dream excursion. The weather was perfect. The animals that roamed the foliage were wild yet tame. The food was delicious, plentiful, and free. All the couple had to do was follow the lead of their travel guide. He promised to take care of all their needs. The only thing he asked was that they keep their distance from a section of the forest that was off-limits.
>
> For what they were enjoying on their expenses-paid adventure, the guide's simple request seemed insignificant. But the couple wasn't satisfied. One day they encountered a disgruntled former employee. He baited them to take their chances and explore the forbidden site, claiming the guide was not trustworthy and was withholding insight. The "new experience" inflamed their desire to go "out of bounds." Ignoring their host's request, they disregarded the "no trespassing" sign. But surveillance cameras captured their disobedience. As a result, they were escorted out of the forest and prohibited from ever returning.

Yes, you *do* know that story. Adam and Eve risked the security and pleasure of paradise for the momentary satisfaction of thinking they didn't have to submit to another's authority. But shortly after nibbling a sweet piece of fruit, they realized just how sour life becomes when you disregard God. Not only did they discover the unimagined angst that alienation from the Creator brings, but all of their offspring were to experience that nightmarish reality as well.

Cut Off from God

The result of Adam and Eve's sin cut off all of humanity from God. The security and pleasure that came with the Creator's constant companionship suddenly became a thing of the past. And now we

> The result of Adam and Eve's sin cut off all of humanity from God.

enter this world subconsciously aware that God exists but lack the ability to locate Him. Being alienated from the eternal God, we feel as though we have a hole in the soul that we know nothing material can satisfy. David said it best when in the depths of despair he wrote, "My God, my God, why have you forsaken me?" (Psalm 22:1).

Cut Off from Ourselves

As we grow up and strike out on our own in the world, we feel an eerie, inner loneliness, as though we are cut off as well from our true selves. A further disconnect stands between the "me I experience and know" and the "me you see," and a battle rages between what we feel is right and what we end up doing. The Apostle Paul put it succinctly when he said, "For I have the desire to do what is good, but I cannot carry it out" (Romans 7:18). None of us has it all together socially, emotionally, mentally, physically, or spiritually.

Cut Off from Others

There is more. Because of what Adam and Eve did, we find ourselves cut off from people around us as well. Ever since those "garden-variety sinners" insisted on their own way, the human family has born the bitter fruit of their self-centered choices. Our great-great grandparents attempted to hide their responsibility for sin by blaming another: "And he said, 'Who told you that you were naked? [Confession requested!] Have you eaten from the tree that I commanded you not to eat from?' The man said, 'The *woman you* put here with me, *she* gave me some fruit from the tree, and I ate it'" [the blame game] (Genesis 3:11–12, italics added). So they tried to cover their sin by blaming each other and hiding their inner hearts from God. We have acted similarly by not owning up to our mistakes (sin) as well as holding others at arm's length. We keep secrets. We act independently. We refuse help. We hide our need for companionship in spite of languishing in private loneliness. "Each of us has turned to his own way" (Isaiah 53:6).

Cut Off from God's Creation

The truth is we are cut off from God, ourselves, those around us, and the perfect world the Creator envisioned for us. Ever since Eve tested Adam with the forbidden fruit and he bit off more than he could chew, we've been severed from our source of eternal life and complete joy. We became subject to the cause and effect laws of a natural order that is prone to disorganization, decay, and death. "For the creation was subjected to frustration" (Romans 8:20).

> "My God, my God, why have you forsaken me?"
> *Psalm 22:1*

> "Each of us has turned to his own way."
> *Isaiah 53:6*

Ours is a world of pollution and dirty politics. We have oil spills and slick televangelists, drought and famine in poor countries, and incest and addiction in rich ones. Mad cow disease and bird flu have taken the toll in the animal kingdom. AIDS and other new diseases threaten the kingdom of humankind. For years the human family held its breath for fear of a nuclear disaster due to a Cold War. Now we are fearful of the effects of global warming. And in the midst of it all, innocent people are often jailed while the guilty get off on legal technicalities.

No wonder we are prone to be cynical and selfish. It appears as though the defective planet on which we spin is doomed. And what is worse, all the consequences of Adam and Eve's sin (spiritual, psychological, sociological, and ecological) contaminate our relationships. Go ahead. Trace the problems you have in your life. Try and understand the components of each crisis. You will see that somehow or someway your problem is a problem because of the way a relationship has been impacted negatively.

> "For the creation was subjected to frustration."
> *Romans 8:20*

The Good News

We long for reasons to have hope. If only we had a way to get back to paradise. The good news found in God's Word is that a return trip into the presence of God is possible. It begins with a personal relationship with Jesus. And in that primary relational healing, all other relationships-gone-bad can be restored.

By getting to know God's Son, the chasm that has separated us from our Creator is crossable. In fact, through that relationship we can draw near to others from whom we have pulled away (or who have pulled away from us). We also find the means in Christ to reconnect with ourselves. The Apostle Paul in Ephesians chapter 2 describes that awesome truth.

> But now you belong to Christ Jesus, and though you once were far away from God, now you have been brought very near to him because of what Jesus Christ has done for you with his blood. For Christ himself is our way of peace. He has made peace between us Jews and you Gentiles by making us all one family, breaking down the wall of contempt that used to separate us. By his death he ended the angry resentment between us, caused by the Jewish laws which favored the Jews and excluded the Gentiles, for he died to annul that whole system of Jewish laws. Then he took the two groups that had been opposed to each other and made them parts of himself; thus he fused us together to become one new person, and at last there was peace. As parts of the same body, our anger

against each other has disappeared, for both of us have been reconciled to God. And so the feud ended at last at the cross. And he has brought this Good News of peace to you Gentiles who were very far away from him, and to us Jews who were near. Now all of us, whether Jews or Gentiles, may come to God the Father with the Holy Spirit's help because of what Christ has done for us. (Ephesians 2:13–18, TLB)

Isn't that incredible? Chances are you've already entered into a personal relationship with Jesus and reestablished a connection with the God who promises to restore paradise for those who are related to Him. Just in case you aren't sure of where you stand with Christ, however, it's not complicated. All that is necessary is to sincerely pray with your heart something like the following:

Lord Jesus, I am sick and tired of being cut off from You and Your plans for my life. I am weary of hiding what I know to be true within me and the struggles within me, of being separated from people around me. I'm done with trying to hide from myself and the need for wearing of masks. I need You, Jesus. Please forgive me of my propensity to serve my selfish passions and pleasures. I accept what You did on the cross as payment for my sin. I accept You as the Lord and leader of my life. Amen.

> It appears as though the defective planet on which we spin is doomed.

Daily Reflection Questions

Day One

1   What about the familiar account of Adam and Eve struck you in a new way as you reconsidered it through a modern-day telling?

2   Read Romans 5:12. How would you paraphrase this verse that illustrates how humanity was cut off from God since the time of Adam?

3 When David felt cut off from God, he lamented, "My God, my God, why have you forsaken me?" What words or actions do people today use to express their sense of separation from their Creator?

Day Two

1 When people use the term "I'm beside myself," what are they attempting to express?

2 Typically people use that expression without picturing the image it implies. It is way of illustrating the fact that one is disconnected from himself or herself and lacks personal wholeness. For example, Adam and Eve were "beside themselves" after they had eaten the forbidden fruit. Look back at the Biblical account of their garden adventure. What suggests that paradise simply evaporated following the couple's disobedience?

3 The Apostle Paul was "beside himself" with frustration because he felt the disconnect between his willful self and his surrendered self. When have the following words recently applied to your spiritual struggle to be a person who is fully surrendered to God? "For I have the desire to do what is good, but I cannot carry it out" (Romans 7:18).

Day Three

1 If you were to keep reading in Genesis, you would encounter individuals alienated from each other (Cain and Abel, Abraham and Lot, Jacob and Esau, Joseph and his brothers, and others). What other incidents of relational distance can you recall from Biblical stories?

2 Why does being cut off from God and cut off from yourself lead to being at odds with other people?

3 Why do you think that this element of separation can still exist after someone has entered into a personal relationship with the Lord?

Day Four

1 What current events illustrate the fact that we live in a fallen world?

2   What do people say or do that demonstrates the longing for hope?

3   What evidences of sin at work or home remind you that heaven is still to come?

Day Five

1   In what ways have you experienced personal healing because of your relationship with Jesus? Healing in other relationships?

2   Complete the following sentence, "In an attempt to explain to my next door neighbor why he (or she) needs a relationship with Jesus Christ, I would begin by saying . . ."

3   Commit to memory the following verses: Romans 3:23, Romans 6:23, and Romans 10:9–10.

CHAPTER THREE

WHAT'S THE BIG PICTURE?

If you've ever traveled as a tourist to New York City, you've most likely taken a Gray Line Tour before attempting to paint the town red. You no doubt walked through Central Park. You drove across the legendary Brooklyn Bridge. You took a boat ride to see the Statue of Liberty. You reflected in silence at Ground Zero. And you also rode an elevator to the observation deck of the Empire State Building. It seemed you could see forever, right? The Big Apple was bigger than you ever imagined, but seeing the big picture somehow made it seem less overwhelming.

From the top of a towering skyscraper, you have a perspective you don't have down below. You can see the intricate network of sidewalks, streets, and highways that connect downtown neighborhoods and distant suburbs. You can appreciate the design that city planners put into place as buildings were laid out. You see a traffic jam that commuters won't discover for ten more miles. You observe a building on fire before the fire department has been dispatched.

It's strange. Despite the enormity of the city, you don't feel dwarfed by it. Based on your bird's-eye view, the traffic and pedestrians below look like miniscule insects, but you are above it all. Because of your vantage point, you feel amazingly in control. You are capable of seeing what others cannot. Curiously, the big picture has given you a sense of peace and purpose.

> Because of your vantage point, you feel amazingly in control.

As if standing atop the tallest building in a major city, the Lord of life has an unobstructed view of our past, present, and future. He sees how all the thoroughfares and detours of our lives fit together. He is not caught off guard by news that sets *us* reeling emotionally. When a phone call in the middle of the night jangles our nerves and shatters our emotions with word of a loved one's death, God is not surprised. When a pink slip at work results in a case of the blues at home, God is not the last to know. When the consequences of some past indiscretion on our part parades down Main Street, God is not otherwise occupied. Instead, He sees it all and has a plan for it all to work out.

What's Wrong with This Picture?

All the same, it's easy to feel as though some things don't make sense. Even after you have gone on record as identifying yourself with the One who identifies Himself with you as Savior and Lord, events happen in your life and feelings fill your heart that cause you to wonder if you are on the right track. You told Jesus you believe He's God and that He died on the cross for your sins, but you still screw up. You still shade the truth when you fear total honesty will make you look inadequate. When push comes to shove, you throw the glove of anger to the ground and take your cuts (at least with words). You still struggle with lust. At times you swear. In fact, when you see several of these indicators of imperfection, you're inclined to wonder if Jesus really did come into your life, and if this is the normal Christian life.

It's obvious what you are thinking at times like that. Maybe you're wondering if you were sincere enough when you prayed the prayer of salvation. Maybe you're questioning if you've held up your end of the bargain, and if more depended on you to receive God's gift than what you were led to believe. Or maybe you wonder if the Lord, for some unknown reason, didn't accept you. Come to think of it, left to your own logic, you can think of a number of reasons why He shouldn't. You understood the basic idea of who Jesus is and what He came to do, but is this all true? And more importantly, did your prayer of repentance and faith stick?

It's Not the Picture, It's Your Perspective

Don't despair. It's time for a metaphorical "elevator ride" to the top of the Empire State Building for some thoughts about perspective—yours and God's. What you need is to grasp the big picture and see what God sees as He observes your life of faith. If you asked Jesus to come into your life, He is there. And He isn't going anywhere. From God's vantage point you can see that change is in fact taking place in your life. What He sees is a view He wants you to have. You are His; you have been bought with a price (1 Corinthians 6:20).

When you understand God's perspective, your anxieties are undermined and your heart fills with hope. In fact, hope in God's ability to bring about continued change will give you the ability to patiently put up with the inevitable struggles and setbacks you will continue to experience. Author John Maxwell says it so well, "Hope is the foundational principle for all change. People change because they have hope." Colossians 1:5 says, "The lines of purpose in your lives never grow slack, tightly tied to your future in heaven, kept taut by hope!" (THE MESSAGE).

The ambivalence to which new Christians are prone (when it comes to assurance of their salvation) is rooted in the inability to see what is going on beyond themselves, their feelings, or their subjective experiences. The following word picture is a way of seeing the big picture that God sees.

What you need is to grasp the big picture and see what God sees as He observes your life of faith.

"The lines of purpose in your lives never grow slack, tightly tied to your future in heaven, kept taut by hope!"

Colossians 1:5,
THE MESSAGE

The Beachhead

Lane Adams, a Presbyterian minister, compared Christ's entrance into a new believer's life to the establishment of a beachhead on an enemy-controlled island. Referring to how the Allied Forces established beachheads to liberate occupied islands during World War II, Adams described a lengthy process.

The very first step was to soften-up an island using whatever was necessary to weaken the resistance. The Allied Forces would take aerial photographs of the island to detect where the enemy was concentrated. Then, based on their reconnaissance, they would shell the island with powerful bombs launched from offshore battleships.

At that point, a small group of Marines would slosh ashore and land on the island in an attempt to control a portion of it. That establishment of a presence was called a "beachhead." Although only a tiny portion of the island, it represented much more. The Allies' presence was the beginning of a process that would eventuate in complete liberation of the island.

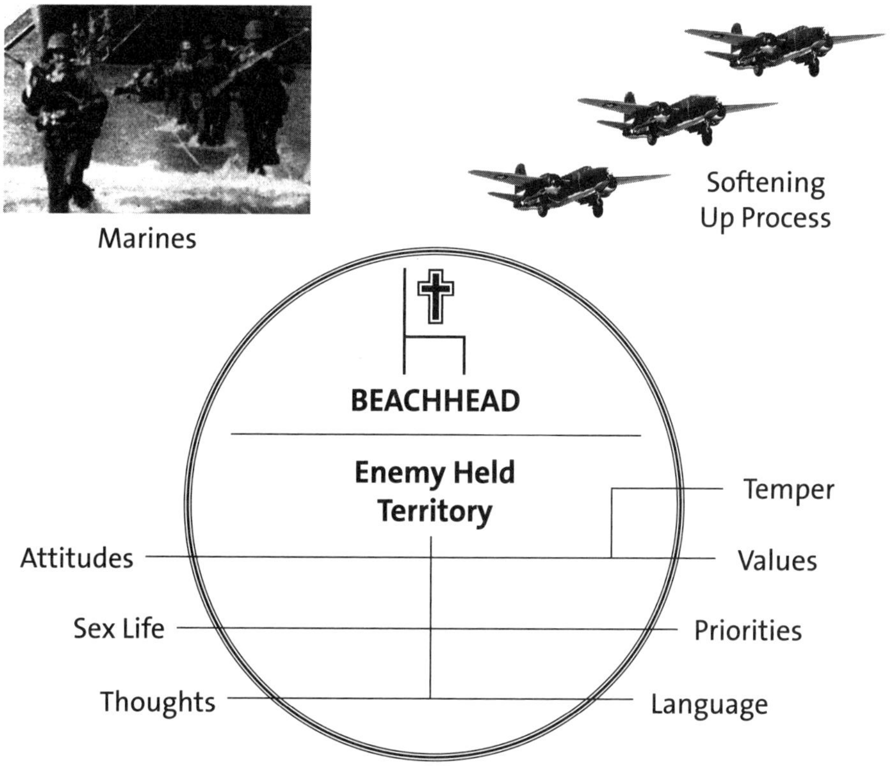
Marines
Softening
Up Process
BEACHHEAD
Enemy Held
Territory
Temper
Attitudes
Values
Sex Life
Priorities
Thoughts
Language

Position Established:

- Personal Invitation
- Permanent
- Benefits = accepted, justified, forgiven

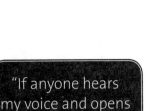

> "If anyone hears my voice and opens the door, I will come in."
> *Revelation 3:20*

Got it? That's what happened to you. When you, by faith, trusted Jesus to be your Savior, He entered your life and established a beachhead. Jesus stated, "If anyone hears my voice and opens the door, I will come in" (Revelation 3:20). The Apostle Paul made it short and sweet in his letter to the Roman Christians, "If you confess with your mouth, 'Jesus is Lord,' and believe in your heart that God raised him from the dead, you will be saved" (Romans 10:9). The evidence of this invasion in your life is a changed heart, changed affections, and a changed identity.

God's bird's-eye view allows Him to see what is in process of taking place. But by understanding His Son's beachhead in your heart, you can see it, too. It's a necessary perspective when the process is taking longer than you think it should and you begin to doubt verses like, "Therefore, if anyone is in Christ, he is a new creation; the old has gone, the new has come!" (2 Corinthians 5:17).

When you continue to trip over the same pitfalls and you wonder why it takes you so long to get better, remember that you are a work in process. The total takeover doesn't happen overnight. And also remember this: your position is secure, although your condition is being conformed to Christ.

J. B. Phillips' translation of the Bible describes the ongoing battle inside of us as Jesus goes about the lengthy process of liberating our hearts. "My own behavior baffles me. For I find myself doing what I really loathe but not doing what I really want to do. . . . I often find that I have the will to do good, but not the power. That is, I don't accomplish the good I set out to do, and the evil I don't really want to do I find I am always doing" (Romans 7:15–19, *PHILLIPS*).

> "If you confess with your mouth, 'Jesus is Lord,' . . . you will be saved."
> *Romans 10:9*

You have to see the Christian life as a process and then cooperate with the process. First, admit your need for a Savior. Most likely, you've already done that. But in the event that you aren't certain, let me invite you to pause right now, put down your book, and pray the "in case" prayer. It goes like this: "Lord, I think you're in my life, but *in case* you're not, I want You to know that I fully trust You with my life and trust You only for the forgiveness of my sins."

And once you've invited the Lord Jesus Christ to come in your heart, He takes the initiative in the rest of the process. Your job is to respond to His takeover initiative and surrender a day at a time (see Romans 12:1–2). That's how an occupied island (and an occupied life) is liberated—a progressive pushing out of alien thoughts, gods, and actions. And the result is gradual growth or maturity. This, then, completes the first phase of the definition of the Christian life: **The Christian life is the life of Christ reproduced in you.**

What's the Bottom Line?

Okay, are you ready for a review? The Christian life is a process. When we acknowledge our need for a Savior, His Holy Spirit enters our lives and establishes a beachhead. It is only the beginning. As was true of the Allied invasions in World War II, Christ's establishment of a beachhead in our lives is hardly the end. It's only the beginning. A beachhead signals the start of countless battles, seemingly endless wins and losses, before the Lord has accomplished His intended purpose for us. At times, the Christian life is one step forward, two steps back.

Gratefully, the Lord isn't put off by our setbacks and struggles. He sees the end from the beginning, and road closures and inevitable detours are no concern to Him. He knows how the traffic jams in our lives will resolve. When we focus on the long-term process of spiritual growth, we begin to see the big picture and trust God with the process. The following inspirational piece by an unknown author illustrates this fact.

> At first, I saw God as my observer, my judge keeping track of the things I did wrong, so as to know whether I merited heaven or hell when I die. He was out there sort of like a president. I recognized His picture when I saw it, but I really didn't know Him. But later on, when I met Christ, it seemed as though life were rather like a bike ride, but it was a tandem bike, and I noticed that Christ was in the back helping me pedal.
>
> I don't know just when it was that He suggested we change places, but life has not been the same since! When I had control, I knew the way. It was rather boring, but predictable . . . it was the shortest distance between two points. But when He took the lead, He knew delightful long-cuts, up mountains, and through rocky places at breakneck speeds. It was all I could do just to hang on! Even though it looked like madness, He said "Pedal!"
>
> I worried and was anxious and asked, "Where are You taking me?" He laughed and didn't answer, and I started to learn to trust. I forgot my boring life and entered into the adventure. And when I'd say, "I'm scared!" He'd lean back and touch my hand. He took me to people with gifts that I needed. Gifts of healing, acceptance, and joy. They gave us gifts to take on my journey, my Lord's and mine. And we were off again. He said, "Give the gifts away; they're extra baggage, too much weight." So I did, to the people we met; and I found that in giving I received, and still our burden was light.

> "Therefore, if anyone is in Christ, he is a new creation; the old has gone, the new has come!"
>
> *2 Corinthians 5:17*

> Gratefully, the Lord isn't put off by our setbacks and struggles

I did not trust Him, as first, in control of my life. I thought He'd wreck it; but He knows bike secrets, knows how to make it bend to take sharp corners, knows how to jump to clear high rocks, knows how to fly to shorten scary passages. And I am learning to shut up and pedal in the strangest places, and I'm beginning to enjoy the view and the cool breeze on my face with my delightful companion, Jesus Christ. And when I'm sure I just can't do anymore, He just smiles and says, "Pedal!"

Simply put, God's purpose for us is not a random spur-of-the-moment idea. Long before we were born, He decided what He wanted our lives to amount to. And it's that purpose that adds meaning to the times we feel like we've blown it or feel buried without a shovel. As the story above illustrates, God never loses sight of the big picture—He is sovereign! It's a picture He alone can see.

Even before He establishes a beachhead in our lives, God's strategy is at work in His mind. And that strategy is this: Once He takes hold of our heart (Ezekiel 11:19; 36:26), He is committed to transforming us into the likeness of His Son. It may take a lifetime, but He is determined to liberate us from ourselves.

What an awesome thought that is. Because of God's plan and perspective, we can better understand how God changes us, about the process of Christian maturity when we begin to wonder if the Holy Spirit is really at work in our lives. God observes (and celebrates) what isn't always evident to us. Because of His ability to weave our lives together into a beautiful tapestry, the knotty or dark threads need not steal our joy or cause us to give up on the process.

While some define the Christian life as the sum and substance of what happens to you when you first trust Jesus Christ as your Savior, that kind of definition sets a person up for disillusionment and despair. A much more Biblical definition of discipleship is not explained by virtue of the starting line, but by the finish line. Whereas we begin the race of faith when we invite Jesus to take possession of our hearts, the Christian life has more to do with a process that has only just begun.

Daily Reflection Questions

Day One

1 Why do radio and television traffic reporters often use the vantage point of a skyscraper as they give regular updates during rush-hour commutes?

2 What about the skyscraper metaphor is helpful to you as you seek to understand God's involvement in your life?

3 Identify some area of your life where you can't see "around the corner" and you dread it. How can you use the concept of God's big picture to stress less about the future?

Day Two

1 List one or two experiences in your life that appeared unredeemable at the time but proved to be stepping stones of faith (Psalm 60:3–4; Acts 14:19–22).

2 Rewrite Romans 8:28 in your own words.

3 Why do you think "all things" are the two most important words in this verse?

Day Three

I Read Hebrews 12:1–3. How does the race imagery here relate to your journey of faith right now?

2 Which do you think is a more appropriate metaphor for the Christian life: a 100-yard dash or a 26.2-mile marathon? Explain.

3 While the Hebrews text calls you to envision a "great cloud of witnesses" in the grandstands watching you progress in your faith, why is God's view from the stands most important?

Day Four

I   In what ways was your life before Christ like an occupied South Pacific island during World War II?

2   Why is the beachhead illustration a good way to explain the starting point of your walk of faith? How would you expand on this idea?

3   How much of your "island" would you say has come under the control of the Holy Spirit? What is some enemy-held-territory that has yet to fall?

Day Five

I   Why should the long-view picture of God's activity in your life encourage you?

2   What season(s) in your life, or present area, represents the idea of "two steps" back? What happened? How did you respond? What did you learn?

3 Spend ten minutes talking to the Lord about this recent setback in your life. Confess your responsibility in this situation. Accept His forgiveness. Then ask Him for the ability to trust that what seems like a loss can be a bridge to a forthcoming gain.

CHAPTER FOUR

WHAT IS THE CHRISTIAN LIFE?

(PART 1)

Pastor Steve Brown tells the story about a guy who played piano at a bar. Every night was the same. He'd play while men and women at various stages of intoxication leaned against the piano listening. Often the inebriated individuals would engage the piano man in conversation. To break the monotony of the nightly routine, the piano player started asking his listeners a provocative question. "What is the meaning of life?" It didn't matter who the people were, he asked the same question night after night. Although some people offered trite clichés, most just smiled and said nothing. One night a guy responded to the question by saying, "I don't know what the meaning of life is, but I know someone who does." The piano man listened with interest and asked for more information. "He's a guru who lives alone high up in the Himalayas."

Several weeks later, when the piano player realized how insignificant it was pounding out meaningless songs he became very depressed. Although he was a gifted musician, those for whom he played were oblivious to his talent because they were self-medicated with booze. He determined he would find a way to discover for himself what life was all about. But where would he start? Then he remembered the comment about the guru.

Booking a flight, he traveled three-quarters of the way around the world. At the base of the Himalayas, he hired a guide to take him to the place where the guru who knew the meaning to life lived. Upon finding this sage, he asked the man "What is the meaning of life?"

The guru sitting in a lotus position did not bother to stand up or even look the musician in the eye. He simply responded, "Life is a fountain."

Unwilling to accept that abstract definition as a final answer, he persisted: "Look, sir, no disrespect intended, but I'm extremely tired. I traveled thousands of miles to find you and learn the answer to the nagging question of my heart."

The guru, still sitting crossed-legged on a carpet, looked up at the desperate man and asked, "Life is a fountain . . . isn't it?"

> "For God so loved the world that he gave his one and only Son."
>
> *John 3:16*

The Meaning of Life

Sadly, millions of people seek answers to the mystery of life from those who aren't really sure of life's meaning themselves. But life can only be fully understood when a person enters into a relationship with the One who created life in the first place. It was Jesus who told an inquisitive seeker by the name of Nicodemus that He was the source of eternal life. "For God so loved the world that he gave his one and only Son, that whoever believes in him shall not perish but have eternal life" (John 3:16). And according to Jesus that quality of life is not reserved for when we die, but begins when we begin a relationship with Him. Jesus later said, "I have come that they might have life, and have it to the full" (John 10:10).

No, it isn't a guru on some snowcapped mountain who has the answer to the meaning of life. Rather, it was a rabbi on the grassy hillside overlooking the Sea of Galilee who said, "I am the way and the truth and the life. No one comes to the Father except through me" (John 14:6). The Christian starts and finishes with Jesus and no one else (Acts 4:12).

> The Christian starts and finishes with Jesus and no one else.

The church will let you down. Finely tuned Christian programs will lose their appeal. People to whom you've looked as spiritual mentors will fail you. Given enough time, even your pastor will disappoint you. And just taking in the pastor's sermons won't bring the abundant life that Jesus promised. The essence of Christianity is not found in imperfect people.

Neither is the abundant life found in simply believing the right facts and doctrines. Christianity is not a statement about a person called Jesus. It's not a set of principals to endorse or a creed to sign-off on. Too many people look at the Christian life as a set of actions they're supposed to do. They see it as a set of propositions they are supposed to memorize or study. But such a vision is shortsighted. By being overly concerned with right beliefs or right behavior, we lose our focus on what really matters. Jesus consistently put down the religionists of His day who were preoccupied with manmade propositions and not a personal relationship with Him, who is the Way, the Truth and the Life (John 14:6).

> "I am the way and the truth and the life. No one comes to the Father except through me."
> John 14:6

Living the Life

No way can you live the abundant life on your own. You just can't do it. It's just not natural. You can't just take a Bible and say, "I'm going to be a Bible-believing Christian." It doesn't work like that. You can't even say, "I'm going to be a good Christian." That's an oxymoron. "Good" Christians don't exist. You never can be good enough. Trying with everything you've got to obey all the Scriptures demand is impossible. You'll just set yourself up for failure. That's because living the Christian life is anything but natural. You have to let Jesus live His life through you. And that's nothing short of *supernatural.*

Still (even after we've begun to follow Jesus), we can't seem to let go of the thought that we have to be good enough somehow or some way for God to accept us. That's simply not Biblical truth! The Bible is clear (and so is our experience of human nature)—we never will be good enough for God to accept us based on our performance. Even on our best day we fall far short of qualifying for God's endorsement.

Amazingly God comes to us anyway. The life He promises is the life He produces. We tend to get it backwards. It's not about what we can do for God; it's all about what He wants to do through us. It doesn't matter who we are, because we are simply the beneficiaries of His sovereign grace. Consider how Eugene Peterson states it in THE MESSAGE (a paraphrase of the Bible):

> Long before he laid down earth's foundations, he had us in mind, had settled on us as the focus of his love, to be made whole and holy by his love. . . . Because of the sacrifice of the Messiah, his blood poured out on the altar of the Cross, we're a free people—free of penalties and punishments chalked up by all our misdeeds. And not just barely free, either. Abundantly free! He thought of everything, provided for everything we could possibly need, letting us in on the plans he took such delight in making. He set it all out before us in Christ, a long-range plan in which everything would be brought together and summed up in him, everything in deepest heaven, everything on planet earth. It's in Christ that we find out who we are and what we are living for. Long before we first heard of Christ and got our hopes up, he had his eye on us, had designs on us for glorious living, part of the overall purpose he is working out in everything and everyone. (Ephesians 1:4, 7–12)

Sadly, most of those to whom God extends grace fail to accept it. They discard it as irrelevant or too-good-to-be-true, or they settle for intellectual knowledge. They are proof that Christianity can't be described if it hasn't been experienced. The life that Jesus espoused in the pages of the New Testament is grounded in a personal relationship with Him. As with any other relationship, it calls for spending time together, conversing, pouring out your hearts to one another, and listening. That's why Christianity isn't really a religion as much as it is a relationship. It's a relationship by which you respond to the risen Christ, living out His life in you.

> "It's in Christ that we find out who we are and what we are living for."
>
> *Ephesians 1:11*
> THE MESSAGE

How Does It Work?

You may wonder how Jesus can reproduce His life in you. An essential part of the answer to this question is the Holy Spirit. **The life of Christ is reproduced in the believer by the power of the Holy Spirit, who makes obedience to the Word of God possible.** The Holy Spirit is one of the three members of the Trinity. The Spirit enabled Jesus to defeat death. The Spirit also is the One who manifests the attributes of the risen Christ among those who follow Him.

When you stop trying to impress God by trying hard to be good, the goodness of His Son takes over. He makes you a more responsible person than you have been before. You start setting priorities that reflect His values and not those of the culture around you (Romans 12:1–2). You're a more dependable husband, wife, leader, or friend than you previously were. You start engaging in the lives of people in effective ways.

It all starts by claiming the free gift of forgiveness that Jesus died to make available to you. Once you've ceased carrying that heavy backpack of guilt, you are free to respond in gratitude and love. And in your response Jesus moves in empowering right choices and Christlike actions. No longer striving to try and convince yourself that you're worthy of being loved, you relax and let the Holy Spirit take over.

> When you stop trying to impress God by trying hard to be good, the goodness of His Son takes over.

Christ in You

So what does it mean that Christ is in you? The Bible says it this way: you are actually *in Christ*. In other words, He locates us in Himself, not in a proposition. He becomes the ground in which you grow. While some people are rooted in themselves and others are rooted in what the crowd thinks, to be in Christ means to pull the roots of one's life out of that soil and transplant them in Him. To be in Christ involves giving up whatever it is you're holding on to and surrendering yourself to His plans and purposes. Once you do, He qualifies you to be used by Him, even when you don't feel qualified.

Unlike all the other major world religions, Christianity is defined by the One after whom it is named. Without the life of Jesus Christ, you have no Christianity. Buddha pointed to his teachings, not his life. Islam is not defined by the life of Muhammad but the Koran. But take away what Jesus did and Christianity crumbles. The great news about the good news of Jesus is that the One on whom Christianity rises and falls is not relegated to a book of teachings. He lives inside those who follow Him.

Does He live inside of you? That is the million-dollar question. Don't take any chances.

Daily Reflection Questions

Day One

1 How would your coworkers answer the question, "What is the meaning of life?"

2 Why is having the answer to that question so important?

3 How well equipped are you to help another person find the answer to that question?

Day Two

1 Why did Nicodemus come to Jesus? (See John 3:1–10.)

2 What was Jesus' answer to him?

3   Jesus said, "I am the way and the truth and the life. No one comes to the Father except through me" (John 14:6). What does that imply?

Day Three

1   Describe a situation when you put your trust in Christian leaders, mentors, or ministries who let you down. What did you learn from that experience?

2   What's the problem with putting our ultimate faith in a human being?

3   In what ways is putting our faith in Christ different?

Day Four

1   Why can't we live the Christian life on our own?

2 Why is it so difficult to let go of the thought that we have to be good enough for God to accept us?

3 What does "grace" mean? What's so amazing about God's grace?

Day Five

1 How does a person grow in a relationship with Christ? How have you grown? What are some of the essential ingredients? (Consider 1 Thessalonians 1 and 2.)

2 What do you need to do to be more like Him?

3 In what areas of your life do you sense the Holy Spirit making changes?

CHAPTER FIVE

WHAT IS THE CHRISTIAN LIFE?

(PART 2)

In the last chapter we said that the Christian life is the life of Christ reproduced in the believer. It's not our attempt to impress God with our best efforts. Rather, it's the way God impacts those who observe our lives as we are increasingly marked by Jesus' values and motives. It's an inside job! The Christian life isn't hard. It's impossible. But thank God He achieves it in us supernaturally. It's all about being connected to the power source by which the current of Jesus' life flows through us.

Suppose you just purchased a new home. You know—the one you've been dreaming about for years. It has all the latest gadgets and conveniences. The extra-large kitchen is fully equipped with state of the art appliances. The master bedroom has a luxury bathroom with a Jacuzzi for two. You have an elaborate entertainment room complete with a big screen plasma TV and surround sound. In addition to the intercom and computerized security system, the backyard features a heated in-ground pool and hot tub.

Everything is as you imagined it except for one thing. After moving in, you discover that you have no power. The lights don't work, neither does the climate-controlled air conditioner. Making the best of an imperfect situation, you sweat it out in the dark without the benefit of all the wonderful gadgets with which your dream home is equipped.

The next day your neighbor introduces himself. During the conversation you learn that he is an electrician with the city utility company. After he leaves, you tell your spouse about your new neighbor and what he does for a living.

Unbelievable! Your home has state of the art conveniences and is wired for power. Your next-door neighbor works for the power company. Yet you still continue to live in the dark without the energy to which you are entitled.

That's like the guy who bought a chain saw at the local hardware store and took it back a week later. He complained to the clerk that he had only been able to cut down three trees when the store manager had told him he would be able to fell dozens of trees with his tool. The clerk examined the saw, looking for a defect, and pulled the starter rope. When the engine started, the customer jumped back frightened and asked, "What's that noise?"

That's what it's like for too many Christians. They say they have a relationship with Jesus and their sins have been forgiven. But they haven't plugged in to the available power that is necessary to live life to the full, as Jesus mentioned in John 10:10.

One of the essential keys for the life of Jesus being reproduced in us is tapping into the power of the Holy Spirit. And in order to get your hand on that key you need to understand something about the Holy Spirit.

Getting Personal

First of all, we need to understand that the Holy Spirit is not an "it." Just as God the Father is a person, and Jesus the Son is a person, so the Holy Spirit is a person as well. Note what Jesus said in John 16:13–14: "But when he, the Spirit of truth, comes, he will guide you into all truth. He will not speak on his own; he will speak only what he hears, and he will tell you what is yet to come. He will bring glory to me by taking from what is mine and making it known to you."

Secondly, we need to understand how we encounter the person of the Holy Spirit. Jesus told His disciples, "You will receive power when the Holy Spirit comes on you; and you will be my witnesses in Jerusalem, and in all Judea and Samaria, and to the ends of the earth" (Acts 1:8). In other words, before we can do something, we have to receive something. Before we can point others to Christ verbally or through our lives, we have to receive the Holy Spirit. In order for Jesus' life to be reproduced in our lives, the power needs to be abiding and then flowing through us.

Here's the good news. If you have accepted Jesus into your life, you've already received the Holy Spirit. When you become a Christian, your life is wired so that you have access to His power. That's one of the ways the Holy Spirit functions in our lives. He enables us to know Christ.

In his famous encounter with Nicodemus (John 3), Jesus explained what being born again is all about. Jesus said, "I tell you the truth, no one can enter the kingdom of God unless he is born of water and the Spirit" (John 3:5). In other words, if the Holy Spirit does not bring you to the point where you see your need for Christ, you'll never invite Him in.

The Holy Spirit also is the One who inspired the Bible writer: "For prophecy never had its origin in the will of man, but men spoke from God as they were carried along by the Holy Spirit" (2 Peter 1:21).

The Spirit and the Word

Still another way the Holy Spirit works in our lives is to open our minds to be able to understand and apply what we read in the Scriptures that

> "You will receive power when the Holy Spirit comes on you."
> *Acts 1:8*

He inspired. Jesus explained that function of the Holy Spirit this way: "But the Counselor, the Holy Spirit, whom the Father will send in my name, will teach you all things and will remind you of everything I have said to you" (John 14:26). It's as if we have a third ear. Call it the "ear of faith." This is the ability the Holy Spirit gives us to understand, comprehend, and then live out what we've read.

The Holy Spirit brings God's Word alive. What seems boring and irrelevant to another is a source of inspiration and instruction to us. Later on Jesus said this about the Holy Spirit: "But when he, the Spirit of truth, comes, he will guide you into all truth" (John 16:13).

The Holy Spirit also calls to our remembrance what we have read and studied. For example, when we find ourselves struggling with pride, the Spirit brings to mind the self-emptying example of Jesus' incarnation to which Paul refers in Philippians 2. And this derails our tendency to focus on "what's in it for us."

Because of that very important function, the Holy Spirit actually keeps us from failing more than we do. He takes principles we've been introduced to and brings them to the forefront of our thinking, so that we find it more difficult to violate what we know God wants.

The Spirit also prays for us (Romans 8:26–27) when we aren't sure what to pray about, or don't know exactly what to say, or when we know what is on our heart but find it difficult to come up with the right words.

The Holy Spirit produces the fruit of Jesus' character in the lives of those who are spiritually alive. Check out Galatians 5:22–23. The qualities of "love, joy, peace, patience, kindness, goodness, faithfulness, gentleness and self-control" marked Jesus. When His life is reproduced in us, those qualities mark us too. The Holy Spirit waters and nurtures that inner orchard. If some of those qualities are not evident in your life, he is the One who can make the change.

For example, if you are struggling with stress or worry, the Holy Spirit can bring about peace in your life. Simply read Philippians 4:4 and ask God to enable you to find reasons to rejoice in Christ's involvement in your life. In the process, you will realize you don't need to be anxious.

Empowered

The Holy Spirit also empowers followers of Jesus to talk about their faith in a sane and sincere way. God doesn't want us to be weird or fanatical, but He does want us to offer valid testimony on His behalf. It's like being on a witness stand in a courtroom. We simply talk about what we've experienced to be true in our lives. The Holy Spirit makes that kind of testifying possible.

> "But the Counselor . . . will teach you all things and will remind you of everything I have said to you."
>
> *John 14:26*

> The Holy Spirit produces the fruit of Jesus' character in the lives of those who are spiritually alive.

Remember, that's what Jesus said would be the natural result of the Spirit coming into our lives: "You will receive power when the Holy Spirit comes on you; and you will be my witnesses" (Acts 1:8). Acts 4 reports that the very ones who heard Jesus speak those words before He ascended into heaven were in a prayer meeting. "After they prayed, the place where they were meeting was shaken. And they were all filled with the Holy Spirit and spoke the word of God boldly" (Acts 4:31).

The Holy Spirit's primary purpose in our lives, however, is to point to Christ. Jesus Himself said so. On that somber night before He was betrayed by Judas, Jesus hinted to His disciples in the upper room that He would be going away: "But I tell you the truth: It is for your good that I am going away. Unless I go away, the Counselor will not come to you; but if I go, I will send him to you . . . But when he, the Spirit of truth, comes, he will guide you into all truth. He will not speak on his own; he will speak only what he hears, and he will tell you what is yet to come. He will bring glory to me by taking from what is mine and making it known to you" (John 16:7, 13–14).

> "He will bring glory to me by taking from what is mine and making it known to you."
> *John 16:14*

Did you get that? Whatever begins with the Holy Spirit always ends with Christ. Even though He manifests Himself with the fruit of the Spirit and the gifts of the Spirit, we need to remember this very important point: The overriding purpose of the Holy Spirit is to point to Jesus, not to draw our attention away from the end by becoming preoccupied with the means.

Most believers have all the information about God and Jesus and the Christian life we really need. What we lack, however, is actually experiencing that knowledge on a firsthand basis. But don't despair. That's what the Holy Spirit makes possible.

Through the Holy Spirit, God has given us the power to be different in our homes, at our places of work, and in our neighborhoods. We have all we need to talk boldly about our faith with those in our spheres of influence. Through the Spirit we have the available resources to be courageously Christ-like in the way we act, decide, and think.

One Step at a Time

But how do we begin to access the Spirit's resources? Good question. According to the Apostle Paul, the answer lies in learning how to walk in the awareness of the Holy Spirit. In his letter to the first century Christians in Galatia, Paul wrote, "Since we live by the Spirit, let us keep in step with the Spirit" (Galatians 5:25).

Keeping in step with the Spirit means learning how to walk a step at a time. Walking in the spiritual realm involves a series of little steps. Just like our kids had to start out by crawling and then taking a few steps and falling, so we have to start out with our arms outstretched to the Lord and head in His direction. In the process of learning to draw on His power, we'll fall flat on our faces. Failure is inevitable when you're learning how to walk. It's part of the process of learning. But it's not that big of a deal.

The Lord knows we'll stumble and fall, but He provides a remedy for getting back up again. Let's take a walking lesson from an old disciple who learned how to crawl and then walk from Christ. John wrote, "This is the message we have heard from him and declare to you: God is light; in him there is no darkness at all. If we claim to have fellowship with him yet walk in the darkness, we lie and do not live by the truth. But if we walk in the light, as he is in the light, we have fellowship with one another, and the blood of Jesus, his Son, purifies us from all sin. If we claim to be without sin, we deceive ourselves and the truth is not in us. If we confess our sins, he is faithful and just and will forgive us our sins and purify us from all unrighteousness" (1 John 1:5–9).

We experience the Holy Spirit's empowering presence in our lives when we are honest with God and admit we have impure thoughts, faulty motives, and selfish attitudes. When we come as needy children to our loving Father, acknowledging that we've messed up, His Spirit picks us up and steadies us so we can start walking again.

In the Holy Spirit you have more energy for living the Christian life than you could possibly imagine. It's as if you are sitting on an undiscovered oil well. Sadly, too many followers of Christ are living below the poverty level when they have unbelievable resources at their availability.

The Untapped Reservoir

Before he died, Dr. Bill Bright loved to tell about a man who lived during the depression. Ira Yates owned a sheep ranch in West Texas. Mr. Yates wasn't able to make enough on his ranching operation to pay the principal and interest on the mortgage, so he was in danger of losing his ranch. He had to live on a government subsidy. Day after day, as his sheep grazed on the rolling West Texas hills, he wondered how he would pay the bills. Then a seismographic crew from an oil company came into the area and told him there might be oil on his land. They asked permission to drill a well, and he signed a contract.

At 1,115 feet they struck oil—big-time! The first well came in at 80,000 barrels a day. Many subsequent wells were more than twice as large. In fact, 30 years after the discovery, a government test of one of the wells showed that it still had the potential flow of 125,000 barrels of oil a day. And Yates owned it all. Actually, he owned it all on the day he purchased the land. Yet he had been living on relief. A multimillionaire living in poverty! The problem? He didn't know the oil was there even though he owned it.

> "If we confess our sins, he is faithful and just and will forgive us our sins and purify us from all unrighteousness."
>
> *1 John 1:9*

Don't overlook the huge reservoir of spiritual riches that needlessly goes untapped. The Holy Spirit is yours for the asking.

Daily Reflection Questions

Day One

1 When have you felt powerless in life?

The Holy Spirit is yours for the asking.

2 What does it mean to be "plugged in" to God? Do you feel "plugged in"?

3 How does a person know that he or she is "plugged in"? How do others know this as well? (Give your observations.)

Day Two

1 What difference does it make that the Holy Spirit is a person, not an "it"?

2 What did Jesus predict His disciples would experience after they received the Holy Spirit?

3   When does a person receive the Holy Spirit?

Day Three

1   How does the Holy Spirit interact with God's Word, the Bible?

2   Why is the Holy Spirit called the "Spirit of Truth"?

3   Why do you think the Holy Spirit is called the "Counselor"?

Day Four

1   Review the list of fruit (Galatians 5:22–23) that the Holy Spirit desires to produce in the lives of believers. Which of those fruits haven't ripened very well in your life? Why do you think this is?

2 What did Paul mean by keeping "in step with the Spirit" (Galatians 5:25)?

3 When we stumble and fall in our Christian walk, what is God's remedy for getting back up again?

Day Five

1 Where, honestly, do you stand in your spiritual walk?

2 What unconfessed sin do you need to talk to God about?

3 Write out a prayer expressing your desire to live in the power of the Holy Spirit.

CHAPTER SIX

An Obedient Response to the Word of God

A friend came to visit W. C. Fields when he was on his deathbed. He was surprised to see the famous comedic actor with a Bible in his lap. It was so out of character for Fields to be leafing through this book, so his friend asked him, "What in the world are you doing?" Fields responded to his uncharacteristic behavior with a most characteristic reply, "I'm looking for loopholes."

If Fields had only opened his Bible sooner, he would have discovered that looking for loopholes is not necessary for those in a right relationship with their Creator. The Bible is a record of what Christ has accomplished on our behalf. It's the good news that allows us to close our eyes on our deathbed with the full assurance of living forever with God. It's also a critical component to understanding what the Christian life is about.

> Obedience is what builds spiritual muscles.

Spiritual Muscles

Thus far we've seen that a basic definition of the Christian life is **the life of Christ reproduced in the believer by the power of the Holy Spirit**. But that definition, in and of itself, is incomplete. The means by which the Holy Spirit brings about Christ's life reproduced in us is this: **An obedient response to the Word of God**.

Obedience is what builds spiritual muscles. What we do with the Bible determines how much we grow in our faith. As an old country preacher once said, "This book will keep you from sin, or sin will keep you from this book." Someone else put it this way, "Dusty Bibles lead to dirty lives." How we incorporate God's Word into our lives determines the degree Christ is reproduced in our lives. We are either allowing the Word to shape our thinking and behavior, or we are allowing the world to squeeze us into its mold.

Most Christians have a sufficient understanding of what the Bible says, but, left to themselves, they have an insufficient desire to obey what they know to be true. Like washed out grainy photographs, too many Christians are overexposed and underdeveloped. For some, the cause is a lack of understanding just how important the Bible really is and a lack of partnership with others in pursuit of His best.

What's the Big Deal?

So what is so special about the Bible? For one thing, the Bible presents itself as God's unique revelation to humanity. Scattered throughout the sixty-six books of this ancient collection of God's revelation are numerous statements that the words and messages are from God Himself. In other words, God guided the writers as they wrote so that their words communicated truth about the human condition that could not be discovered any other way. The writers were not taking dictation. God used the culture, personality, and vocabulary of each contributor.

The Bible not only claims to be God's Word, the evidence points to the fact that it has a divine origin. For one thing, all sixty-six books, written over fifteen hundred years display an amazing unity. Just think of it, the forty some Bible writers included kings, statesmen, poets, fishermen, farmers, and physicians. They wrote independently of each other, yet their writings all tell the story of Jesus.

The Bible has survived intact. Some of the earliest portions of it were written more than three thousand years ago. Actually, we have more evidence for the authenticity of the books in the Bible than for any other ancient literature.

Historical authenticity aside, the message of the Bible continues to be timeless as well as timely. It addresses the origin of life as well as its meaning and purpose. It points to ethical issues of justice and mercy in this life. It also points beyond the grave to what we can expect in the life to come. Obviously the Bible was never intended to be read as a scientific, philosophical, or psychological textbook. When understood in its historical and cultural setting, the Bible's claims are consistent with scientific findings.

And we can't overlook the influence attributed to the Bible throughout history. It has cast a pervasive shadow over every imaginable area of life. From promiscuity to politics and from academics to the arts, the Bible's message has changed lives and challenged opinions. Amazingly more has been written about the Bible than any other book. It's still the number one bestseller of any book ever published.

> Actually, we have more evidence for the authenticity of the books in the Bible than for any other ancient literature.

A Truly Unique Book

The reason for the Bible's undiminished popularity is clear: it is unlike any other book. Just by reading the Bible you get the sense that it is supernaturally inspired. For one thing it is remarkably accurate. Archaeology continues to consistently substantiate the Bible's claims even though critics have repeatedly attempted to undermine them.

For example, historians used to think that the Bible was wrong when it spoke of Abraham taking camels with him to Egypt (Genesis 12:16), asserting that camels were not present in that part of the world at that time. But archaeologists later discovered the skull of a camel, dating back to 2000 BC (when Abraham had traveled to Egypt).

The Bible's numerous prophecies also indicate its supernatural nature. Critics have to acknowledge that humans living hundreds of years before a predicted event took place could not take credit for what they prophesied.

For example, centuries before Christ's birth a Hebrew prophet by the name of Micah said the Messiah would be born in Bethlehem (Micah 5:2). Isaiah said He would be born of a virgin (Isaiah 7:14). Zechariah told of His riding into Jerusalem on a donkey while people hailed Him as king (Zechariah 9:9–10). Isaiah also gave an unbelievably accurate description of Christ's passion (Isaiah 53).

The Benefits of the Book

The value of the Bible is not just seen in its divine origin but in the practical way it benefits our lives. First, it is a light that provides illumination about the human condition as well as God's plan for the world (Psalm 119:105). The Bible is also a mirror. Not just any mirror, mind you, but the kind of looking glass that reflects our personalities and souls rather than our physical appearance. Through God's Word we have the opportunity to see ourselves from God's perspective and determine what in our lives is in need of change (James 1:23–24).

The Bible is also an essential source of food that sustains our souls. Call it spiritual nourishment, if you like. Its simple direct instruction, when acted upon, results in growth with essential benefits of fruitfulness, areas of wisdom, character, love, integrity, and courage.

The Word of God provides appropriate weaponry to respond defensively as well as offensively (Ephesians 6:10–18). It is a shield that protects us from assaults on our emotions, our self-esteem, and our faith—not to mention doubt, guilt, fear, insecurity, and feelings of inferiority (see Psalm 119:114). But the Bible is also a sword that defends the man or woman of God from the lurking enemies of false truths or half-truths lying in wait ready to ambush us (Hebrews 4:12).

Furthermore, the Bible is the means by which we understand how to access the presence of the living God. As we read words He inspired, it is as though we have a private audience with the King of Kings. His words counsel us (Psalm 73:24). A daily reading of God's Word provides us with the awareness that He is good, powerful, and sovereign in directing our lives. In it we learn that He has expectations of us and resources for us.

> The Bible is also an essential source of food that sustains our souls.

It is possible, however, to know both the uniqueness of God's Word and the benefits of it, without benefiting from its unique revelation. You have to understand what it says, and you have to act on what you understand for the Bible to impact your life. The more you respond to the Word of God, the greater your capacity to understand it. And that's why we must do more than merely read the Bible—we must put it into practice. Obedience to God's Word means wrestling with the challenges and implications that a cursory reading of Scripture will not bring about.

The Benefits of Bible Study

Many Christians just absorb information. But what does that accomplish? Here's an illustration that might explain the superficiality of mere Bible exposure. Did you know that 93 million miles away from earth there is a star called the sun? Its diameter is 109.3 times the diameter of the earth, and its surface is 12,000 times the earth's surface because hydrogen in the sun is heated to 27 million degrees Fahrenheit. Because the hydrogen is heated to the point that it changes into helium, tremendous energy is generated. This energy bursts out into space and reaches the earth at a rate of four million horsepower per square mile. Pretty amazing, huh? Fascinating stuff. But it probably won't impact the way you go about your day, right?

That's the way many deal with the truths they read in the Bible. A person reads an interesting passage. It's information that he had never heard before. After scratching his chin and opening his mouth to yawn, he closes the book. He can check off that he read that section of Scripture on his read-through-the-Bible-in-one-year-chart, but that's about all.

Meanwhile, back to the science lesson dealing with the sun. The sun's energy is ultraviolet radiation. If it hits unexposed skin, those UV rays penetrate your skin. Some call the result of that exposure a beautiful tan. If you get too much of a beautiful tan, you may get something that's not so beautiful—skin cancer. The sensible action would be to avoid prolonged exposure to ultraviolet radiation.

Do you understand the progression being illustrated here? Once a correlation is made between the truth and how that truth impacts your life, you pay better attention to the topic in question and you will likely act on what you understand. That's the essence of what it takes to study the Bible. You ask questions of the text and you ask questions of yourself.

Here's a simple way to visualize the process. Draw a triangle on a sheet of paper. Draw two parallel horizontal lines inside the triangle. On the top line write, "Truth Stated." On the second line

> Obedience to God's Word means wrestling with the challenges and implications that a cursory reading of Scripture will not bring about.

write, "Implications from the Truth." On the final line (the base of the triangle) write, "Applications for My Life." That's an easy-to-remember and very effective way to study the Bible.

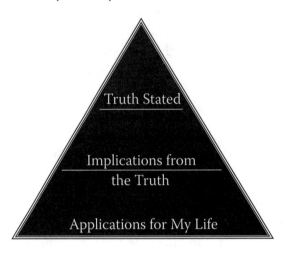

After reading a passage ask yourself, "What did I just read? What did the passage say?" Then go ahead and look to the text through the lens of understanding. This may require the use of a dictionary to make sure you understand the meaning of a word that you don't normally use. It also may require accessing a concordance in the back of your Bible to see how the word is used elsewhere in Scripture.

On this second level you are basically asking yourself, "What is the implication of this truth when taken at face value? What are the conditions, promises, or consequences of this verse? To whom does it apply? How are those people like me?"

Finally, ask yourself, "If I were going to put this truth into practice, what would I have to do or say or choose? What impact would this reality have on my marriage, my job, my character, my relationships, or the goals that I'm currently pursing?" That's where obedience to God's Word shows up. First you have to know what is expected. Then you have to know what it means. Finally you are in a position to act on what you understand to be true.

To try your hand at this simple Bible study method, turn to the sample study in the Appendix at the end of this chapter.

As you can see, reading the Bible and studying the Bible are related, but they are not the same. Obviously, you need to read God's Word before you can study it. But reading it is not the same as studying it. An obedient response to the truth it contains assumes study. Determine today that you will not just crack open the book and skim. If the Bible is as unique and timeless as you've read earlier in this chapter, it is worthy of in-depth study and application. As Chuck Swindoll says, "The Bible is irrelevant only to those who don't read it!"

Daily Reflection Questions

Day One

1 How often do you read the Bible?

2 How does obedience build spiritual muscles?

3 Why do many Christians, who know the Bible, find it difficult to do what it says?

Day Two

1 What's so special about the Bible?

2 What's significant about calling the Bible "God's Word"?

3 What is the unifying theme of the Bible?

Day Three

1   Why is it important to realize that the Bible was never intended to be a scientific, philosophical, or psychological *textbook*?

2   In what ways is the message of the Bible "timeless" and "timely"?

3   What evidence points to the fact that the Bible has a divine origin?

Day Four

1   How would you answer someone who claims that the Bible is riddled with errors and contradictions?

2   What are a few of your favorite Bible passages?

3 How, specifically, has God spoken to you recently through His Word?

Day Five

1 What changes do you need to make in your schedule to be more consistent in your Bible reading?

2 What Bible study tool(s) will you obtain to help you understand God's timeless truths?

3 In your recent Bible reading, what have you felt the Holy Spirit prompting you to do?

4 What steps will you take to do it, to obey?

Appendix: Sample Bible Study

Read Psalm 1

What Does It Say?

What two kinds of persons is the psalmist writing about?

1.

2.

In what ways are their lives distinct?

What are the outcomes of each person's pursuits?

What Does It Mean?

Who does the righteous person avoid?

In what does he or she delight?

What characterizes the unrighteous person's life?

What is the law of the Lord?

What does the progression symbolized by walking, standing, and sitting suggest?

How does the metaphor of the tree explain a life of devotion to God's Word?

What Does It Mean to Me?

With whom do you spend most of your discretionary time?

Are these individuals a healthy influence?

Do they encourage you to take God's Word seriously? Why or why not?

If you were to start meditating on Biblical truth, what would you do? When would you do it?

Begin today by starting to memorize Psalm 1.

CHAPTER SEVEN

THE CHRISTIAN LIFE: HOW IT WORKS (PRAYER)

If you've seen Mel Gibson's epic movie "The Passion of the Christ," you probably recall one or two scenes that really made a lasting impression. One of those unforgettable scenes was when Jesus' mother watched her son stumble under the weight of the cross and fall. She flashes back to when He tripped as a boy and she ran to His side to comfort Him. It brought tears to my eyes.

There's another scene that is hard to get out of your head. It's the poignant one right at the beginning. Underneath the overarching branches of olive trees, we see Jesus stooped in the shadows. His haunting moans make it clear that all is not well. He is overwhelmed with sorrow. The words He painfully blurts out are in Aramaic, and although the English subtitles are provided, they aren't really necessary. It is obvious that the Son is pouring out His heavy heart to the Father. In an agonizing monologue Jesus admits His desire to be kept from the cross as well as His willingness to fulfill His foreordained destiny.

When it seems His conversation with His Father has concluded, a snake slithers from a nearby bush. With a confident resignation to imminent suffering and death, Jesus does not draw back in fear. With a calculated stomp, He guides His leather-sandaled foot and crushes the serpent's head as He walks through the trees toward the cross, a powerful reminder of the first promise of God's redemption recorded in Genesis 3:15.

> It was in the context of prayer that Jesus chose to respond obediently to His Father's plan.

It was in the context of prayer that Jesus chose to respond obediently to His Father's plan. In the atmosphere of prayer, we also learn to breathe the air of obedience. Prayer is a critical component for all those who want the life of Christ reproduced in them. Oswald Chambers says it powerfully: "Prayer is not getting things from God . . . prayer is getting into communion with God; I tell Him what I know He knows in order that I may get to know it as He does"

Practicing the Presence of Jesus

That kind of communion with the Lord is best illustrated in the life of a monk who lived in a monastery outside Paris more than three hundred years ago. As a member of the Carmelite community, Brother Lawrence served his Lord and his brothers in the kitchen as a cook. Because he was convinced that Jesus was with him at all times, he viewed everything he did in that little room as an act of prayer. He called his unorthodox definition of prayer practicing the presence of Christ. In Brother Lawrence's words, "God is here, close beside me. Because He is everywhere, I can never again be out of His holy presence." For this remarkable man, prayer was nothing more than communing with the Lord and bringing every detail of his life into His available presence.

With a view of prayer like that, the intimidating ideas of what it takes to communicate with God no longer are an excuse. If prayer is nothing more than practicing the presence of Christ, it is as simple (and natural) as breathing.

Why Is Prayer Important?

The best reason anyone can give for why we should take prayer seriously is because Jesus told us to pray. He encouraged His followers to ask, seek, and knock. He told His disciples that certain kinds of interventions could only be successful if prayer preceded them. He insisted that they pray for increased numbers of persons who would cooperate to evangelize the world.

Jesus assumed that His disciples would pray. He didn't say *if* you pray. Rather, when He introduced His followers to a pattern of prayer, He said, "When you pray, say: 'Father, hallowed be your name'" (Luke 11:2). You know that prayer, often referred to as the Lord's Prayer. In reality, however, it is the *disciples'* prayer.

More than Words

But Jesus didn't just command us to pray, and He didn't just provide a verbal example of how to pray. He gave us a living example as well. According to the New Testament, Jesus made prayer a personal priority. Luke makes note of the fact that "Jesus often withdrew to lonely places and prayed" (Luke 5:16). Mark records a time when "very early in the morning, while it was still dark, Jesus . . . left the house and went off to a solitary place, where he prayed" (Mark 1:35). In fact, Jesus taught His friends the "disciples' prayer" because they were so impressed with the pattern of prayer that characterized His life that they wanted to follow His lead.

At the beginning of Jesus' public ministry, He spent forty days in the Judean wilderness. It was a boot camp of sorts. He encountered spiritual temptation and learned to listen with His heart. Living in the empty, windswept desert and dealing with an empty stomach, the Son of God filled His days talking to His Father. And, as we saw at the beginning of this lesson, Jesus concluded His ministry by pouring out

> "When you pray, say: 'Father, hallowed be your name.'"
> *Luke 11:2*

His heart to the heavenly Father in a garden in the shadow of olive trees. Then as He hung on the cross in utter agony, He used His final ounce of energy to pray. Yes, prayer punctuated Jesus' life.

Is it too obvious to suggest that if Jesus recognized the need for regular communication and communion with His Father, we should as well? After all, healthy growing relationships demand ongoing contact. It's an essential quality in lasting friendships. It's critically important in a marriage. It's also an indispensable part of our relationship with the Lord. In the process of talking to God and listening to Him, we are reminded of His presence with us at all times. We are also in a position to sense His direction and guidance. It provides the opportunity to acknowledge need and ask for help.

What Should We Pray For?

Prayer is a powerful privilege. It ushers us immediately into the presence of the Lord of the universe. No waiting required.

What is more, He gives us His undivided attention. So that being the case, what kinds of things should you bring to Him? What should we pray for?

Well, for starters, ask God to provide you with growth options and opportunities that will enhance your relationship with Him. Ask the Lord to give you a willingness to obey what you know He desires. Ask Him for the faith to trust Him when you're tempted to worry or doubt (Matthew 6:31–33). Jesus said that when we pray according to God's will, we can be sure that He will answer (Matthew 7:7–8). And you can be sure that God wills for you to mature in your relationship with Him.

Praying for your own personal growth is also appropriate. How are things at your job? Most likely you have issues there that concern you. Bring those to the Father. Are there those with whom you have difficulty working? Don't pretend with God that all is well. Talk to Him about those relationships. Are you apprehensive about your job security? Tell the Father.

Ask God for insight into situations that overwhelm you. In his little epistle, the Apostle James states, "If any of you lack wisdom he should ask God" (James 1:5). Also, acknowledge your desire for physical health to the Lord. When you are sick, ask for His healing touch. Confess your need for rational thinking. If you are prone to depression, ask the Lord to bring into your life people and treatment options that will stop the emotional spiral.

In addition, pray for family members and close friends. If they do not yet know the Lord, ask Him to surround them with Christians who will share their faith (Colossians 1:6) and stir them with

> "If any of you lack wisdom he should ask God."
>
> *James 1:5*

questions of eternity to whet their appetite for spiritual matters. If they are believers, ask the Father to open their eyes to evidence of His faithfulness in their lives and their dependence upon Him.

Don't stop with family and friends—pray for your church family. Ask God to encourage your pastor as he guides the congregation. Name those who teach your kids and request that the Lord would reward their commitment with creativity and patience.

If we take our cues from Jesus' model prayer, we should talk to God about everything that matters to us (or Him). We should feel free to ask Him for bread. More than food, that's whatever it takes to survive day to day. We should ask the Father for forgiveness because acknowledging our spiritual indebtedness to God and cashing in on His forgiveness prompts us to be more patient and forgiving toward others. We are to call on the Lord for strength when tempted and for deliverance when we find ourselves kidnapped by calamity.

Leighton Ford puts it this way: "Prayer is recognizing that I have needs, for bread and clothing and shelter—and a need for His Holy Spirit. As a human being I am not self-sufficient; I am incomplete and insufficient. So I must ask."

> Jesus tells us to ask, seek, and knock.

How Does God Answer Prayer?

Someone once said, God answers every prayer. Sometimes He says "yes." Sometimes He says "no." And sometimes He says "wait." That's good. The One to whom we pray is always online. He never deletes our instant messages. He downloads the attachments we've forwarded to Him.

Jesus told great stories to illustrate God's inclination to respond to our supplications. They concern children in need of bread, a widow in need of justice, and a neighbor in need of supplies. In every case, Jesus reiterated how much the Father loves to come through on behalf of those He considers His children. Jesus tells us to ask, seek, and knock.

Ever heard of King Hezekiah in the Old Testament? He was diagnosed with an incurable disease and was devastated. He didn't want to die. The sick king turned his heart to the Lord in prayer and asked that his life be spared. And the Lord answered his prayer by adding fifteen years to his life (2 Kings 20:1–11). Most likely you remember about Daniel from your days in Sunday school. He was sentenced to sure death in a den of lions for his uncompromising practice of prayer. And God answered his prayers too. Amazingly, Daniel spent the night in feline jail without incident.

The Apostle Paul was plagued with an undisclosed ailment. He called it a "thorn in the flesh." By his own admission he said that he pleaded with the Lord for healing. But God did not answer in the way Paul had hoped. Instead, the Lord responded, "My grace is sufficient for you . . ." (2 Corinthians 12:9). In that case, the answer to Paul's prayer was "no."

The Bible also reports those occasions when people who were praying for God's deliverance learned how to wait. Isaiah wrote to such folks. He knew that freedom from Babylonian bondage would come. The Lord had given him a preview of coming attractions. But he also knew that the motion picture of God's redemption would not be released in the near future. No wonder he wrote, "They that wait upon the Lord shall renew their strength" (Isaiah 40:31, KJV).

God answered prayer in the days of the Bible, and He still does. Wendy Steven was rushed to a Southern California hospital struggling to get a breath. An examination of the twenty-seven-year-old elementary school teacher determined she was in the throes of anaphylactic shock. While in the emergency room, Wendy's lungs collapsed. As doctors attempted to diagnose a treatment, her systems began to shut down and she was placed on life support.

Her frightened parents huddled in the fourth floor waiting room stunned by this unexpected turn of events. Just the day before Wendy had been seated at the family table, laughing and entering into conversation. The unfamiliar room in which they felt like hostages fueled feelings of fear.

As a doctor approached them, they could tell by his downcast countenance that the news was not good. "If you are praying people, I'd advise you to pray," he said. "We've done everything we know to do to help your daughter, and we're losing her."

What he didn't know is that Hugh and Norma Steven, missionaries with Wycliffe Bible Translators, had a network of prayer partners that literally circled the globe. As they put out their emergency request, they knew that thousands would be holding Wendy (and them) on the wings of prayer.

Within five days, Wendy's condition made an unexpected turn in the right direction. It was determined she had experienced a severe allergic reaction to a common antibiotic. Although a pharmacist friend of the family is the one who traced the symptoms to their cause, it was obvious God had intervened at just the right time.

How Do You Pray?

For the follower of Jesus, prayer is not some religious ritual. It is candid conversation with Someone we care about Who cares for us. As a result, we don't need to be overly concerned about parroting someone else's words or attempting to sound religious. We aren't praying for

> "They that wait upon the Lord shall renew their strength."
> Isaiah 40:31, KJV

the benefit of anyone other than the One who can already read our thoughts before we verbalize them. So we can relax and be creative.

One man in Illinois actually prays with a pencil. He writes his thoughts in a journal as if writing a letter to the Lord. Taking his cue from David, he is brutally honest with his emotions. Doubt and anger are as welcomed in his scribbles as praise and gratitude.

Praying Without Constraints

If kneeling makes you feel close to God, take a knee (or two). A case can be made that bowing or kneeling helps us assume a posture of reverence and humility. But Jesus taught us to talk to God as if He were our papa or daddy, not a king (Matthew 6:9). If closing your eyes helps you concentrate what you are saying and to Whom you are speaking, then go for it. If you can close out distractions while keeping your eyes open, then by all means *watch* and pray. After all, that's Biblical. It's also a safety precaution if you are attempting to pray while commuting to work. Remember—no occasion is inappropriate for talking to the Lord.

Once again, Leighton is right on the mark when he suggests, "Don't limit your prayers to a formal act once a day. Get in the habit of sending *flash* prayers to God many times a day. Pray when you wake up; pray before meals; pray as you walk or ride or wait; pray when you can't sleep. Even doing your work or your recreation to the glory of God can be a prayer."

About the only restrictions Jesus placed on prayer had to do with words spoken without thinking or with wrong motives. He really got on the religious leaders of His day for mindlessly babbling religious sounding words that had become a ritualistic exercise (Matthew 6:7). Jesus warned against equating prayer with vain repetitions. The words may be valid, but if they are offered from an insincere heart, they have no value. And praying as a means to impress others is just as worthless.

A Simple Formula for Revived Faith

So don't be overly concerned with how you pray as much as being prayerful in all you do. At times you simply will need to offer an SOS prayer. That's what Peter did when he accepted Jesus' invitation to walk toward Him on the water. When the big fisherman took his eyes off the Lord and began to sink, he simply called out, "Lord, save me!" (Matthew 14:30). That's an SOS prayer. With no time for a lengthy explanation, you only need to call out to Christ to come to the rescue.

> So don't be overly concerned with how you pray as much as being prayerful in all you do.

At other times you simply will want to uplink your concerns that relate to yourself or other people. You request God's help to stay calm in a stressful meeting at work. You request His intervention for a friend's marriage that's gone south. Listing those petitions and then reading that list to God, mindful of His presence and concern, is a kosher way to pray.

If prayer is really the interaction between friends, however, it should not be seen as motivated solely by need. Praying that is always looking for a handout is nothing more than verbal coins inserted in a cosmic vending machine. The kind of communication Jesus calls us to is primarily relationship building. That means talking to the Lord about issues that have a tendency to come between Him and us. It also has to do with asking forgiveness when we know wrong choices or willful actions have created a distance between us.

Relationship building prayer involves protracted periods of time conversing about little things—admiring the beauty of a sunset, commenting on undeserved blessings, or letting the Lord know how special He is to you. You know, the glue of commitment is the stickiness of what we used to call "sweet nothings."

In other words, it is important that we talk to the Lord about crises in our lives. It's important that we petition Him about issues that are beyond our control. And it's important that we relate to Him as to a cherished friend.

Every kind of prayer is necessary to sustain your spiritual life. When your heart seems dead toward life (and God), you need to have CPR to get it beating again.

> **C (crises centered)**
>
> **P (petition grounded)**
>
> **R (relationship based)**

> Every kind of prayer is necessary to sustain your spiritual life.

Daily Reflection Questions

Day One

I Who taught (and modeled for) you the importance of prayer and how to pray?

2 When, during the day, are you most likely to pray?

3 Why should we take prayer seriously?

Day Two

1 What did Brother Lawrence mean by "practicing the presence of Christ"?

2 In what ways was Jesus a living example of the importance and place of prayer?

3 Why is prayer said to be *two-way* communication with God?

Day Three

1 Why is prayer a powerful privilege?

2　For what is it appropriate to pray?

3　What are your normal or usual prayer categories?

4　About what do you find yourself praying the most?

Day Four

1　How does God answer prayer?

2　What powerful answers to prayer can you remember from your own experience?

3 When have you struggled to trust God and accept His answer when He seems to be answering "no"?

Day Five

1 What changes will you make to your praying pattern to be more consistent?

2 What changes will you make to your prayers to make them more meaningful?

To help improve your relationship with God?

To help you listen more to God?

3 On what pressing needs and concerns will you focus your prayers?

CHAPTER EIGHT

THE CHRISTIAN LIFE: HOW IT WORKS (WORSHIP)

Like hundreds of thousands in the Bay Area, Tony Martin is an avid San Francisco Forty-niners fan. For the past twenty years he's been a season ticket holder. Tony is proud of the fact he has not missed one home game in that time. His wife will also attest that he has only rarely missed an away game on their giant TV.

Tony literally eats and breathes 49er football. He scours the *San Francisco Chronicle* every morning for news that relates to the coaches, players, or management. Those who follow him on the freeway in the daily commute to the office can know from his vanity license plate what occupies his heart: 49ERFAN.

Every Sunday, from August through December, Tony religiously follows a set routine. Unlike most days, he showers but doesn't shave. "Bad luck," he tells his kids. Without fail he pulls on his Sunday best: his red and gold official NFL 49er jersey. While eating breakfast, he watches ESPN *Game Day* to prepare himself to watch his team.

On days when the 49ers are at home, he packs bratwursts, buns, chips, and beer in the back of his Jeep and heads to the ballpark. There, in the parking lot, he joins the same eight guys with whom he has tailgated for twenty years. On days that his watching is limited to his living room, Tony plays Tony Bennett singing "I Left My Heart in San Francisco" on his obsolete record player while arranging folding chairs in rows in front of the giant screen. On these days his neighbors know they are welcome to spend the afternoon at the Martin home watching the game with him.

If you were to follow Tony to 3Com Park, you would see a sea of red and gold. Fans equally as fanatical as Tony fill the stadium. They have their own rituals and traditional observances that make their game-watching experience extra-ordinary. Complete with radio headsets and binoculars, logo water bottles and blankets, these diehard followers of the 49ers are a congregation of sorts. They hang on every word the public address announcer utters as if it were from God. They stand together to sing the national anthem. Their emotional response to third down conversions, touchdown passes, and game winning field goals resembles the fervor of an old-fashioned tent meeting revival.

> They have their own rituals and traditional observances that make their game-watching experience extra-ordinary.

The Essence of Biblical Worship

Yes, our culture knows all about worship. Unfortunately, the object most Americans worship is not what the Bible calls us to. We worship sports teams and sports personalities. We worship movie stars. We worship golden ladders whose rungs promise promotion and big paychecks. In fact, the god of a personal career is the deity before whom more people bow than their favorite football team.

Gordon Dahl once said that we are "a people who tend to worship our work, work at our play, and play at our worship." In other words, we have succeeded in putting the right em*phasis* on the wrong syl*lable*. Work is good. So is play. Worship is essential. But how we embrace these three activities is critical.

The thrill of being in a 50,000-seat stadium while bonding with fellow fans is a legitimate joy. Being committed to a cause and being part of a corporate effort fulfills a need God placed in every person. Likewise, the aura a person feels being dwarfed by something larger than himself is unexplainably meaningful. But that fulfillment we seek can only be found when we are focusing our energies toward someone worthy of our worship. And that's not a professional football team (no matter how great a season they might have).

For those who are committed to having Jesus live out His life in them, doing worship right is a must. It's a non-negotiable. Here's why: Your concept of God will be shaped by your worship of God. If you only worship on your own, your God will be limited to your understanding of Him. Chances are, that's not very big. A theologian by the name of J. B. Phillips wrote a book a few decades ago entitled *Your God Is Too Small*. In it he denounced our tendency to force God to fit in a box of our own making. Someone else described that tendency this way: "In the beginning God created us in His image, and ever since we've attempted to return the favor."

When we join others for public worship the context of our contemplation about the Creator is multiplied exponentially. As with a crowded sporting event, the atmosphere is charged with expectation of how we will experience the Lord of the universe. But whereas the presence of others raises our experience of God to a new level, worship ultimately does not have to do with other people.

Worship also doesn't have to do with the externals we often associate it with. It really doesn't matter whether we hold a hymnbook in our hands and sing lyrics written two hundred years ago or we sing songs that were composed two months ago. It doesn't matter if the church has a worship team up front holding microphones or a choir in a loft wearing robes. Meaningful public worship isn't dependent on

> Work is good. So is play. Worship is essential. But how we embrace these three activities is critical.

stained glass windows. It can take place in high school gymnasium. The reason is this: Worship has to do with spending time in the presence of the Lord to acknowledge His greatness and express our gratitude. Our focus and affections are on Him.

Pointers for Public Worship

Just like the guy who wouldn't think of heading to the 3Com Park without a warm blanket, his headphone radio, and a bag of peanuts, the avid worshiper of God has a punch list of things to be mindful of before heading out to a worship service. Here's what to bring.

Come with a positive attitude. That means expecting that something significant is going to happen. Obviously this will involve spending time in private worship between Sundays so that you will be in the habit of hearing from the Lord, with that frequency fine-tuned. Come with the intention of interacting mentally with what is heard (James 1:23–25).

Come with the necessary gear. If you were headed to a baseball game, you might take binoculars as well as a radio. A serious fan would have a scorecard and a pen to track the progress of the game. For the serious worshiper, this means bringing a Bible, a notebook, and a pen. You're not a passive bystander. You're the primary participant. Sören Kierkegaard, a Danish theologian, suggested that in terms of a drama our view of worship often spotlights the preacher as the star performer and ourselves as the audience. He contended, however, that worshipers are the performers, with the pastor, choir, and other participants the prompters. But God is the audience.

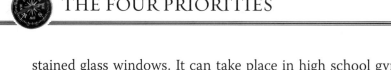

> To offer God the praise, imagination, and worth that He deserves demands that we are capable of creative thought and energetic participation.

Arrive at worship rested. To offer God the praise, imagination, and worth that He deserves demands that we are capable of creative thought and energetic participation. That isn't likely to happen if we have been out past midnight on Saturday. We also are apt to be out-of-tune or blurred in our focus if we have filled our minds with entertainment that undermines the kind of life we are attempting to live out. Filtering our thoughts during the week and going to bed at a decent hour the night before Sunday (or whatever day you worship) is a must.

Don't be late. Those who lead worship at your church have taken great pains to plan a seamless experience in which one element builds on another. If you show up ten minutes late, you will have missed a foundational aspect to the service that will prevent you from experiencing the desired impact. In addition, tardiness distracts those you have to step over to find your seat. It's also discourteous to those who are speaking or leading when you barge in.

Be alert. This means working at your worship. And that's more apt to happen if you've had a good night sleep and a good breakfast. Don't simply be reactionary. Be proactive. Be intentional. Read over the order of service ahead of time so you will know the flow of the morning before it begins. You may want to mark pages in your hymnal or Bible that will be referred to.

Prioritize the pattern of weekly worship. If you recognize the importance of public worship celebrations, factor them into your week. Make it habit-forming. You tend to value what you accommodate. Jesus put it this way, "Where your treasure is, there your heart will be also" (Matthew 6:21). The person who wrote the first century epistle to persecuted Jewish Christians put it this way, "Let us not give up meeting together, as some are in the habit of doing, but let us encourage one another—and all the more as you see the Day approaching" (Hebrews 10:25).

Finally, *be a learner.* Don't come to church as though you know it all. As indicated previously, a big reason for gathering with other believers is to place ourselves in a setting where we stretch our understanding. If the living Christ is present whenever His people are gathered in His name (and that's a here and now implication of the reality of Easter), we had better believe that Jesus can bring us to a place of understanding that is deeper than we've known before.

Why We Worship

Our culture is preoccupied with being entertained. We've been conditioned to ask "What's in it for me?" or "Does it move me?" But worship is not intended to entertain. It has to do with giving ourselves to the object of our worship. As such, we must continually guard against that tendency to enter the sanctuary with inappropriate expectations. Although at times our experience in worship will profoundly impact us, we don't come into God's presence primarily to be "wowed."

We must also resist the subtle temptation to exploit worship to serve our personal or professional needs. It's only natural to be aware of those who are seated around us on a Sunday morning. And we may feel the need to be seen by someone we admire or make a good impression on someone who could benefit our career advancement. Our pragmatic nature that always attempts to make the best use of our time sees Sundays as an optimal opportunity for networking (from hawking our daughter's Girl Scout cookies to passing out a business card). But looking at worship as a means of networking flies in the face of why we are there.

Quite simply, we worship to bring the Lord pleasure by revering Him, thanking Him, and celebrating His goodness and power. The words to an old gospel song say it well: "Turn your eyes upon Jesus.

> "Where your treasure is, there your heart will be also."
> *Matthew 6:21*

> "Let us not give up meeting together, as some are in the habit of doing, but let us encourage one another."
> *Hebrews 10:25*

Look full in His wonderful face. And the things of earth will grow strangely dim in the light of His glory and grace."

The Benefits of Worship

As stated previously, "What's in it for me?" is an inappropriate question to ask as you come into a worship service. A better question is "How can I give myself to the Lord today?" All the same, those who focus on Jesus in the singing, praying, contemplating in silence, or listening to the sermon experience a tangible payoff. Consider the following benefits:

When you gather with other believers on a regular basis *you have the opportunity to release your cares and concerns.* The founder of the Vineyard movement wrote a praise song that contained these words: "O let him have the things that hold you and His Spirit like a dove will descend upon your heart." Doesn't that sound inviting?

When you enter into the Lord's presence in a place or a time set apart for the express purpose of considering His attributes, *something significant occurs.* Even though you've come to worship with unresolved issues and intimidating challenges in your life, those problems are dwarfed when contrasted to the answer of Whose presence you're keenly aware.

When you exercise your faith in the context of worship, *you discover long-term results.* Just as with physical muscles, working your faith muscles makes them stronger. No wonder the person who wrote Hebrews felt so strongly about maintaining a core value of regular worship. The inner strength that is derived from consistently being in corporate worship is not an exercise in vanity. Those well-chiseled faith muscles aren't intended for showing off or gaining a sense of fulfillment while looking at yourself in the mirror. They have a practical benefit. They allow you to lift the responsibilities that come with maturing in your understanding of the Christian life.

When you make worship a priority, *you discover you are not a solitary pilgrim on the path of faith.* Rather, as you are surrounded by others confessing the same creeds, singing the same lyrics, and facing the same cross on the back of the platform, you are relieved to realize there is an entire congregation headed in the same direction you are. Chances are, you need to be reminded of that sense of community (and unity) at least once a week.

Finally, it's in worship that *your doubting, anxious heart is infused with confidence and hope to face the uncertainties that await you during the week.* It's as though faith (like a focused ray of sunshine through a magnifying glass) ignites into contagious trust and courage in light of what lies ahead. There's a moving scene near the end of that

> "What's in it for me?" is an inappropriate question to ask as you come into a worship service.

great Civil War epic movie *Glory*. The Union's first black regiment has enthusiastically volunteered to lead an assault on a Confederate fort. Given the circumstances, many of the regiment are highly likely to be killed. The night before the invasion, the soldiers gather around a fire worshiping Jesus. As they sing and pray aloud, their obvious fears give way to an inexplicable confidence that God is in control.

Choosing a Local Church

You don't have to dress up in a suit to attend a worship service. Our culture is a whole lot less formal than it used to be. But finding a local fellowship that suits you is vitally important. You will be more inclined to worship regularly if you like the way a given congregation "does church." And no two congregations "do church" the same way.

You have a unique personality, and so do local churches. Some are quite traditional. Some are more free-flowing. Some sing hymns. Some sing choruses. Some incorporate puppets (as a way of relating to children), while others incorporate liturgical dance as a way of visualizing Biblical truth. Some aim for a quiet meditative atmosphere, while some strive to be high-energy and vocal. Because there are so many different personality types, every kind has its place. As author and speaker Jay Kesler says, "Choosing a church should be like selecting items at Old Country Buffet. Feel free to choose what you like, and just pass on what you don't. There's no need to spit on what you aren't drawn to."

Look around you on a given Sunday morning. It's obvious not everybody is engaged in a meaningful way. Have you ever tried counting those who are nodding off? If you took all the people who fall asleep in a church service and laid them end to end, do you know what would happen? Well, for one thing they'd be a whole lot more comfortable.

Seriously, the sleeping sickness epidemic in most churches is most likely an issue of faithful attendees who are tired of going to a place that is at odds with the way they think, feel, and process truth. The kind of worship an individual will embrace (and stay awake to enjoy) is one that is framed in the "language" that person speaks. So don't be afraid to seek out a pastor and congregation that communicate in a way you understand and relate to your personal culture.

Here are some suggestions on how to go about selecting a place to hang your Sunday morning hat:

1. Find a way to determine if this group of Sunday morning gatherers believes that Jesus is the Son of God. If they simply say He was a great moral teacher, keep looking.

> Look around you on a given Sunday morning. It's obvious not everybody is engaged in a meaningful way.

2. Figure out as best you can if the pastor preaches from the Bible or is inclined to offer popular psychology from the pulpit. If God's Word is esteemed as trustworthy and authoritative, that's a good sign. If the sermon and other Christian education programs offer ways to apply the Bible, you'd do well to take a closer look.

3. As you visit around, you'll likely pick up clues that indicate how people are treated. If they are valued and their needs addressed sensitively, you can expect you'll be treated the same way. As Martha Stewart used to say, "That's a good thing!" You'd do well to connect with a gathering of the Body of Christ that views people as important because they are made in the image of God.

4. Yet another key indicator of a congregation worth tying into is one that is up-front about the mission of Christ beyond their four walls. As you visit, allow your antennae to pick up signals that would indicate there is a concern for winning spiritually lost people to Christ, bringing justice to the oppressed, and caring for the physical needs of the poor. If you also sense the church goes to great lengths to involve individuals in these kinds of worthy projects, you will have found a fellowship that's worthy of a second look.

5. As you visit a second and third time, you probably will be able to tell if this is a setting where you could grow in the Four Priorities. If you determine it's not, keep looking.

> The landscape of Christianity in our country almost resembles the Mall of America in the Twin Cities.

The landscape of Christianity in our country almost resembles the Mall of America in the Twin Cities. Even after filtering out those congregations that don't measure up to the five categories just listed, chances are there's something for every imaginable taste within a reasonable driving distance from where you live. And speaking of the largest mall in the world, church shopping is appropriate. As a matter of fact, it's recommended.

Church hopping, on the other hand, is not a healthy practice. When you make your choice of a home church a matter of prayer (and ask the Lord to guide you in the selection process), don't be apt to up and move on. Sink roots. Make a commitment. With the same commitment you express to members of a biological family, live out unflinching loyalty to this group of people who are, in actuality, members of Christ's family and thus people to whom you are related.

Sadly, sometimes the difficult decision must be made to leave a church. But those decisions should be rare and extremely painful.

Far too many people bail out and break their membership vows to a congregation when working through issues of preference or personality, when staying might have resulted in a deeply meaningful experience of Christian growth and joy.

Daily Reflection Questions

Day One

1 What is worship?

2 What do your non-religious friends "worship"?

3 What do the object of a person's worship and his or her style of worship say about that person and God?

Day Two

1 In what ways do people put God "in a box"?

2 Why is "doing worship right" a non-negotiable for followers of Christ?

3   What is the essence of true worship of the one, true God?

Day Three

1   What do you usually receive from a typical local church worship service? (Psalm 73:17)

2   How does your home church's worship services help your life of worship?

In what ways do they hinder your worship?

3   In what ways is your worship hindered or impaired by what you bring to the services?

Day Four

1   What could you do before the service to be better prepared for worship?

2 What could you do during the service to worship more effectively?

3 What could you do to help your family get more out of worship?

Day Five

1 What factors have you considered when choosing a home church in the past?

2 What makes a local fellowship part of the *true* church?

3 What will it take for you to be more committed to your local assembly?

CHAPTER NINE

THE CHRISTIAN LIFE: HOW IT WORKS (OBEDIENCE)

Obedience—now there's a word with which we have a love/hate relationship. When it comes to a puppy that has chewed a pair of $300 Bruno Magli shoes, we'll pay a small fortune to enroll the confounded canine in obedience school. When it comes to insisting that our toddlers or teenagers comply with our wishes (be it not putting a finger in an electrical outlet or being home by midnight), we're unflinching advocates of the importance of obedience. But when it comes to us obeying the speed limit or the handicap-only sign, our advocacy is a bit less impassioned. The same holds true when it comes to doing what we know God wants or avoiding what He prohibits. Obedience is something we're all for except when complying with what is demanded of us seems to inconvenience us.

Obedience Defined

> "Only he who believes is truly obedient and only he who is obedient truly believes."

Dietrich Bonhoeffer was a brilliant young Lutheran pastor in Germany who lived during the first half of the twentieth century. When Hitler attempted to hypnotize pastors and church leaders into thinking his regime was consistent with the teachings of Christianity, this stocky, blond, bespectacled theologian could not ignore what he saw as a gross violation against people created in God's image. Bonhoeffer led a courageous resistance movement that resulted in an underground church. In the process, he gained a first-hand knowledge of what it means to take God's values seriously. He identified the price tag associated with obeying the law of love. He referred to it as "the cost of discipleship." This thirty-something cleric was arrested and sent to a concentration camp where he was executed just two weeks before the allied forces liberated his cell. Before his death, Bonhoeffer wrote, **"Only he who believes is truly obedient and only he who is obedient truly believes."**

Even though obedience, or submission, is difficult for many Christians, it is at the heart of being a joyful Christ-follower.

That's why when we return to Howard Hendricks's basic definition of the Christian life, we find the "O" word: "Christianity is the life of Christ reproduced in the believer by the Holy Spirit through an **obedient** response to the Word of God invading every area of human experience."

What You Do with What You Know Matters Most

Obedience is the key to our ability to grow spiritually. Does that surprise you? After considering the importance of personal and public worship, you might get the idea that those activities are most important. But you would be wrong. Reading, studying, and meditating on God's Word is undeniably important too. But it doesn't guarantee growth like obedience will. Somehow we think that just exposing ourselves to the Bible will bring about the life it describes. Not so.

"Do not think of the holy life in all of its immensity, but about a moment of obedience in its individuality, because a holy life is simply the succession of these moments." – Ed Goodrick

Jesus' half-brother James wrote an epistle to first century Christians who would score high on book knowledge but low on street smarts. He wrote, "Do not merely listen to the word, and so deceive yourselves. Do what it says." He then explained the problem in a way that they (and we) could picture: "Anyone who listens to the word but does not do what it says is like a man who looks at his face in a mirror and, after looking at himself, goes away and immediately forgets what he looks like. But the man who looks intently into the perfect law that gives freedom, and continues to do this, not forgetting what he has heard, but doing it—he will be blessed in what he does" (James 1:22–25).

> "Do not merely listen to the word, and so deceive yourselves. Do what it says."
> *James 1:22*

To become a healthy follower of Christ, simply reading God's Word isn't adequate. Anyone can do that much, and many Sunday service attendees, who would call themselves "Christ-followers," do just that. Sadder still, many of these never read a word from Scripture except on Sunday. But reading the truth does not translate into doing what is right. Neither does understanding the truth. Only those who look into the mirror and then respond to what the reflection indicates are living the truth.

Just imagine the silliness of the following scenario. You have just finished lunch in a nice restaurant with someone you hope to win over as a client. The food was outstanding. Your interaction was even better. But too many cups of coffee have taken their toll. So you excuse yourself to visit the restroom before closing the deal. While washing your hands, you glance in the mirror above the sink and see you have a piece of spinach lodged between your teeth. You hadn't felt anything odd in your mouth so didn't know it was there. Instead of picking it out, however, you simply return to your potential customer at the table and carry on as if all is normal. Not the best way to impress a client!

Obviously, you never would do that with spinach in your teeth. But it's amazing how often people look into God's Word and see a reflection of their lives and simply refuse to act on what they know they should do. For example, if someone you know claims to be a Christian but consistently cheats on her taxes, something is terribly wrong. She knows what God thinks of deceit and corrupt business dealings, but she chooses not to alter her actions in accordance with what she knows is right. As you might guess, in spite of what she might say, if Christ lives in her, even as she disobeys Him, she is in inner turmoil and sicker than she realizes.

Disobedience leads to spiritual anorexia. The person becomes weak and lifeless and running on empty. King David wrote about a time when he had disregarded God's laws for his life. "When I kept silent, my bones wasted away through my groaning all day long. For day and night your [God's] hand was heavy upon me; my strength was sapped as in the heat of summer" (Psalm 32:3–4).

In stark contrast, a life of obedience brings inner joy. When we act in keeping with what we know God expects, we have no low-grade guilt or remorse or the need to try and fake what we feel inside. The deep, indescribable satisfaction that comes with honoring God by complying with His wishes is one of the obvious benefits of living a life of obedience.

> "When I kept silent, my bones wasted away through my groaning all day long."
> *Psalm 32:3*

Why Obey?

Obedience is a way to prove one's love for another. When your child purposely chooses to do what you have asked him to do (even though his little heart would rather do the opposite), what is going on? Compliance probably goes beyond simply valuing what you think. It's more than obeying in order to avoid discipline. More likely, your child's obedience flows from his love for you.

The same goes for you and your mate. The laws of Christian marriage prohibit infidelity. While standing before a preacher and a packed church you had agreed to God's demands. But after every wedding comes a marriage. That's when the "I do's" simply fall to the floor and break or are faithfully lived out so that they eventually become "I did's." Chances are you have found (or will find) yourself tempted to disregard the promises pledged at the altar. When you choose to keep your word and do what your mate expects (and longs for) you are proving that you really do love that person.

> "If you love me, you will obey what I command."
> *John 14:15*

The night before Jesus was betrayed, arrested, and crucified, He provided a litmus test of love for His followers. He said, "If you love me, you will obey what I command . . . Whoever has my commands and obeys them, he is the one who loves me. He who loves me will be loved by my Father, and I too will love him and show myself to him . . . If anyone loves me, he will obey my teaching. My Father will love him, and we will come to him and make our home with him. He who does not love me will not obey my teaching. These words you hear are not my own; they belong to the Father who sent me" (John 14:15, 21, 23–24). For Jesus, actions spoke louder than words. Anyone can profess to love another, but the one who complies with what is requested is more likely to be believed.

In fact, the quality of compliance is an indispensable factor that marks those who say they are loved by God and love Him in return. In that same conversation with His friends, Jesus said, "As the Father has loved me, so have I loved you. Now remain in my love. If you obey my commands, you will remain in my love, just as I have obeyed my Father's commands and remain in his love" (John 15:9–10).

For Jesus, a person's willingness to obey was the primary indicator of whether that person was truly committed to Him. Why else do you think Jesus would say, "You are my friends if you do what I command" (John 15:14)? There is no way to minimize the importance Jesus places on doing what is expected.

Obedience is a way of coming under the promises of God. Back in the days of the Old Testament, God made a covenant with the nation of Israel. This set of promises had to do with protection from enemies and plagues, guaranteed provisions, a reminder of His presence, and success both politically and economically. The only condition of the covenant was that the people of God continue to honor Him with obedient lives. God would do the work; all they had to do was remain in a committed, contented, and compliant relationship with Him. Although the promises God has given to us have more to do with our spiritual success, they require a walk of faith—acting on what we know to be true (see John 14:13–14).

> . . . as we obey God's commandments, His activity in our lives changes us.

In other words, as we obey God's commandments, His activity in our lives changes us. Obedience is a fertilizer that promotes healthy growth. It enables us to fully benefit from God's process of growing us into the likeness of His Son. The Apostle Paul thought deeply on that when he wrote, "Therefore, I urge you, brothers, in view of God's mercy, to offer your bodies as living sacrifices, holy and pleasing to God—this is your spiritual act of worship. Do not conform any longer to the pattern of this world, but be transformed by the renewing of your mind. Then you will be able to test and approve what God's will is—his good, pleasing and perfect will" (Romans 12:1–2). Becoming a living sacrifice means sacrificing our own whims and wants in order to obey what God wants. In the process of learning to do that, however, we begin to think more and more like Jesus and gain an even clearer understanding of what brings God pleasure (Hebrews 13:20–21). In fact, joy increases as we have an increased desire to do it.

We aren't the only ones who benefit from our obedience. Others who might not yet be Christians do as well. As you might guess, if we are consistently following the moral map God has laid out for us in the Bible, those who observe our lives will take notice. The reason is obvious. Such uncompromising devotion and loving commitment to others is uncommon in our culture. We will stand out. Jesus hinted at the fact that when we obey His command to make His glory and the love of others the overriding aim of our lives, people will know that we are different.

What Good Is Obedience?

Can't you hear the reaction of some? "Obey, obey, obey. Just what's the big deal with obedience? I thought Christianity was all about grace. Obedience smacks of legalistic performance. I don't get it."

Those who think that way are looking at obedience the wrong way. God isn't out to make our lives miserable by insisting on meaningless demands. His requirements dealing with sexual purity, fidelity, integrity, generosity, forgiveness, justice, and worship are not onerous have-to's meant to make life difficult. Instead, they are keys that unlock the secrets to happiness and fulfillment. The owner's manual that you get with your new car doesn't complicate your life. Those instructions (like changing the oil every 3,000 miles) are given to extend the life and performance of your car. The same is true with God. Everything He asks us to do is grounded in His love for us.

As stated earlier in this chapter, obedience to God's law is liberating. When we do what God expects, we are freed from guilt. That's the negative way of putting it. Try the positive spin. When we choose to obey the Lord, we feel good, joyful, and stress-free. Obedience simplifies life. If we are committed to always do what the Lord wants, we save ourselves having to make decisions about what to do all the time.

How Do We Obey?

Obedience may be the very best way to show that we believe. It is also one of the most difficult choices to make. A life of obedience isn't something we wake up one morning and decide to live out. It's a process of going three steps forward and two steps backward. Remember, as the beachhead metaphor illustrates, each person is still an enemy occupied island that is in the process of being liberated. The takeover takes longer than we had hoped. Though we belong to the Father and have been cleansed of our sin, we still have a sinful nature that resists doing what we know we should (1 Corinthians 9:27). Barreling down

> When we choose to obey the Lord, we feel good, joyful, and stress-free.

the freeway of faith toward a destination of *God's* choosing, we find ourselves choosing the nearest exit in order to do what seems more freeing for the moment.

If you are serious about learning obedience, you have to be honest with yourself and God. That means admitting that you have left the freeway. It means coming to the bottom of the exit ramp and asking yourself, "What am I doing here? I really don't want to be here. I blew it by blowing off God's desires in order to serve my own momentary needs." Once you have recognized your mistake by getting off the freeway, the next step is easy. Find the nearest on-ramp, get cleaned up, and gather speed (1 John 1:8–9).

In Psalm 32, David describes how he felt when he had willingly disobeyed God's directives. He explains how awful life was when he chose not to obey. But then comes the contrast when he chose to admit his folly and own his disobedience. He writes, "Then I acknowledged my sin to you and did not cover up my iniquity. I said, 'I will confess my transgressions to the Lord'—and you forgave the guilt of my sin" (Psalm 32:5).

Eugene Petersen (who wrote THE MESSAGE, a paraphrase of the Bible into modern language) wrote a book some time ago regarding the values required for a faith that has preserving quality. The title is priceless—*A Long Obedience in the Same Direction.* That's how we have to look at learning to obediently respond to the Word of God. It's a marathon not a sprint. It takes a lifetime, not a couple of tries. Hebrews 3:14 reads, "If we can only keep our grip on the sure thing we started out with, we're in this with Christ for the long haul" (THE MESSAGE). And as John Murray said just prior to going to be with the Lord, "Thank God for the active obedience of Christ."

Peter stands as another example of one who learned to obey. Before he was broken of his self-sufficiency, the formerly brash, overly confident fisherman struggled to understand and had not the power to follow Jesus' instructions. Even after he had received the promise of the Spirit and had grown in his faith, becoming a leader in the Jerusalem church, he struggled to obey what he knew to be God's will. In one situation, the Lord gave him a dream assuring him that Gentiles were no longer off-limits for Jews, but part of God's original master plan. But Peter and Paul got into a verbal battle royal when Peter refused to eat with Gentile converts. After years of sticking his foot in his mouth, a broken and wiser Peter wrote a couple of postcard-size epistles that today bear his name. In 1 and 2 Peter, we find the aging apostle now in pace with God's kingdom and much more inclusive in his manner of living before God and man.

> "I said, 'I will confess my transgressions to the Lord'—and you forgave the guilt of my sin."
> *Psalm 32:5*

The Consequences of Disobedience

When we choose to disregard the owner's manual that comes with our car, stuff happens. Not good stuff—bad stuff. The same is true when we choose to ignore God's directions when it comes to the sanctity of the marriage bed. We live in a cause and effect world. Even scientists who claim that God doesn't exist are willing to accept certain laws. Newton's Third Law indicates every action has an equal and opposite reaction. The Apostle Paul spoke of a similar law. He called this the law of the harvest: We reap what we sow.

Ultimate salvation from judgment does not eliminate the consequences of disregarding God's dictates. Those consequences are sadly called "wasted opportunities," "blown chances," "wounded family members," "compromised health," "disqualification for public ministry," and sometimes result in a shortened life.

Just as the Apostle Peter illustrates one who stayed with the process of learning how to obey God, Israel's first king illustrates the opposite. According to what we read in 1 Samuel 9:2, Saul is said to have stood head and shoulders above his peers in more ways than one. He was tall, handsome, and gifted. He had a heart for the Lord. He had a brilliant advisor in Samuel the prophet. Saul knew what he was supposed to do. He knew what God desired, and he knew he had the means to honor the Lord's wishes. Saul seemed to have it all.

But Saul struggled with pride and jealousy (1 Samuel 18:8). When Samuel advised the young king to wait for him before beginning a ceremony, Saul grew impatient and began slaughtering animals for the sacrificial offering (1 Samuel 13:9ff.). Saul who was tall in stature was a Pygmy when it came to humility. His ability to rationalize why it wasn't prudent to obey Samuel's orders proved to be his downfall. When Samuel finally arrived and realized that Saul had gone ahead without him, he undressed the king with a sharp tongue and a word from God. "To obey is better than sacrifice" (1 Samuel 15:22). Sadly for Saul, his inability to embrace obedience as a core value cost him his throne. It was after this willful transgression that the Lord prompted Samuel to anoint David as Saul's replacement.

Yes, disobedience has consequences. It might not be the loss of your job, but it could be. One thing is certain—not taking God's Word seriously will rob you of the joyful sense of God's presence He desires for you. On the other hand, the more you respond to the Word of God with appropriate action, the greater capacity you will have to understand the truth contained in His Book (Matthew 25:15ff.; Luke 12:48). In other words, when you act on what you know, the Lord opens your eyes and your heart to experience even more.

> "To obey is better than sacrifice."
> *1 Samuel 15:22*

That's what Jesus was getting at with His friends in the upper room. The love relationship that exists between the Father and the Son and the Son and His followers is maximized when those involved respond with faith and action.

Daily Reflection Questions

Day One

1 Why do we have a love/hate relationship with the word "obedience"?

2 Dietrich Bonhoeffer said, "Only he who believes is truly obedient, and only he who is obedient truly believes." What did he mean?

3 Why is obedience so important for Christians?

Day Two

1 What's wrong with simply reading and studying the Bible? Isn't that enough?

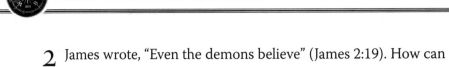

2　James wrote, "Even the demons believe" (James 2:19). How can that be?

3　So what's the relationship, then, between faith and works?

Day Three

1　How can a life of obedience to God bring joy?

2　What does a person's obedience say about his or her relationship with God?

3　How does obedience position you to receive God's promises?

Day Four

1　If obeying God's commandments changes us, what is He changing us into?

2 What does being a "living sacrifice" entail?

3 How do obedience and grace relate?

Day Five

1 If you are serious about learning obedience, what should be your first step?

2 What do you need to confess to God about your disobedience?

3 What two or three actions do you need to take, today, to obey what you know God is telling you?

CHAPTER TEN

WHY DO I NEED TO GIVE?

Happiness is not so much having as sharing. We make a living by what we get, but we make a life by what we give.

Norman MacEwan

Charles Swindoll tells the story of a man named Davis. During his ninety-two years of life, this reclusive farmer outside Lincoln, Nebraska, amassed a considerable fortune. He worked his way up from a hired hand to a successful rancher. In the process, however, he alienated himself from neighbors and extended family. Davis was so embittered when he learned that his in-laws thought their daughter (his wife) had married beneath her, he vowed that he would never leave them or their other children any of his estate.

When his wife died, the old man spent an incredible amount of money on monuments in her memory. He hired a sculptor to create a stone loveseat on which were perched the likeness of both his wife and himself. Then he commissioned another monument of himself kneeling at the grave of his wife, laying a wreath. After that he had a statue created of his wife with angelic wings depositing a wreath at his future grave. As more and more ideas came to his mind, he commissioned more and more works of art until he at last had spent more than a quarter of a million dollars.

However, when civic leaders approached him for a major contribution for a hospital, park, or swimming pool, Mr. Davis slammed the door in their faces, complaining that the community had never done anything for him. He continued to live detached and depressed, grieving for his deceased wife. By the time his miserly heart quit beating, he had exhausted his estate. He died broke and alone in the poorhouse. According to a published report, only one person even bothered to attend his funeral. You guess it—the tombstone salesman.

Sadly, he ended up a bitter man who never learned the joy of sharing with others, having lost scope on an eternal key to legacy investing (Matthew 16:26). In fact, those cherished monuments on which he wasted his money fell into disrepair as they gradually sank into the black Nebraska soil. Mr. Davis failed to realize that the secret to an abundant life is giving generously from what you have received.

> Mr. Davis failed to realize that the secret to an abundant life is giving generously from what you have received.

A Sign of Life

If you've ever traveled to the Holy Land, you belong to a special fraternity. You are among a minority of humanity. You've risked your life and limbs in a corner of the world with continuing political instability in order to see landmarks and landscapes of places mentioned in the Bible. If you were part of a fast-paced tour group that packed two weeks worth of excursions into seven days, you know what it's like to *run* where Jesus walked. You most likely saw the Church of the Nativity in Bethlehem and the Garden Tomb in Jerusalem.

Christian tourists on pilgrimage to Israel also make note of the stark contrast between the Sea of Galilee and the Dead Sea. The Sea of Galilee is fed by fresh water from the far north with the melting snows of Mount Hermon. The deep blue lake is only thirteen miles long and seven miles across, but it teems with a wide variety of fish. As was the case in Jesus' day, fishing boats continue to harvest a bounty that helps to fuel Israel's economy.

At the southern end of the Sea of Galilee, the famous Jordan River flows freely as it winds its way southward, separating Israel from its neighbors to the east. Eventually the Jordan empties into the Dead Sea—1,300 feet below sea level. It doesn't take a Rhodes scholar to understand how this sea got its name. The Dead Sea is so-called because no fish or organisms live in it. The salt concentration, six times that of the ocean, prevents the possibility of life.

The Sea of Galilee receives fresh water and it gives off fresh water. The Dead Sea receives fresh water but passes nothing on. Curious, don't you think? It is a great metaphor for life. People who have learned how to pass on their God-given resources to others are fresh and vital. Those who don't are stagnant and "dead."

You may have experienced the principle of "receiving and giving" firsthand in the context of a local church. Those who attend on a regular basis soak in what the pastor dishes out Sunday after Sunday. Bibles get marked up, and notebooks fill up. If you are blessed to have a gifted communicator of God's truth, each sermon is an anticipated feast. You eat it up and long for more. But you may be oblivious to the weekly notices in the bulletin crying out for the need for volunteers in the nursery, teachers in Sunday school, or attendants in the parking lot. After all, you go to church to get your tank filled, right?

Continually on the receiving end, we can grow indifferent toward the needs of others. In time this apathy is joined by a critical spirit toward others. What seemed to satisfy our appetite no longer does. A sweet spirit that once flowed through us like the Jordan River becomes bitter and disgusting like the Dead Sea.

> People who have learned how to pass on their God-given resources to others are fresh and vital.

This syndrome can happen with our finances as well. When we soak up the teachings of the local church without sharing in the ministry, we are apt to become sour and mildewy sponges that no one enjoys being around. The blessings that should flow through us to others become like stagnant water.

Pastors are criticized for preaching about money. In some cases this might be emphasized too often, but Jesus talked about money more than He did about heaven or hell. Much of Jesus' teaching dealt with stewardship: one sixth of the Gospels and one third of the parables deal with what people do with their money—and what that says about them and their priorities. As James Moffatt has said, "A man's treatment of money is the most decisive test of his character . . . how he makes it and how he spends it!" Or, as Fred Smith, Sr. has said, "I determine my life-style; my money doesn't." Jesus' teaching comes with a warning. Peter Marshall has well said, a man ought to "give according to his income lest God make your income according to your giving!"

The Savior knew that greed shrivels a person's heart and soul. Looking for more and more ways to get more and more money prevents a person from seeing the truth of life. (Think about it. Have you ever met someone who admitted they were too wealthy?) A preoccupation with income has a predictable outcome. It blinds you from seeing God's best for your life.

> "Give, and it will be given to you. . . . For with the measure you use, it will be measured to you."
> *Luke 6:38*

A Good Investment

Jesus also understood that sharing one's shekels liberates the heart from the prison of self-interest. The freedom that comes with being a conduit of blessings (whereby what God allows to flow into our lives is passed along to others) is only superseded by increased blessings. In other words, any attempts at generosity will be rewarded in kind. Jesus said, "Give, and it will be given to you. A good measure, pressed down, shaken together and running over, will be poured into your lap. For with the measure you use, it will be measured to you" (Luke 6:38). Would you call that incentive giving? You might just call it the way God wired His world.

If you grew up in Nebraska or Kansas, you know the truth of that principle. If you plant corn, you won't harvest pumpkins. You harvest what you sow. When you prepare the soil and then plant wheat, you will harvest wheat, not soybeans. A person doesn't have to grow up on a farm to understand the Law of the Harvest. The Bible puts it this way: "Do not be deceived: God cannot be mocked. A man reaps what he sows" (Galatians 6:7).

In terms of the Sea of Galilee, it's "fresh water in—fresh water out."

In terms of friendship, it's "A man who has friends must himself be friendly" (Proverbs 18:24, NKJV).

In terms of prayer, when you spend time talking to God, you are more capable of hearing God's still small voice speak to you.

With money, the Law of the Harvest means that a believer will always gain a return on what he or she gives away. Give to a person in need, and you will not go needy yourself. A life marked by a habit of being generous will be richly rewarded. That's right—*richly rewarded*—not necessarily in cash but in contentment and joy and with an amazingly clear perspective of just how abundant life really is. When you develop a pattern of giving you are making an investment in tomorrow.

> "A man who has friends must himself be friendly."
> *Proverbs 18:24, NKJV*

Joyful Life of a Faithful Steward

The inevitable benefits of investing in this "futures market" are but one practical reason to give your hard-earned income away. There's also a spiritual reason: God requires that we give of our wealth. In the Old Testament, God made it clear that His people should dedicate ten percent of their income and return it to Him (Genesis 14:20; Deuteronomy 14:22; Malachi 3:8). This contribution of first fruits was called a tithe (which means a tenth). For the Hebrews, first fruits were literally that—fruit, grain, and livestock. The currency of their agrarian lifestyle was not coins and cash but what they would grow and gather or raise and offer.

God's insistence that His people contribute a portion of what they produced was God's creative way to remind the Hebrews that they were tenants on earth. Their tithe was much like a rent check, regularly reminding them that they could not live independent of their Creator. When they gave a percentage of what they had worked hard to amass, they were forced to come to terms that all they had ultimately had come from God. As it says in Psalm 24:1, "The earth is the Lord's, and everything in it, the world, and all who live in it." Giving a tenth of their livestock and produce helped the people learn to revere God's holiness and recognize His ability to provide for them. We catch the purpose of tithing in this edict from Moses: "Be sure to set aside a tenth of all that your fields produce . . . that you may learn to revere the Lord your God always" (Deuteronomy 24:22–23).

> "The earth is the Lord's, and everything in it, the world, and all who live in it."
> *Psalm 24:1*

For God's people today, the principle of the tithe is a good beginning point but, not obligatory. When reading the New Testament, you can't help but understand that all of our possessions belong to God, not just ten percent (Psalm 24:1; 104:24). We are stewards of what God has entrusted to us. It is all at His disposal and we must hold loosely what we claim as hard earned. When we are convinced that what we have isn't ultimately ours, we can let it go a little bit more easily and properly live as a steward (the manager of another's property).

Giving What Is Not Owned

One golfer in the Seattle area refuses to play with new golf balls. For one reason, his modest salary causes him to grimace at the rising cost of green fees let alone dole out additional dollars for the extras. Gregg just can't bring himself to pay $10 for a sleeve of three balls. While his thrifty approach to the game that originated in Scotland seems strangely appropriate, the cost of new golf balls is not the only reason he balks at doing what most golfers consider normal. For Gregg, if you pay full-price you are more apt to psyche yourself out hitting over a water hazard. After all, you are aware of how much you spent on that silly ball and you sure hope it doesn't end up in the bottom of the lake because that would be a waste of money. Thus preoccupied, you aren't free to simply swing away. Time and time again, that expensive ball takes a swim. The same is true of losing a ball in the rough or out of bounds. If you've just plopped down good money, you feel obligated to look for the lost ball. Not only does such a search break the rhythm of your game, it frustrates the foursome behind you.

So what does Gregg do? Following a round of golf (or on another day off), he'll wander through the woods bordering the golf course in search of balls that others have lost. By building up a stockpile of almost-new used balls, this golfing cleric has discovered a new freedom in swinging away. Since he didn't buy the ball to begin with, he isn't overly upset when he is forced to part with it. When we view what we have as something we've inherited from someone else, the power of possession loses its grip on us. As a result, we lessen our grip on it.

But it's not just the promise of reward or our place as stewards that should motivate our generosity. Perspective should make a difference. That is, in light of how little life we have left to live, why not give away more than our inbred, selfish hearts are inclined to? We need a realistic view of what really matters in life and in death. Have you ever seen a hearse pulling a U-Haul trailer? No way. You can't take any of your earthly possessions with you when you move from a 2,800 square foot brick front Georgian home to a three by seven foot box six feet beneath the grass. As Oswald Chambers has said, "You can't take it with you, but you can send it on ahead!"

Don't be like old Mr. Davis. He spent a fortune on gravestones that marked the final resting place of his wife's decaying body. Instead, determine today to be a generous person who gives freely of the good things God has enabled you to acquire, that the borders of His kingdom might be increased.

... in light of how little life we have left to live, why not give away more than our inbred, selfish hearts are inclined to?

Giving Guidelines

By way of suggestion, you might want to order your giving to Christian causes as follows:

1. Give to the ministries that you and your family have benefited from and that depend on your generous partnership (Galatians 6:6). Here is a way to evaluate the value of a good spiritual investment—look for places where they are attempting to make Christ known in a variety of ways, looking in the areas of (1) Scope of Outreach, (2) Growth of Missions, (3) Multiplication, (4) Urgency, and (5) Impact. That is investing in good soil!

2. Prayerfully ask God what missionaries you should invest in. This would include those who serve overseas as well as those with para-church or local organizations.

3. Be responsive to causes in your community that benefit those who have physical needs and are disadvantaged.

4. Why not get into the habit of carrying a $20 bill in your pocket each day. Designate that as God's money. When you encounter someone who is in dire need or someone you feel impressed to give that money to, offer it as a gift from God (not from you).

Daily Reflection Questions

Day One

I Who reminds you of Mr. Davis?

In what ways?

2   What did Mr. Davis lose by how he spent his fortune?

Day Two

1   What's the main difference between the Sea of Galilee and the Dead Sea?

2   What makes the Dead Sea dead?

3   In what ways are people like the Dead Sea?

Day Three

1   What is the principle of "receiving and giving"?

2 What happens to a person who constantly gives but doesn't receive?

3 What results in the life of a person who continually receives but doesn't give?

Day Four

I Why does sharing of our finances liberate our hearts from the prison of self-interest?

2 What is the "Law of the Harvest"?

3 What does being a good steward of God's resources involve?

Day Five

1   What giving goals have you set for yourself?

2   What do you need to do to be a better steward of God's resources?

A more generous giver?

3   What steps will you take in the next month to move you in that direction?

PRIORITY
TWO

A Personal, Progressive Commitment to Yourself

This seems like a self-serving priority, to be committed to yourself. After all, doesn't Jesus present the ideal follower as one who lives out the teaching of the Beatitudes or the Sermon on the Mount? Those who are a part of His kingdom are blessed when they are poor in spirit, mourning, meek, merciful, peacemakers, and willing to suffer as one of His disciples. That sounds like the opposite of being committed to self.

This priority is not about being self-centered or selfish. It is about seeing yourself as God sees you, near the apex of His creation. "What is man that you are mindful of him?" (Hebrews 2:6). "God created man in his own image, in the image of God he created him; male and female he created them" (Genesis 1:27).

David was overwhelmed when he realized how special he was in the eyes of God (Psalm 139) and though he knew how easy it was to be offensive in His sight, it never changed the fact that God loved him and adored him as one of His children.

It takes a long time to really believe what David proclaimed. Our lives are a composition of both happiness and sorrow, accomplishments and defeat, obedience and horrid behavior. It also takes an understanding of how to grow spiritually, physically, mentally, emotionally, and socially.

All of us, at some point in our lives, have been profoundly impacted by another human being who pulled us out of a pit or shined a light in the darkness. They did so because they had something to offer. There was a reservoir of strength; there were assets they could draw on. At some point they made a personal commitment to grow and so they learned how life works with the faculties God equipped us. We are complex people with bodies, minds, emotions, and the need for social interaction. We aren't all full of strength in each of these areas by accident. In fact, many Christians find that their love for Christ hasn't made them a positive person or one who never battles depression or who has the ability to automatically forgive someone who as hurt them deeply.

It only happens when we deliberately and regularly add deposits of knowledge and experience that transform us into a person who can serve and minister to others out of the wealth of our own transformation.

That's what **Priority Two** is about. We never fully arrive, but that's why we say it is a personal, *progressive* commitment. Join us on this journey to personal growth and watch what happens.

CHAPTER ELEVEN

PHYSICAL ASSETS: THE AGING PROCESS—EXERCISE AND REST

Man's days are determined; you have decreed the number
of his months and have set limits he cannot exceed.

Job 14:5

How long do you want to be productive? Be truthful, now. Many people think they want to be active and engaged in meaningful work into their eighties. Sounds good, but they either fail to realize what it will take to reach such a goal, or they are unwilling to pay the price.

Louis is the president and CEO of a Fortune 500 company, who is nearing retirement. He has lots of energy and a passion to make a significant contribution, and he is seeking the next assignment God has for him. He thinks it will be with a Christian organization and eagerly waits to shift his focus from bottom-line issues to meeting the needs of people who are having a difficult time in life.

This is a common venture for those in the second half of life. They are in the process of moving from success to significance. They have made their mark, now they want to serve their Maker.

This approach has several pitfalls. One is to assume that making one's mark in the corporate world is not significant. For many people, God's will is that they serve Him faithfully in the offices of business, education, industry, or government. Joseph was called to the upper echelon of the Egyptian hierarchy and saved both the Egyptian people from starvation and also his Jewish family who was threatened by the famine.

The second pitfall is to assume that one will have the health, energy, money, and passion to pursue a second career in the nonprofit world. It would be good to take a look at the aging process and understand the physical changes that take place over time. Many people anticipate what it will take to survive financially over many decades but pay no attention to the toll of time on their bodies.

So let's ask a few questions. The answers are from Finn R. Amble, M.D, of the Carle Clinic in central Illinois, who received his training at the Mayo Clinic. He provided current research for this chapter as well as chapter 12.

> How long do you want to be productive?

When Does Aging Begin?

"Senescence," or aging, is the progressive deterioration of virtually every bodily function over time. If we view our bodies as personal laboratories, we can see one of the first signs of physical decline is joint-stiffness. As Peter Medawar, the Nobel Prize-winning immunologist, once put it, "What lays a young man up may lay his senior out." While this is referring to age and immunity in specific, it can be used to describe physical performance in general.

Dr. Amble asks, "At what point do you think your body begins to age? 40 years old? 50 years old?" In reality the body begins to age much earlier, at about 10 or 11 years of age, or just before puberty. After age 25, the body has a decreased ability to keep up with the deterioration process. **We also know that physical decline, once begun, is followed by a decline of 1 percent per year up until the elderly years at which time the rate of decline accelerates.**

Virtually all components of performance capacity decline with age. The slowest rate of decline involves the nervous system's ability to transmit signals while higher rates of deterioration are seen in other functions such as lung capacity and muscle strength. Wisdom is one function that increases with experience, but wisdom does not help us hit a ball farther or jump higher.

The maximum human life span has remained consistent at 115 to 120 years. Despite this, the average life expectancy has increased with each generation. In the twentieth century, average longevity increased from 48 years to more than 75 years in the United States. Over this span, however, the rate of aging has not changed significantly. What changed in the past century is our ability to combat infectious disease, the quality of our water, the sanitary conditions in which our food is stored and prepared, and a host of other public-health measures. Therefore, while our likelihood to live to an older age is greater than in years past, we are unable to affect the rate at which our bodies deteriorate.

Are genetics important? "My grandparents lived into their nineties so surely I can expect to live at least as long, right?" Not necessarily. Approximately 25 percent of the aging process is genetic. A study of several hundred Danish twins born between 1870 and 1880 who survived at least to adulthood found that about 20 to 30 percent of the variability in life span could be attributed to genetic effects. To put this in perspective, height is about 65 percent heritable and IQ studies typically find that genes explain 40 to 80 percent of variability. So the effects of genetics on longevity are not huge, but they are present. **The good news is that we have the opportunity to affect**

> Virtually all components of performance capacity decline with age.

approximately 75 percent of the aging process. In other words, genetics does *not* equal physical destiny!

What Is Happening to Us as We Age?

Many normal physiological changes occur during aging. The most significant change is probably that of body composition. Lean body mass includes such components as bone, muscle, and connective tissue. Lean mass can be viewed as what is left of the body after all water volume has been removed. What we experience with this lean body mass reduction over the years is primarily a result of skeletal muscle loss. This loss in muscle mass accounts for age-associated decreases in the body's metabolic rate, muscle strength, and activity levels. Unfortunately, our decreasing caloric needs are not always associated with a decreased caloric intake (see chapter on diet and weight control). Subsequently, the body learns to convert this extra energy to fat. Thus, resistance exercise plays such an important role in optimal physical health, in tandem with aerobic training.

> Genetics does *not* equal physical destiny!

How Can We Impact the Aging Process?

Any financial advisor will be quick to show that the sooner one begins to save money, the greater the ultimate result. But often this advice is neglected. How many of us have learned about 401Ks or the stock market and regret not having invested earlier? If financial health is important, how much more so is our physical and mental health? Clearly, the earlier we start, the better. The adage "Today is the first day of the rest of your life" holds particularly true here. On the other hand, if you have not begun to address your health until later in life, you can start now. **Remarkable improvements in fitness are being proven daily in the elderly who begin weight training, regardless of their age.**

Aging with Grace: What Happens as We Age?

Someone has said, "Age is a high price to pay for maturity." But what does aging *gracefully* mean? That question has many answers. Such definitions will take on personal characteristics unique to our individual perspectives. Aren't you inspired by elderly individuals who appear to be in good physical, as well as mental, shape? Finn Amble met an 84-year-old former naval petty officer and current pilot who is riding his 32nd motorcycle in addition to keeping physically active farming with his son. When asked his secrets for staying so mentally sharp and physically fit, he replied, "Well, the Bible has a lot to do with it." Then he added, "I used to do barbells until my arthritis got me.

And I try not to eat enough to give me a belly." Dr. Amble's personal hero of the aging process is his 75-year-old mother. Over the past seven years, she has vigorously climbed the second highest mountain in Norway, has taken a 32-mile day hike and has completed her first half marathon. Her youthful outlook on life is a key component to her physical youth.

So how can we *stop* the effects of aging on our bodies? The answer is that we cannot. Any text or video program that says otherwise is wrong. But there is much we *can* do.

Exercise and Effects on Aging

Think about how long it has taken for our bodies to reach their current state. Adam and Eve were not placed into the garden to e-mail one another business transactions. From the beginning of humanity, ours has been a very physical existence involving strength and endurance. Now we struggle to find time for physical activity in our frequently sedentary work life. With time increasingly scarce to achieve such an important goal, we must therefore address health intelligently. Does that mean that it is bad if we decide to just get outside and take a long walk? Absolutely not. But we should ask, "Just what types of exercise should we pursue?" Do we jog, or walk for hours on end? Do we attack weight lifting like a body builder? Does it make sense for a twenty-year-old male to pursue yoga or a sixty-year-old woman to pump iron?

We might wonder: "Does exercise make a difference in how long we live?" If we were rats, the information would be clear. A number of studies have examined rats that typically live to about two years of age. In one experiment, rats were randomly assigned to exercise or sedentary groups at early ages and life span was recorded. Voluntary running in a cage wheel increased life span of rats, both male and female, by 15–20 percent (according to studies by David Lamb, *Physiology of Exercise, Response and Adaptations*). One can speculate about the results of the same type of study involving humans. We can safely assume that humans would have similar results.

So what type of exercise is helpful for aging gracefully? We now know that *both* aerobic and strength conditioning are important. That just makes sense. What good is being stronger when we cannot walk a mile? Similarly, strengthening the many muscles we have that are not gravity dependent is crucial to joint stability and optimal metabolism. Are we getting too old to think about a true commitment to exercise? The answer is NO. **There is no general point at which we are "too old" to benefit from exercise.** When physical therapists are asked if those suffering from arthritis can safely participate in an exercise

So how can we *stop* the effects of aging on our bodies? The answer is that we cannot.

program, they are quick to answer that regular, moderate-level exercise brings little risk of damage to joints. Safe physical activity such as that in an aquatic environment actually protects against the development of chronic disease and disability. In spite of well-documented evidence that physical activity is beneficial, only 30 percent of individuals over the age of 65 report exercising regularly. On January 13, 2005, *USA Today*'s front page featured the Dietary Guidelines for Americans 2005, published by the U.S. Department of Health and Human Services and Agriculture. In these pages was found the recommendation of *one hour of exercise per day.*

We are clearly blessed, therefore, with the ability to improve our physical status at any age and set the stage for an improved aging experience. A veteran tennis coach, Jack Sanford, once stated, "There is no such thing as a self-motivated athlete." This might explain why there is such a lack of exercise around us and perhaps we even experience it ourselves. The question then is, what better motivator can we have than our Lord, and how would He want us to take care of ourselves?

What about Rest?

A missionary once said, "I'd rather burn out than rust out." But are those our only options? People ready to burn out attach their spiritual significance to their self-importance and take pride in whizzing through life without taking a breath. Those who "rust out" are either lazy or have no plans that are engaging their energy. They may live a long time, but so what?

> "God blessed the seventh day and made it holy, because on it he rested."
> *Genesis 2:3*

God knew we needed breathing room, or space between vitality and exhaustion. He called it a "day of rest." "By the seventh day God had finished the work he had been doing; so on the seventh day he rested from all his work. And God blessed the seventh day and made it holy, because on it he rested from all the work of creating that he had done" (Genesis 2:2–3).

Jewish rabbis refer to this as a day to let our souls catch up with our bodies. In fact, "Sabbath" actually means, "to catch one's breath."

Some Bible teachers refer to the importance of having a *balanced life.* That is, we are to be balanced physically, socially, mentally, and spiritually. A more accurate metaphor, however, is rhythm.

Scripture says, "There is a time for everything, and a season for every activity under heaven: a time to be born and a time to die, a time to plant and a time to uproot" (Ecclesiastes 3:1–2). Let's stop there. Farmers know they have a narrow window of opportunity to get the seed in the ground. At that point, they don't need to balance their physical and social life; they need to work, and for long hours. Once the job is completed, then they can rest; in fact, they need rest. That rhythm is taught in Scripture. Remember, Jesus said, "The Sabbath was made for man, not man for the Sabbath" (Mark 2:27).

It's also interesting to watch the pace at which Jesus lived. Even though He was in constant demand, we never read "Jesus ran over to Samaria," or "Jesus jogged to Bethany." He had a mission, and He knew where He was going. But He also knew that from time to time He needed to get away. Like any human, Jesus could be both physically and spiritually drained.

Like one preacher said, "If you don't come apart to rest a while, you will come apart."

> "The Sabbath was made for man, not man for the Sabbath."
> *Mark 2:27*

Daily Reflection Questions

Day One

1 With which of the pitfalls do you most identify?

2 What physical changes have you noticed in yourself over the past few years?

How do you feel about those changes?

3   When do you most feel your age?

Day Two

1   In what ways has your wisdom grown through the years?

2   How do you feel about your diminishing physical abilities?

3   How have you seen your life reflect your genetic heritage in the physical area?

Day Three

1   What does the adage, "Today is the first day of the rest of your life" mean to you?

2 What does it mean to age gracefully?

3 What's the opposite of aging gracefully?

Day Four

1 What is your regular exercise routine?

2 How do you get needed rest?

3 What's wrong with the statement "I'd rather burn out than rust out"?

Day Five

1 Why is taking care of the body a spiritual issue?

2 Why is "rhythm" a good metaphor for how we should take care of ourselves?

3 What changes do you need to make in exercise and rest?

CHAPTER TWELVE

PHYSICAL ASSETS: DIET AND WEIGHT CONTROL

America is obsessed with talking about food and weight control. The food channel on cable TV creates mouth-watering cuisine so enticing you can almost smell the aroma coming through your set.

Those who have succumbed to these tempting recipes, however, are soon discussing the latest diet fad in the company break room. Who has the best formula for losing weight? Is it South Beach or Mediterranean? Atkins or Ornish? Weight-Watchers or the Caveman Diet? It's all so confusing.

In the opinion of physician Finn Amble, who wrote this chapter, doctors create even more tension by being overweight themselves and experimenting with a variety of diets. The starting point for clarity on the subject is to determine what is known and what is not known.

> America is obsessed with talking about food and weight control.

What We Know

Calorie Intake

The often used crude analogy states, "There are no overweight products of concentration camps." Just dropping the pounds is not helpful or a positive goal. On the other hand, as one physician-colleague, Dr. Bina Patel, says, "It's simple. If it doesn't go in, it doesn't stay on." Though appearing to be overly simplistic at first glance, that concept has significant merit. Caloric restriction is a fundamental principle in most diets. One reason many people lose weight on diets is that they pay more attention to how much they eat. Often we'll hear that diets don't work. That's usually true. The fundamental "take home point" is, weight management needs to be a *lifestyle change*, not a "quick fix." Caloric restriction is a cornerstone principle towards this end.

Metabolism and Muscle Mass

Beginning at approximately age 25, we lose 1 percent of muscle mass per year. That means that if we are at the same weight at 45 years as we were at 25, we are many pounds the fatter. If we exercise well and regularly, we can decrease the rate of muscle loss. This is not only important for personal well-being but also for weight control. Your muscular system is a major driver of metabolism. The better your muscular system, the better your ability to burn fat.

Exercise and Diet

The two must go hand-in-hand to effectively control weight. At a national cardiology meeting held in Chicago, conclusive evidence was produced to show that exercise has a dose-dependent benefit on cardiovascular health. Furthermore, the more we exercise, regardless of the time intervals, the more our overall health, as well as weight management, is benefited.

What We Do Not Know

That is a bold heading. Dr. Phil, Bill Philips, and others seem to *know* the answers to weight loss. The beauty of science is that, generally speaking, there is *one* truth. For example, either insulin helps diabetes or it does not. Granted, a spectrum may be involved, but we know that the scale has positive and negative ends. Either vitamin E is worthwhile using at a certain dose in the prevention of Alzheimer's disease, or it is not. Go to any bookstore and look at the plethora of books on diet. Do they express doubt about their approaches? No. Can they all be the perfect answer? It would seem unlikely. The Mediterranean Diet favors whole wheat breads and fruit, for instance. In the Atkins Diet, these are to be shunned. What is the truth? Is there a "truth"?

What Do the Experts Say?

One medical director for a weight-loss program of a major clinic said: "Diets don't work." More insightful comments included: "Obesity is a chronic illness. Our (intensive medical) approach is a high protein, modified fast. It has nothing to do with Atkins. Behavioral changes are important, and it has to be a long-term program. If you don't continue with something, the weight will go right back. People need more than to do the diet themselves."

A dietician at the same clinic stated, "Beware of a diet that takes an entire food group totally out of the picture. We are having good results with high protein, actually moderate protein diets, but they are not for everyone . . . for example, vegetarians. Diets need to go along with resistance exercise. Our approach keeps vegetables and grains. You need to balance proteins and carbohydrates. Caloric restriction is still important."

Already we see a divergence within the same medical center. What do physicians do for themselves? A personal survey of a number of physicians revealed a greater emphasis on proteins in addition to caloric restriction. Over two-thirds of this small group of physicians have kept their weight down. Obviously, others have not. Sound familiar?

Age does not help. During adolescence, just thinking of doing a

> What is the truth? Is there a "truth"?

sit-up could melt away the unwelcome "handles." As an adult, such an accomplishment takes three weeks with caloric restriction, careful food selection, and increased exercise. At the pivotal age of 40, it takes four weeks. In the meantime, what information do we have available to us? Let's take a look at what the experts have to say:

Andrew Weil, MD

In a book entitled *The Healthy Kitchen*, Dr. Weil does a nice job summarizing the present state of knowledge: "You can lose weight on any kind of a diet; the trick is to keep it off by finding a healthful way of eating you can live with and a regimen of physical activity you can stick to. For initiating weight loss, more people find a low-carbohydrate regimen easier and more satisfying than a low-fat one, and medical research strongly supports the idea that many people are carbohydrate sensitive as a result of their genetic makeup. Carbohydrate-sensitive individuals are particularly susceptible to weight gain if they eat refined carbs—that includes products made with flour or sugar, for example. But that does not mean they should follow the Atkins diet, which is overloaded with meat and deficient in fruits and vegetables. I do not recommend it for more than short-term dieting—six weeks or less. As a long-term strategy, this way of eating puts too much of a workload on the kidneys and undermines body defenses against cancer and other chronic diseases that tend to show up later in life." He goes on to advocate a vegetarian approach with care to avoid deficiencies of essential fats, proteins, and micronutrients.

The Mediterranean Diet

In her book on this topic entitled *The Mediterranean Diet Cookbook*, author Nancy Harmon Jenkins quotes the famous Harvard 1993 study advocating: "Plentiful fruits, vegetables, legumes and grains; olive oil as the principal fat; lean red meat consumed only a few times per month or somewhat more often in very small portions; low to moderate consumption of other foods from animal sources, such as dairy products (especially cheese and yogurt), fish and poultry; and moderate consumption of wine (primarily at meals)." What name will you not find in the index of this particular book? (Hint: see next paragraph.)

Dr. Atkins' New Diet Revolution

Is a "boast" the way to start? He does so to get your attention in his book by the same title. "Atkins is the most successful weight loss—and weight maintenance—program of the last quarter of the twentieth century." Other statements include, "Most obesity is the result of metabolic disturbances, not over-consumption of fats; low-fat diets

Let's take a look at what the experts have to say:

are in effect high-carbohydrate diets and bring on the very problems that they were intended to protect us from. The Atkins approach is composed of protein and fat—even if you are not trying to lose weight, avoid the typical high-carb breakfast choices such as toast, muffins, bagels and cereal." Many have had success with this approach in the short term. The longer term remains to be seen.

Mayo Clinic

The *New Mayo Clinic Cookbook* does not delve in great detail into the debate between various approaches. Its approach is really more akin to the Mediterranean diet approach, recommending "the Mayo Clinic Health Weight Pyramid." As noted in the foreword: "Although the Pyramid was designed as a weight-control tool, it can easily be put to use by everyone interested in eating wisely for better health." The Pyramid emphasizes vegetables and fruits followed by carbohydrates with the smallest portions being fats, then sweets. Protein and dairy products fall in the middle, with a strong and appropriate emphasis on daily physical activity. Further wisdom is imparted as follows: "Without an eye to how much we eat, it's easy to take in too many calories, the food energy that fuels our bodies. Excess calories turn to excess weight, a health concern of its own. To maintain a healthy weight, try to eat only as much food as your body can burn in a day—1,600 to 2,800 calories for most adults." Fundamental principles include, "Think variety and balance; favor vegetables and fruits; eat more whole grains; choose smart proteins; use good types of fat; save sweets for treats."

Weight Loss Kit for Dummies

While addressing many erroneous thoughts about the topic of weight loss, the book comes up thin in clear comparison of the different approaches. But guess what shape you will find to dietary recommendations? Hint: found in Egypt and the shape you do not want for your own body. In this case, it is the Food Guide Pyramid. The book has a general review of multiple approaches as well as many salient pieces of advice such as whether you even need to lose weight, as well as having the correct mind-set, both of critical importance.

Confused yet? What does Bob Greene of Oprah fame have to say on the topic? The back of the book jacket has a picture of strawberries, oranges, a pear, olive oil, water, and healthy bread—if that gives you an idea. His take on proteins? "I wish I had a pat answer, but the truth is that how much protein you need is a very individual issue." What does Dr. Arthur Agatston, author of the South Beach Diet, have to say about the competition? "The major problem I have with the Atkins Diet is the liberal intake of saturated fats . . . the biggest problem that

I see in the Ornish approach is one that he readily acknowledges: It is very difficult to follow." And the view of Bill Philips, author of *Eating for Life* as well as *Body for Life*? "Don't let protein pushers, who proclaim the power of their 'source' to be superior to any other, persuade and override your intuition. The power of protein is in the variety, the satiety, the health-enhancing, muscle-strengthening effects . . ." Do the premier athletes have a clear answer? Michael Jordan would have a steak and potato dinner before games, while Lance Armstrong weighs his whole grain/complex carbohydrates prior to training. And the Macrobiotic Diet? When a book about this diet begins by explaining its principles with the "Order of the Universe" as well as the "Dietary Order According to Yin and Yang," this reader's universe rapidly falls out of order.

So What about the Medical Literature?

Let's assume you have restricted your calories. What should those calories be made up of? The observations beginning in this chapter were made from following this subject over the past twenty-four years with an interest in athletics, heart disease prevention, and staying in overall good shape. These do not a research scientist make. So what does a physician do when there are questions? Go to the medical literature.

The World Health Organization estimates that 1.2 billion people worldwide are affected by overweight and obesity, and the numbers are increasing at an unprecedented rate.

Ninety percent of long-term weight maintainers consume a diet with 20 to 30 percent of energy from fat, restrict total energy intake, and participate in regular physical activity. Only 9 percent of the National Weight Registry sample maintain weight loss by diet alone, and only 1 percent achieve weight maintenance by physical activity alone.

Basic treatment of overweight and obese patients requires a comprehensive approach involving diet and nutrition, regular physical activity, and behavioral change, with an emphasis on long-term weight management rather than short-term extreme weight reduction.

Increasing evidence suggests that obesity is not a simple problem of willpower or self-control, but a complex disorder involving appetite regulation and energy metabolism.

Some individuals may become overweight or obese partly because they have a genetic or biologic predisposition to gain weight readily. In most cases, however, the increasing prevalence of overweight and obesity reflects changes in society and behaviors over the past 20 to 30 years.

The World Health Organization estimates that 1.2 billion people worldwide are affected by overweight and obesity, and the numbers are increasing at an unprecedented rate.

To maintain a healthy weight, good dietary habits must be coupled with increasing physical activity, and these must become permanent lifestyle changes.

Obesity should be considered a chronic disease that can cause serious medical complications, an impaired quality of life, and premature mortality. Approximately 61 percent of adults (ages 20–74 years) in the United States are overweight or obese.

The prevalence of obesity has increased markedly among children and adolescents. **Obesity is caused by regularly ingesting foods containing more energy than is expended over a long period of time.** A very small but chronic positive energy balance can lead to an increase in body fat.

An expert panel convened by the National Institutes of Health (NIH) and the North American Society for the Study of Obesity has developed treatment guidelines for obesity. An initial evaluation is needed to identify which patients need obesity management and to determine what form of therapy is most appropriate for each individual.

Meal replacements can enhance weight loss by helping control portion size and energy intake. Obese persons tend to underestimate their energy intake because they underestimate serving sizes or they fail to identify "hidden" calories from fat and sugar in the food.

The use of low-carbohydrate (high-protein and high-fat) diets has received renewed interest as a potential weight-management tool. Although such diets were introduced more than 100 years ago to treat obesity, no randomized controlled long-term trials have evaluated the safety and efficacy of this dietary approach.

Many different dietary programs are available, but the patient should find the approach practical, sustainable, enjoyable, and healthful. Studies show that people who keep diet records are more successful at weight loss than those who don't keep track of their intake.

The exercise chosen should be enjoyable, made a priority in the schedule, and most importantly, performed consistently over time.

Keys to success include creating an individualized approach based on each patient's specific health risks and habits, using various resources (for example, support groups and registered dieticians), and encouraging and empowering patients to become active participants in their weight-loss program.

> Many different dietary programs are available, but the patient should find the approach practical, sustainable, enjoyable, and healthful.

Conclusions

Where does all of this bring us? The satellite image shows clearly that obesity in the United States is at a crisis level as is being experienced in other countries as well. The U.S. Surgeon General has appropriately declared obesity an epidemic.

As to each of us as individuals, what is the clear answer? Can we tell the future? In five to ten years from now, we will know much better how best to optimally pursue weight loss/control in a healthy manner. Caloric restriction will remain a fundamental cornerstone to optimizing the temples we know as our bodies. The ultimate answers will steer us away from processed foods, and long-term healthy weight control will include vegetables and fruit. Remember the age-old maxim "everything in moderation." Fish will remain a good idea, likely followed by poultry and pork. Other predictions? We can likely tolerate more protein than has been classically taught, and exercise will largely retain a dose-dependant relationship to good health. As a general observation, similar to addictions, a person with weight control problems needs to decide that he or she is serious about addressing the problem and then become committed to a lifestyle change. At that point, pursuit of the guidelines above has a significant chance for long-term success. Just reading about physical fitness will clearly not achieve it.

What is your specific situation? Talk to your physician (for example, are you prone to diabetes or do you have a history of cardiovascular disease?). If standard measures are not getting you to your goal, consider a monitored, reputable weight loss clinic with medical oversight. **This has to be a lifestyle change.** Surgical options are increasingly being refined, but these are reserved for those who have clearly shown that they are unable to have success with aggressive dietary changes.

The old adage is true. "You only live life once. But if you live right, once is enough." Is it not time to adopt this approach with our own bodies? As the wise Solomon said in Ecclesiastes 9:10, "Whatever your hand finds to do, do it with all your might."

> The old adage is true. "You only live life once. But if you live right, once is enough."

Daily Reflection Questions

Day One

I What diet programs have you tried?

2 Why are diets so popular these days?

3 Why is weight control important for a Christian?

4. Why is this a spiritual issue?

Day Two

1 Why is it so difficult to restrict our caloric intake?

2 When did you begin to notice the changes in your metabolism rate and in your muscle mass?

3 How has your activity level and exercise routine changed through the years?

Day Three

1 Why would a weight-loss director say, "Diets don't work"?

2 What makes it more difficult to keep weight off than to take it off?

3 Why are lifestyle choices more important than dieting for controlling weight?

Day Four

1 When were you most successful at weight management?

2 When were you least successful?

3 What made the difference?

Day Five

1 How do you feel about your weight and overall physical condition?

2 What have you learned from this chapter that can help you in this area?

3 What lifestyle changes will you make?

CHAPTER THIRTEEN

PHYSICAL ASSETS: SEXUAL CONTROL

Dave's vulnerability to an extra-marital affair was obvious to those who knew him. As the head of his corporate empire, he had reached the pinnacle of success by his mid-thirties. His employees admired his leadership savvy that had resulted in the company's unprecedented dominance. All the same they were jealous of his boyish looks and athletic physique that the women were drawn to.

His senior management team knew something wasn't quite right when Dave announced he'd be spending time alone at his lake cottage instead of accompanying the newest recruits on their field trip of Wall Street. "What's up with Dave?" they asked. "He never misses the opportunity to lead the troops to the frontlines of corporate warfare. He must be battling burnout."

That was exactly what was going on. Twenty years of climbing up the ladder of success had taken their toll. Dave sent his wife and kids home while he stayed at their vacation place. He told them he just needed time alone. In spite of the fact that he was a success in every imaginable definition of the word, Dave wasn't satisfied. His wife's aging body no longer provided him the sexual turn-on it once had. To make matters worse, she complained of a headache more often than she used to when he was interested in after-hours pleasure. She blamed her lack of desire on menopause.

With the family gone, Dave surfed the cable channels on the cottage plasma TV. He sipped a glass of wine after landing on an adult channel with minimal dialog and maximum skin. Feeling aroused and guilty at the same time, the half-drunk, burned-out executive decided to take a walk along the lake. Within a hundred yards he saw his neighbor's wife in their beachfront Jacuzzi. He called out a greeting to Beth. She smiled and gestured for him to join her.

As enjoyable as a midnight walk along the beach would have been on this balmy autumn night, sitting in a hot tub with a beautiful woman seemed an even more attractive option. When Beth offered him a glass of wine, he didn't indicate he'd had too much already.

"My husband is back in the city doing battle with the corporate bosses," she explained. Dave knew all about Uri's job. The two families had owned vacation homes next to each other for eight years. Although Dave and his wife and Beth and her Israeli-born husband had shared

> In spite of the fact that he was a success in every imaginable definition of the word, Dave wasn't satisfied.

many a festive evening in one another's spas, this was the first time Dave and Beth had been alone.

Before too long too much booze and too little clothing resulted in a recipe for adultery. What Dave had watched two hours earlier on the adult channel in his home was being played out in his next-door neighbor's bedroom.

Oh, yes. You know the rest of the story. What you've just read is a modern-day telling of a familiar episode in the life of Israel's most celebrated king. You can read the actual account in 2 Samuel 11:1–5.

Sadly, the David and Bathsheba story is not an isolated one. It is being played out over and over again among Christians and non-believers. The awesome (and beautiful) gift of sexual intimacy that God invented for His creature's pleasure is being abused and perverted. Unlike the gifts of art, music, and imagination, the sex drive is one that resists control. This gift almost has a life of its own.

The Beast Within Us

In the words of author Frederick Buechner: "Lust is the ape that gibbers in our loins. Tame him as we will day-by-day, he rages all the wilder in our dreams by night. Just when we think we're safe from him he raises up his ugly head and smirks, and there's no river in the world that flows cold and strong enough to strike him down. Almighty God, why dost thou deck men with such a loathsome toy?"

Men aren't the only ones who struggle with the issue of sexual control. Consider Darla (not her real name). Her dad walked out on her and her mother when she was a preschooler. Following the divorce, Darla longed for her daddy's affection, but she was most often disappointed. Her unemployed father rarely picked her up on weekends when he was entitled to visitations. As a result, Darla projected her need for affection on her stepfather. But since she was not his biological daughter, he didn't go out of his way to lavish love or attention on her.

As Darla entered adolescence, the reflection she saw in the mirror began to surprise her. Her flat chest transformed almost overnight into a full-figure like her mother. The boys at school began to notice as well. Soon Darla recognized that when she wore tight-fitting sweaters she received a lot of looks. Starved for attention, Darla soon played into the hands of those who seemed sincere in their expressions of love. From the back seats of Firebirds and Hondas the prelude to a life of sexual promiscuity could be heard against the backdrop of crickets chirping along a rural road outside of town. She knew what to wear (or not wear) to solicit the affection for which she longed.

Although Darla became a Christian through a campus ministry

> Men aren't the only ones who struggle with the issue of sexual control.

in college, she would be the first to say that her appetite for sex was stronger than most women she knew would admit to. She would readily acknowledge that casual sex did not provide the security of commitment and unconditional love that she had been denied as a child. She also knew the pleasurable satisfaction to which she had become accustomed. Darla's "easy" reputation won her many dates, but her attempts to win the battle with promiscuity didn't succeed until she got married.

After ten years of marriage and three kids, Darla has maintained a physical appearance that turns heads. When men take a second look at her in the grocery store or at the city pool, she feels a certain sense of excitement. When she watches soaps on TV, the bedroom scenes can trigger her own imagination. On more than one occasion she has found herself fantasizing about romantic getaways with men she has seen across the sanctuary at church. Amazingly, Darla's dysfunctional past and her overactive libido have not resulted in her having an affair. But unless she takes steps to release the stranglehold lust has on her thoughts, it's only a matter of time.

The Gift of Sex

> "How beautiful you are and how pleasing, O love, with your delights!"
> *Song of Solomon 7:6*

Lust may be an uncaged ape, but sex is heaven's gift. The Creator Himself gave it to us. But its guiltless pleasure can only be enjoyed within the appropriate boundaries of commitment. Lust prompts us to monkey around, but leaves us stranded at the zoo. Sex invites us to explore the unclothed dimensions of unconditional acceptance. The result of such delightful entanglement is becoming one in flesh and spirit without regrets or fear of getting caught.

The longing for sexual pleasure and unrestrained intimacy is wired into the psyche of the human soul. The obvious reason that God factored the sex drive into our DNA was to propagate the human race. God's instructions to replenish and multiply were aided by the inner urge to let our hormones play. But the gift of sex was given for more than just population purposes. Reading the Song of Solomon indicates that it was also designed for pleasure.

"I have taken off my robe— must I put it on again? I have washed my feet— must I soil them again? My lover thrust his hand through the latch-opening; my heart began to pound for him. I arose to open for my lover, and my hands dripped with myrrh, my fingers with flowing myrrh, on the handles of the lock" (Song of Solomon 5:3–5). "How beautiful you are and how pleasing, O love, with your delights! Your stature is like that of the palm, and your breasts like clusters of fruit. I said, 'I will climb the palm tree; I will take hold of its fruit.' May your breasts be like the clusters of the vine, the fragrance of your breath like apples, and your mouth like the best wine" (Song of Solomon 7:6–9).

Solomon's amazingly candid exposé of the love of a husband and a wife is definitely R rated. Its erotic poetry has an aura of mystery. The spiritual component of the sex act is celebrated. No wonder the writer of Genesis describes the process by which a man and a woman leave their families of origin and become a union of two spirits in terms of sexual intercourse. "And they will become one flesh" (Genesis 2:24).

But sexual passion is a powerful force that pulsates within men and women regardless of their marital state. It doesn't just show up on the wedding night. It is a primal instinct that begs to be noticed and lobbies to be satisfied. And because sex is such a dominant desire, it has been known to bypass the logic center of the brain. Otherwise responsible individuals have been branded as mindless fools by giving in to sexual temptation. Without thought for anything or anyone than themselves, men and women have lost jobs, reputations and marriages—all for the rush of a fleeting sexual high.

The Scriptures make it clear that the gift of sexual intimacy and pleasure is to be unwrapped by those who are committed to one another in a lifelong bond of marriage. Ignoring the instructions provided by the Giver renders the gift less valuable and less appreciated.

Caging the Ape While Enjoying the Gift

Countless individuals have shipwrecked their potential on the reef of indiscretions. You most likely could name several. Some quite possibly were those you once considered mentors. You also are acquainted with the pain they have both endured and caused by their selfish choices. But the fact that people you once admired could fail morally should give you cause for pause. As Paul wrote to the Christians in Corinth, "So, if you think you are standing firm, be careful that you don't fall" (1 Corinthians 10:12).

> "So, if you think you are standing firm, be careful that you don't fall."
> *1 Corinthians 10:12*

The following are a few tried and true ways you can be careful.

Be aware of your vulnerability. Although you might think you are incapable of sexual sin, think again. Take a personal inventory. Make note of what is going on in your life when you are most liable to sexual temptation. You know what tends to cause your sexual engine to increase its rpm—perhaps certain magazines or movies or the influence of certain people. Identify your personal escape route. Determine to put it down, turn it off, or leave the room.

Peter advised those being shaped by the promiscuous culture of the first century to "abstain from sinful desires, which war against your soul" (1 Peter 2:11). Even though our culture may wink at one-night stands or indiscretions, you know too much to close your eyes to what God thinks.

If you are not married, ask God to give you the ability to remain sexually pure. If you have blown it, confess your sin and ask His forgiveness. Nonetheless, when it comes to temptation, you're not out of the woods. You need to be proactive. Paul's concern for his young unmarried friend Timothy is good advice. "Run from anything that stimulates youthful lust. Follow anything that makes you want to do right. Pursue faith and love and peace, and enjoy the companionship of those who call on the Lord with pure hearts" (2 Timothy 2:22, NLT).

Guard the marriage bed. If you are married and have an active sex life, you can't assume you're impervious to sexual temptation. The Enemy of our souls will try to convince you you're bored and attempt to entice you with what is curvier, more muscular or younger. But don't give in. The Bible says, "Marriage should be honored by all, and the marriage bed kept pure, for God will judge the adulterer and all the sexually immoral" (Hebrews 13:4).

A wise Hebrew writer suggested a way that those who are married can maintain the integrity of their bedroom. It has to do with avoiding envy and practicing gratitude. Be content with what God has given you to enjoy. He wrote, "Drink water from your own cistern, running water from your own well. Should your springs overflow in the streets, your streams of water in the public squares? Let them be yours alone, never to be shared with strangers. May your fountain be blessed, and may you rejoice in the wife of your youth. A loving doe, a graceful deer— may her breasts satisfy you always, may you ever be captivated by her love. Why be captivated, my son, by an adulteress? Why embrace the bosom of another man's wife? For a man's ways are in full view of the Lord, and he examines all his paths" (Proverbs 5:15–21).

Another way to derail the train of sexual temptation is to continue to court your mate. Express your love regularly. Take time for walks and hugs. Make time for sexual intercourse even when the "need" for sex is not as obvious as it once was.

Guard your thoughts. The power of suggestion is mind-boggling— and mind-controlling. We become what we think about. We do what we ponder. With that in mind, don't allow sexual fantasies to fill your thoughts. Obviously, you can't prevent lustful images or urges from gaining entrance into your brain. But you can limit the focus you give them. As Martin Luther stated, "You can't keep the birds from flying over head, but you can keep them from building a nest in the branches."

When Paul wrote to the Christians in Philippi, he gave them a formula for living above reproach. "Do not be anxious about anything,

> "Run from anything that stimulates youthful lust. Follow anything that makes you want to do right."
>
> *2 Timothy 2:22, NLT*

> "If anything is excellent or praise-worthy—think about such things."
>
> *Philippians 4:8*

but in everything, by prayer and petition, with thanksgiving, present your requests to God. And the peace of God, which transcends all understanding, will guard your hearts and your minds in Christ Jesus. Finally, brothers, whatever is true, whatever is noble, whatever is right, whatever is pure, whatever is lovely, whatever is admirable—if anything is excellent or praiseworthy—think about such things. Whatever you have learned or received or heard from me, or seen in me—put it into practice. And the God of peace will be with you" (Philippians 4:6–9).

Accountability

Establish accountability checkpoints. Don't underestimate the power of confession when it comes to keeping your nose (or other body parts) clean. Admitting your failure and your tendency to stumble is a strong deterrent to sinning. Ask one or two people to be part of an accountability small group with you. Meet regularly. Allow each person to express areas of temptation for which they would like to be held accountable.

Chances are, if you have someone asking you on a periodic basis how you are doing with your struggle with lust, you will be less apt to give in to sexual promiscuity. Just knowing that someone (to whom you've confessed your struggle with lust) will be asking you how you are doing should cause you to think twice. If you are a businessperson who spends as many nights in a hotel room as you do in your bedroom at home, you know the availability of adult entertainment on in-room televisions. If you are tempted to watch such programming, ask someone from your church to pray for you to have strength. Invite this person to ask you upon your return if you avoided the trap.

When Chuck Swindoll was pastor of First Evangelical Free Church of Fullerton, California, he had a list of questions he asked his staff on a weekly basis. Although the questions dealt with more than issues of sexual temptation, his checklist certainly touched on that area.

> Don't underestimate the power of confession when it comes to keeping your nose (or other body parts) clean.

1. **Have you been with a woman anywhere this past week that might be seen as compromising?**

2. **Have any of your financial dealings lacked integrity?**

3. **Have you exposed yourself to any sexually explicit material?**

4. **Have you spent adequate time in Bible study and prayer?**

5. **Have you given priority time to your family?**

6. Have you fulfilled the mandates of your calling?

7. Have you just lied to me?

We would do well to come up with a similar list of questions for use in our accountability groups.

Daily Reflection Questions

Day One

1   What were you thinking as you read the opening story about "Dave"?

2   Why is the sex drive called the "beast within us"?

3   Why is lust such a problem, especially with men?

Day Two

1   Why is sex called "heaven's gift"?

2 What's so good about sex?

3 Why did God give us such a powerful drive anyway?

Day Three

1 What are some ways we can guard ourselves sexually?

2 When are you most vulnerable to sexually temptation?

3 How has your sex life changed in the last few years?

Day Four

I What can a married person do to maintain the integrity of the bedroom?

2 How can someone "court" his or her mate?

3 How does a person guard his or her thoughts?

Day Five

I About what area of your sex life do you need to talk to God?

2 What will you do to limit lust?

3 Who will you ask to hold you accountable in this area of life?

CHAPTER FOURTEEN

MENTAL ASSETS: IMPORTANCE OF THE MIND

If most of us are ashamed of shabby clothes and shoddy furniture,
let us be more ashamed of shabby ideas and shoddy philosophies.

Albert Einstein

For I can testify about them that they are zealous for God, but their zeal
is not based on knowledge.

Romans 10:2

A mind is a terrible thing to waste. Yet the hectic lives of twenty-first-century families and the access to unlimited amusement opportunities have reduced both Christians and non-Christians into culturally perceptive but clueless robots who have surrendered their minds to whomever has the jazziest jargon and the slickest presentation.

> "'Come now, let us reason together,' says the Lord."
> *Isaiah 1:18*

We have become victims of pop-up Internet ads, propaganda (whether political or commercial), urban legends, and a secular mind-set, whether overtly marketed through media outlets or subtly infiltrated into the Church with all of its sources of distribution.

One chapter will not solve the problem of how to get Christians to think Christianly, but we have to start somewhere. So we will ask two questions to kick-start the dialogue.

Question 1: Why Use Our Minds?

We use our minds because ideas, whether good or inane, are shaped by the mind. In 1849, Lord Palmerston made a statement to the British House of Commons on this subject: "Opinions are stronger than armies. Opinions, if they are founded in truth and justice, will in the end, prevail against the bayonet of infantry, the fire of artillery, and the charges of cavalry."

Scripture states, "'Come now, let us reason together,' says the Lord" (Isaiah 1:18). God knows that opinions come from a reasoning process. To reason is not automatic with all people, even though we were created with the capacity to think. We are different than the rest of the animal kingdom in that they respond to instinct and environment, while we make cognitive choices.

Educators use a term to describe when true learning takes place, when the mind is reshaped. It's called *cognitive dissonance.* We live with a set of assumptions about life until something causes a serious disruption and shakes up our world, forcing us to think or reason differently. An example of this in a horribly negative sense was the terrorist attack against the United States on September 11, 2001. Along with the Twin Towers collapsed the assumption by most Americans that we are invincible and sheltered from foreign attack by two large oceans. That was cognitive dissonance (knowledge disruption) for all Americans and a reshaping of our minds.

From a positive standpoint, the Apostle Paul wrote a letter to the Romans saying, "Be transformed by the renewing of your mind" (Romans 12:2). His assumption, like all of the Bible writers, is that although sin has corrupted or darkened the thinking process, thinking God's thoughts can transcend every aberrant view when the scales fall from our eyes after searching God's Word.

Paul said "the righteous will live by faith" (Romans 1:17), but we have to first settle the issues of what is meant Biblically by the word *faith.* It is not blind optimism; it is not a positive mental attitude. Instead, according to Jesus, faith is a *reasoning trust* (see Matthew 6:30–31). Jesus says faith is making the rational deduction that the same God who provides for nature will provide for you if you seek Him as your primary source of provision.

This is also true regarding how God will guide your life. Some are looking for a hotline to heaven or a divine tap on the shoulder. Scripture speaks of two kinds of "God's will": His *general* will, living by sound principles of faith (treating one another in love, the need to study, pray, and worship) and His *particular* will. In most cases, God expects you to find His particular will by using your mind and common sense after it has been immersed in His Word and the principles contained therein.

> "Be transformed
> by the renewing
> of your mind."
> *Romans 12:2*

Question 2: How Does a Christian Think?

Harry Blamires, in his book *The Christian Mind,* highlights the following marks of the Christian mind or evidence that a person is thinking Christianly.

The first mark is to think supernaturally. This means having an eternal perspective. When a person who thinks supernaturally looks at nature, that person sees the complex yet beautiful design of a Creator. When this individual looks at the events of life, he or she sees the sovereign hand of providence. When looking at insurmountable problems like illness or financial setback, this person sees prayer as a life-changing resource. A supernatural perspective sees aging and death as the inevitable journey of mortal flesh but without succumbing to despair because of the promise of eternal life in Christ.

Johnny Cash, the famous "man in black" country/ballad singer, along with his wife, June Carter Cash, entertained millions through their albums, concerts, and TV performances. Johnny's life on the road to perform before presidents and prisoners was not an easy journey. He battled addiction to painkillers and wound up in the hospital several times, with his survival in question.

Toward the end, he knew that diabetes and asthma were taking its toll. His wife was already in God's presence. In August 2003, he held his last recording session. He brought a sheet of paper that contained the words for a new song, but he had no melody in mind. He left the paper on the table and walked out of the room. Here is some of what he wrote:

My Lord has gone to make a place for me.

I heard that it's a mansion that will stand eternally....

He called down from heaven just for me.

He said, "Your mansion's ready as soon you will be."

(From "My Lord Has Gone," © 2003 by John R. Cash)

Johnny Cash died several weeks later. These words reveal the heart of a man who was thinking supernaturally about his approaching death. He was a man with hope and profound faith.

Those who think supernaturally also see the resources of talent or wealth as a means to help others or as an investment in eternal matters, such as the work of evangelism and the mission of the church. The supernatural mind-set says, "What you see is not all that is there and not all you will get." They hold lightly to things that will disappear.

The second mark is to be aware of evil. Humans can be remarkably cruel to other humans, the animal world, or the environment. Lurking in the shadows of every seemingly upright person is the capacity to do very ugly things. Wars have a way of making this point. Where does the capacity to exterminate a whole ethnic group of people come from? Where does the selfish behavior in all of us arise? What is the source of the vanity and pride often displayed in the religious profession? Rather than learned behavior, these are constantly reverberating echoes of a fallen world and the prompting of the Evil One and all his schemes.

The third mark is to focus on truth. Every culture has interpretation of values, prejudices for certain appetites, philosophical assumptions, and interpretation of reality. Thus, people can be lured

> The super-natural mind-set says, "What you see is not all that is there and not all you will get."

by mass-preference and ideas without questioning whether those preferences and ideas are true. Most people become quite comfortable with society's values, premises, and assumptions without questioning their validity. "Mass-preference" societies allow for individual preferences as long as no one claims to have absolute truth.

In contrast, Christianity is comprised of acts and facts. These acts and facts are the foundation for our faith and they transcend all time, all cultures, and all personal preferences. Christianity is a religion of events that actually happened and a God who lived among us and taught us what truth looks like. Truth is the way things are, not the way we want them to be. Truth stands the test of time and will always be supported either directly or indirectly by Scripture. Not all truth comes from Scripture, but all that Scripture teaches and supports is true.

The fourth mark is to accept authority. Any monarch has the option of being benevolent or a tyrant. The Christian mind asserts that God is benevolent; that is, He wants to be followed and worshiped voluntarily rather than forcibly. The Christian, thinking Christianly, not only bows his knees before a sovereign Lord but also does so eagerly and willfully.

> The Christian does not take a pick-and-choose approach to obedience.

The Christian does not take a pick-and-choose approach to obedience. The old cliché "God said it, I believe it, that settles it!" applies. That is not the statement of an idiot leaping blindly into the dark but of a grateful child acknowledging the authority and security of a loving parent.

This mark of the Christian mind can be difficult to accept at times. The Scriptures contain commandments that can seem impossible to follow: "Love your neighbor," "Return good for evil," "Don't commit adultery," "Give and it will be given unto you." Yet the Christian with a Christian mind-set will not question that he or she needs to respond to every admonition of Scripture. Like the Apostle Paul, this person will not always do everything that he or she wants to do (Romans 7:14–20), but the intent is to do so.

The fifth mark is to have concern for the individual. Tension will always exist between goals, agendas, systems, and productivity and a concern for the human beings who make all those things happen. Our society has been extremely successful in creating crowded cities with roaring traffic, accompanied by modern technical innovations that speed up communications through the Internet, cell phones, and other media. At times, however, an eerie loneliness pervades this progress from a lack of real connectedness with other humans.

In many ways, we have been reduced to be sub-human slaves of the mechanization that has been created and the energy it takes to try to succeed in the various systems that have been created. Many parents, when asked what values they are trying to instill into their children, fill their answers with references to competing with others in order to go to the best school, to make the best grades, to get the best job, to make lots of money, to buy lots of things so they can have children who will do the same thing. That's OK, if those parents deal with their children as unique individuals and consider their individual dreams, aspirations, and gifts and then try to find a personalized pathway to the future. Often, however, they often just throw the kids into the system, leaving them to survive on their own.

In many respects, Christians and non-Christians exhibit little difference when it comes to these values. But when Jesus was on earth, He paid virtually no attention to the organizational systems. Instead, He dealt with people in relationships, who they were as family members, their eternal values, and the way they worshiped God and treated their fellow human beings.

Christians can be consumed with the hierarchy and the machinery of the church. They can begin to enjoy the bureaucracy more than the Beatitudes. The only difference at that point between the church and a corporate institution is a steeple and a cross. Somehow people with their joys and pain, their struggles and their victories, fall through the cracks.

A person with a Christian mind-set knows how to step back from the functions that consume him or her and to think about ways to treat everyone more humanly. According to the Catholic Church, 8,000 people a day go into St. Patrick's Cathedral in New York City. Many are there as tourists, but many are also seeking a reprieve from the chaos and noise of life for solitude and spiritual renewal that makes them feel more alive as human beings.

> Somehow people with their joys and pain, their struggles and their victories, fall through the cracks.

Daily Reflection Questions

Day One

1. How do you rate your intelligence and ability to think?

2 What evidence do you see of the lack of thinking in society?

3 Why is using one's mind so important?

Day Two

1 What is "cognitive dissonance"?

2 When have your life assumptions been shattered or at least rearranged?

3 What does Romans 12:2 mean by "renewing" our minds?

Day Three

1 What is the relationship between rational thinking and faith?

2 What does it mean to think "supernaturally"?

3 How can we do that?

Day Four

1 Why do people seem so unconcerned about the truth?

2 Why is knowing the truth important?

3   What other differences do you see between the Christian perspective and the world's?

Day Five

I   In what areas—perspective, awareness of evil, focus on truth, acceptance of authority, and concern for the individual—does your mind need renewal?

2   What steps can you take to make that happen?

3   What can you do to help others (children, fellow believers, and so forth) think Christianly?

CHAPTER FIFTEEN

Mental Assets: Positive and Negative Influences

The Bible says more about emotional well-being than sanitation, hygiene, or diet. It must be important, so important that a person with a positive outlook could overcome some of the diseases associated with all cultures for all time.

For instance, heart attack patients who are depressed have a risk of death five times greater than heart attack patients who are not (research from the Health Emotions Research Institute at the University of Wisconsin).

> "A cheerful heart is good medicine, but a crushed spirit dries up the bones."
> *Proverbs 17:22*

- Emotions, not events, cause stress-related illnesses.
- Emotions affect our immune system and the ability to resist disease.
- Thoughts can cause physical problems like ulcers, indigestion, and high blood pressure.
- In some cases, depression is a better detector of heart problems than physical measurements.

We all have heard of the old acronym GIGO. It stands for Garbage In, Garbage Out. Your life produces whatever goes into your mind, whether negatively or positively. Let's look at each.

Negative Thinking

The Mental Health Today website identifies seven common cognitive distortions. These are distorted, self-defeating patterns of reality. Like a fun-house mirror, they reflect a distorted image that is often assumed to be real but isn't. As a result, they lead to anger, fear, guilt, and other emotions that accelerate the negative image rather than help it.

Here are the Seven Cognitive Distortions as summarized by Brenda Polk of Lifeway Christian Resources.

1. **All-or-Nothing Thinking:** If your performance falls short of perfect, you see yourself as a total failure.

2. **Overgeneralization:** You see a single negative event

as a never-ending pattern of defeat. The extreme form of over-generalization is called Labeling or Mislabeling. When a single event or error leads to a negative label of yourself: *"I'm a loser."*

3. Jumping to Conclusions: You make a negative interpretation even though there are no definite facts that convincingly support your conclusion.

4. Magnification (catastrophizing) or Minimization: You exaggerate the importance of things (such as a minor goof-up) or you inappropriately shrink things until they appear tiny (your own desirable qualities).

5. Emotional Reasoning: You assume that your negative emotions necessarily reflect the way things really are: *"I feel it, therefore it must be true."*

6. Should Statements: You try to motivate yourself with "should's" and "should not's," as if you had to be punished before you could be expected to do anything. "Must" and "ought to" statements are also offenders. The emotional consequence is guilt. When we direct these statements toward others, the emotional consequence is anger, resentment, and frustration.

7. Personalization: You see yourself as the cause of some negative, external event, which in fact you were not primarily responsible for.

Positive Thinking

The Bible tells us that physical health and emotions are connected.

✖ "A cheerful heart is good medicine, but a crushed spirit dries up the bones" (Proverbs 17:22).

✖ "A heart at peace gives life to the body, but envy rots the bones" (Proverbs 14:30).

✖ "Pleasant words are . . . sweet to the soul and healing to the bones" (Proverbs 16:24).

> "Pleasant words are . . . sweet to the soul and healing to the bones."
>
> *Proverbs 16:24*

Boldness, confidence, diligence, zeal are all great approaches to life. They are also great for your health. If you want these characteristics to be in your life, start with 5 strategies offered by the Bible for a mental (extreme) makeover (also taken from Brenda Polk).

Strategy One: Take every thought captive. "We demolish arguments and every high-minded thing that is raised up against the knowledge of God, taking every thought captive to the obedience of Christ" (2 Corinthians 10:4–5, HCSB). To overcome the continuous pattern of negative thinking, listen to your thoughts and realize when they do not match up to the truth of God's Word. Write down the negative thoughts, and ask God to show you His truth that counters it. List the truth beside the negative thought; then, when that thought comes to mind, replace it with the Scripture or truth you have discovered. Avoid trying to conquer every thought at once. Begin with one negative thought and when you have replaced it several times with the truth, move to the next one.

Strategy Two: Release condemning thoughts. "Therefore, no condemnation now exists for those in Christ Jesus" (Romans 8:1, HCSB). Thoughts that belittle are destructive and compound the negative conclusions we draw. Avoid condemnation by admitting mistakes and errors that are common in life. Remember, only Jesus was perfect. Ask for forgiveness when necessary from God, others, and yourself and move on without continuing to belittle or berate yourself.

Strategy Three: Realize you are powerless to change on your own, but you can change through Christ's power working in you. "I am able to do all things through Him who strengthens me" (Philippians 4:13, HCSB). Ask for God's help in making these mental changes. Seek help from another qualified person who can also help you work through the negative thoughts. A Christian counselor or your pastor may be helpful in making changes in your mind, attitude, and habits. A trusted accountability partner who understands your struggles can help to keep you on track.

Strategy Four: Renew your mind. "Do not be conformed to this age, but be transformed by the renewing of your mind" (Romans 12:2, HCSB). Negative thoughts are developed over many years and often a lifetime. Many times these thoughts began from someone else's comments that stuck and made an impression. Other outside influences to our thoughts are television, books, magazines, pictures, advertisements, and music. Transform your mind by learning and meditating on God's truth. Commit to turning off the outside influences that most strongly impact your thinking.

Strategy Five: Think on these things. "Finally brothers, whatever is true, whatever is honorable, whatever is just, whatever is pure, whatever is lovely, whatever is commendable—if there is any moral excellence and if there is any praise—dwell on these things" (Philippians 4:8, HCSB). Test your thoughts against this checklist. If your thoughts do not match up to the criteria God has provided, release the thought as unworthy of your mental energy.

> "I am able to do all things through Him who strengthens me."
> *Philippians 4:13, HCSB*

> "Do not be conformed to this age, but be transformed by the renewing of your mind."
> *Romans 12:2, HCSB*

Changing your mind will not happen overnight.

As you gradually realize and change the way you think about yourself, you will change your attitude and then your actions. Even with a mental makeover, you will continue to need "attitude adjustment" work. Trust God for the consistent renewal of your mind and reap the benefits from making daily, sometimes small, but significant steps from a negative to a positive frame of life.

Case Study

Leadership gurus and psychologists use different terms to describe the condition where a person has hit a personal barrier that will not allow him or her to move any further in a positive direction.

This person may want to be promoted within the company, but it won't happen. He or she may want more meaningful personal relationships, but that seems impossible. The person may want to be successful financially, but all he or she can see on the horizon is debt and a looming catastrophe.

John Maxwell calls this the "law of the lid." Psychologist Flip Flippen refers to it as a "constraint." Each term makes you feel restricted, boxed in, or bound up. Now the lid can be lifted; the cords of restraint can be loosed. The process starts by being honest with oneself and having a willingness to call a lid a lid.

Richard was the President and CEO of one of the nation's most prestigious and successful non-profit service organizations. He was recognized as a rapidly rising star early in his career, due to his public charisma, natural speaking ability, intelligence, and photographic memory.

For nearly twenty years his career was stellar, and his organization flourished with national attention and admiration. As a result, he was in great demand to tell his story and to instruct others who wanted to model both their personal careers and their organizations in the same pattern.

Little did people know that behind the scenes, all was not well. Richard's flaws took time to surface, but like a cancer they were spreading undetected, until one day, he no longer had the credibility or influence he needed to lead. Sadly, he not only was rendered ineffective, but he nearly destroyed his organization.

What flaws were so toxic that it slammed the lid down on such a promising career? One was Richard's perception that any disagreement on direction, programs, or policy was a personal threat to his leadership. The second flaw was a volatile temper that would scorch his staff and others who seemed to be in opposition.

When Richard's closest acquaintances realized what was

> The process starts by being honest with one-self and having a willingness to call a lid a lid.

happening, they tried to reason with him, to help him see that if he didn't recognize and deal with this lid in his life, he would destroy everything for which he had worked so hard. He refused to believe that such a lid existed, and eventually he was gone. In fact, he walked out of one of those meetings where he was being confronted, went home, packed his suitcase, and along with his wife, got in the car and left the state. No one knew where they were for many weeks, nor when they would return to sell their home. At that point, his life was in shambles.

Another person who faced a number of lids or constraints in his life was King David. Author John Maxwell identified at least four constraints, adapted here from the *Maxwell Leadership Bible.*

1. His family. David's limitations started at home. When Samuel asked Jesse to gather all his sons so God could reveal the next king of Israel, no one thought to invite David. His brothers thought no better of him than did his father. When David visited the battlefront, they scorned him. When David spoke out against Goliath's blasphemy, his brothers insulted him and told him to go home.

2. His leader. Saul continually tried to sabotage David's leadership and effectiveness. When David offered to fight Goliath, Saul told him, "You are not able to go out against this Philistine and fight him" (1 Samuel 17:33). Then Saul tried to put his heavy armor on the boy—Saul certainly wasn't going to use it! For many years, Saul tried repeatedly to kill David.

3. His background. David came from a family of poor shepherds. His father, Jesse the Bethlehemite, lacked both lofty lineage and powerful position. David wasn't even the eldest son in his family; seven older brothers all came before him.

4. His youthfulness and inexperience. At the time Saul anointed David, the boy had no experience leading anything but sheep. When he stepped forward to fight Goliath, others considered him "only a youth," and he had never fought a wartime battle. Time and again, people underestimated and disrespected him.

This is not an easy process. Admitting to a flaw that needs to be fixed or circumstances that are beyond our control can be a blow to our pride. But the results are worth the pain. Many people have been unloosed, set free to soar to unbelievable levels because of a new identity, an identity freed from negative thoughts, history, and other kinds of baggage. *What about you?*

> Admitting to a flaw that needs to be fixed or circumstances that are beyond our control can be a blow to our pride. But the results are worth the pain.

Daily Reflection Questions

Day One

1 Which of the "cognitive distortions" did you see in your life?

2 Why do some people seem to be so negative all the time?

3 When do you tend to be most negative?

Day Two

1 What fights against positive thinking in your life?

2 In what situations do you condemn yourself?

3 Why do others' negative comments affect us so much?

Day Three

1 What thoughts do you need to "take captive"?

2 What can you do to turn off the negative outside influences?

3 In what area do you need an attitude adjustment?

Day Four

1 When have you experienced the "law of the lid"?

2 Why is it difficult to be honest about our "lids"?

3 With which of David's constraints do you identify?

Day Five

1 How has your family been a "lid"?

2 Why is it so difficult to admit our flaws?

3 From what baggage do you need to ask God to release you?

CHAPTER SIXTEEN

EMOTIONAL ASSETS: GRIPING OR GRATITUDE

God wants us to be just like Jesus. Isn't that good news?
You aren't stuck with today's personality. You aren't condemned to
"grumpydom." You are tweakable. Even if you are worried each day of
your life. So what if you were born a bigot? You don't have to die one.

Max Lucado

You need to ask the question, "What is it like to live with me every day?" When you come home from work, does your family brace themselves for an earthquake or embrace you for the joy you bring in the door? What are you like at work? Do people want to drop by your office for an uplift, or do they tiptoe past trying to avoid a downdraft?

All of us would like to forget the cranky way we have responded both inside and outside the home. We would also like to defeat crankiness before it hijacks our personality and then no one wants to be around us.

John Maxwell sponsors an annual *Maximum Impact Simulcast* where the nation's top gurus of industry and leadership gather to give their top three or four ideas about being a success in life. All of them agree that attitude is one of the most important characteristics.

Southwest Airlines has a slogan: "We hire attitudes." What do they mean by that? They hire people who listen to others, who smile, and know how to say thank you.

King David said: "You turned my wailing into dancing; you removed my sackcloth and clothed me with joy" (Psalm 30:11). Southwest Airlines would have offered David a job.

Jesus said, "I have come that they may have life, and have it to the full" (John 10:10).

> "You turned my wailing into dancing; you removed by sackcloth and clothed me with joy."
> *Psalm 30:11*

The Model

So how does this happen? We know it doesn't come by gritting our teeth and promising to be a better person tomorrow. It comes from having a model we want to emulate and a power to change that is greater than our internal motivation.

The ultimate model is Jesus. He wants to rule and reign over every aspect of our lives. For a while the wrist bracelet WWJD was fashionable because certain Christian, professional golfers wore it. Anything that is overexposed can become trivialized, but the core message of that wristband was true: "What Would Jesus Do?"

What would Jesus do when someone takes advantage of you at work? What would Jesus do when someone cuts into your traffic lane? What would Jesus do when your 5-year-old throws a temper tantrum?

We may not know what He would do in every situation, but we know He would transform our lives and attitudes.

Several years ago, the pastor, Randy Pope, and several church leaders of Perimeter Church in Atlanta decided to try and purchase a special piece of property in order to create another congregation as a part of their master plan. The lady who owned the property had a reputation for being hard to deal with, and they anticipated that their request would be met with negativity.

When they laid out their plans, she said, "I think you are just the right group to buy it." They were shocked. They told her they had expected her to resist. She said that would have been her response until she trusted Christ, but now she was a different person. She didn't use the phrase, but she was asking and answering, "What would Jesus do?"

Learning what Jesus would do takes some time but the first step is to make Him first in your life. Jesus said, "Seek first his kingdom and his righteousness, and all these things will be given to you as well" (Matthew 6:33). If He is first, then grumbling can be transformed into gratitude. He also wants us to deal with our motivations, the reasons for doing what we do. That is the first step to change—taking a hard look at why we have become so negative.

> "Seek first his kingdom and his righteousness, and all these things will be given to you as well."
>
> Matthew 6:33

Possible Reasons for Griping

One of the primary causes for griping is *spoilage*; that is, like a child, the person may be spoiled. People who usually get what they want find it difficult to handle things that are less than perfect. Life is all about them, and that runs contrary to what Jesus taught about priorities. Generally speaking, the more we have, the less grateful we are. "Keep falsehood and lies far from me; give me neither poverty nor riches, but give me only my daily bread. Otherwise, I may have too much and disown you and say, 'Who is the Lord?'" (Proverbs 30:8–9).

Another cause for griping is negative friends. The writer of Proverbs 13:20 observes, "He who walks with the wise grows wise, but a companion of fools suffers harm."

Complainers tend to flock together and feed off of one another. They exaggerate, contaminate, and sour life's experiences for everyone. They can't wait to share bad news with each other. It becomes such an ingrained personality disorder that good news threatens their stability and undermines their identity.

If you are being poisoned by the company you keep, it is time to run. Far better to incur the displeasure of your friends than to waste your future.

A negative, griping attitude can also be caused by spending time comparing one's self to others. Paul wrote, "We do not dare to classify or compare ourselves with some who commend themselves. When they measure themselves by themselves and compare themselves with themselves, they are not wise" (2 Corinthians 10:12).

Comparing oneself to others is a by-product of ingratitude. We can look at the talents or possessions that others have and become either jealous or intimidated. Some enjoy good health while others suffer from sickness or a handicap. Some are born into wealth; others struggle to make ends meet. Some are born with natural good looks, and others are not. Some have a boatload of charisma, while others struggle to attract friends.

Measuring one's self against others is a losing proposition. We can always find someone richer, healthier, better looking, and more successful. Therefore it is both spiritually defeating and an act in futility to gripe about what is or what is not.

> "We do not dare to classify or compare ourselves with some who commend themselves. . . . They are not wise."
>
> *2 Corinthians 10:12*

Grumbling and God

God doesn't like grumbling. When the Israelites fled the iron grip of Pharaoh in Egypt and wandered around Sinai, they eventually joined the grumblers chorus and whined, "Why have you brought us up out of Egypt to die in the desert? There is no bread! There is no water! And we detest this miserable food!" (Numbers 21:5).

God's response seems to be overly harsh, but it puts grumbling into a category of "untolerated" behavior.

James, the brother of Jesus said, "Don't grumble against each other, brothers, or you will be judged" (James 5:9).

The Bible is filled with examples of grumblers. These are people of ingratitude—ingratitude toward God (2 Timothy 3:2), ingratitude toward others (2 Timothy 3:1–4), and ingratitude toward Jesus (Luke 17:12–18). They get into a grumblers' rut. Most people want to avoid people who are in ruts. They are no fun. They are what Gordon MacDonald calls VDP (very draining people).

Thanksgiving gives us the opportunity to pause and reflect on why we are grateful. The traditional Thanksgiving list includes family, health, good fortune, material blessings, and so forth. Real gratitude goes much deeper, however; it relates to how we view the world and can be summarized in three areas.

Gratitude for the Capacity to Understand

Not everyone can look at his or her personal situation or the awful mess the world is in and understand what is happening. A Christian is not surprised when either good or bad things happen. Like we learned in Chapter 14, the Christian, who has read Scripture and used his or her mind, understands that God is ultimately in control but that the "fallenness" of humankind creates unimaginable evil. There seems to be no limit to the vicious ways of human beings. Just watch a TV report of a mother who kills all of her children—that's evil.

We can find peace, however, in having the capacity to understand these things, especially when we see others who are emotional wrecks because they have no clue what is going on.

Gratitude for the Capacity to Care

Not everyone is touched by the needs of others. Some have experienced a sort of "compassion fatigue" by viewing too many villages devastated by earthquakes or wars, too many abused children, too many victims of crime, or too many starving people.

So if you can look at any form of human need and still find a place in your heart to care about the plight of others, you are a fortunate person. You are not emotionally dead. You still have the capacity to respond. God can still use you. That is worth celebrating, and you can thank God that you haven't become completely calloused by the overload of negative communication coming from the media.

> So if you can look at any form of human need and still find a place in your heart to care about the plight of others, you are a fortunate person.

Gratitude for the Compassion to Get Involved

It's one thing to see what needs to be done and another thing to respond. We usually have to overcome the inertia created by the overwhelming number of needs and the thought that one human being makes little difference.

Ask those who have gone on a short-term mission trip how they felt about the experience. They usually are deeply grateful that they took the time and effort to make the trip. In fact, they usually respond that it meant more to them and their personal growth than to the people they were helping.

Daily Reflection Questions

Day One

1   How would you describe a grouchy person?

2   What does Southwest Airlines mean by "We hire attitudes"?

3   What causes bad attitudes?

Day Two

1   Why is Jesus our ultimate model?

2   Why would following what Jesus would do transform a person's life?

3   What will it take to make Jesus first in your life?

Day Three

1   When you slip into griping, what is the usual cause?

2   When have you seen complainers feed off of each other?

3   Why do people compare themselves with others?

Day Four

1   What does God think of ingratitude? Why?

2 Why should we be grateful to God?

3 What experiences have helped deepen your gratitude?

Day Five

1 For what are you most grateful to God?

2 How can you show your gratitude?

3 Take a few minutes and write a prayer of thanksgiving.

CHAPTER SEVENTEEN

EMOTIONAL ASSETS: BITTERNESS OR FORGIVENESS

Bitterness is the poison you swallow hoping the other guy dies.

More lethal than a car bomb, more toxic than sarin gas, is bitterness to the human spirit. It is the corrosive chemical that denies our peace; it is the spiteful sourness that lurks in the shadows when you have been maliciously wronged; it is the acid in the mind that destroys relationships.

The author of Hebrews warned of this corrupting influence and its aftermath: "See to it that no one misses the grace of God and that no bitter root grows up to cause trouble and defile many" (Hebrews 12:15).

Bitterness shows itself in three ways:

First, bitterness can be directed against God. A child resents that his father loves his work more than his own flesh and blood, so the child becomes angry with God. A wife feels trapped in a loveless marriage, so she walks away from her faith. A man is fired from his job or is overlooked for the third time for a promotion, so he cries out against God in the night. In so many words they all say, "If you answer prayers, God, why didn't you answer mine?"

Second, bitterness can be directed against other people. A person may not blame God for his circumstances, but thinks he knows whom to blame so he looks for ways to make them pay for the pain they have inflicted. One event, forever seared on our minds, depicts what bitterness can do to others—the photos of airplanes flying into the World Trade Center towers on 9-11-01.

Third, bitterness can be directed against one's self. A person finds it difficult to forgive himself for being so stupid and doing something so dumb. In doing this, he throws away the key that allows someone to unlock his heart and help him process his confusion and pain. This person may even feel deserving of God's harsh treatment and go through life with a big lid over his head that he cannot remove. It is a lid of bitterness. Until this lid is dealt with, this person will make everyone around him miserable.

The analogy referred to in Hebrews for bitterness is a root. Where is a root? It is underground. You may not know the root exists because you can't see it, but it is there and growing nevertheless.

> "See to it that no one misses the grace of God and that no bitter root grows up to cause trouble."
>
> *Hebrews 12:15*

Roots can burrow under an asphalt road and crack the surface. If the roots are ignored, they can cause cracks and holes large enough to threaten traffic. Likewise in life, the roots of bitterness can detour all normal patterns of human interaction or bring them to a screeching halt.

The roots of bitterness cause all kinds of trouble—at least four problems.

Physical Problems

Dr. S.I. McMillan's classic work, *None Of These Diseases*, showed both the health and the hazards of following or ignoring what the Bible says about sanitation, diet, and the mind. He reported that anger, if not handled properly, would contribute to at least 50 diseases.

Dr. Norman Wright, professor of psychology at Biola University, says that God has constructed us with a tube about 30 feet long that begins at our throat and runs to our rectum. Colitis, diarrhea, and ulcers are produced in that tube when it is disturbed by bitterness and anger.

Mental Problems

One thing is certain. An angry and bitter person has no joy, creativity, and positive influence. Eventually, bitterness can lead to a borderline personality disorder (BPD)—a serious emotional disturbance characterized by unstable personal relationships and fears of abandonment leading to a constant state of emotional turmoil (www.MayoClinic.com).

What triggers BPD is not the same for everyone; however, most causes can be linked to perceived or real neglect and abuse during childhood. Such abuse was never adequately dealt with, and the bitterness took an enormous toll.

Relational Problems

A person can camouflage bitterness for only so long. Eventually it will "defile" others (Hebrews 12:15). The Greek word for "defile" means, "to stain." No wonder we see so many separations and divorces—broken homes.

Steve had always felt neglected by his wife during the years the children were at home. He had tried, but to no avail, to talk to her about getting the emotional leftovers from the love and attention she showered on their three kids. Even though this barren relationship was painful, he endured for the sake of the children—that is, until the youngest one left for college. Steve left then, too, his bitterness a parting gift that stained those who were closest to him.

> One thing is certain. An angry and bitter person has no joy, creativity, and positive influence.

Spiritual Problems

A bitter attitude is so serious that Jesus said you should stop whatever religious "thing" you are doing and go settle the matter with the one with whom you have a problem. "Therefore, if you are offering your gift at the altar and there remember that your brother has something against you, leave your gift there in front of the altar. First go and be reconciled to your brother; then come and offer your gift" (Matthew 5:23–24).

Both your relationship with Christ and your influence for Him are at stake. Pastor and author Charles Stanley understood this when he reflected on his relationship with his children:

> Not long ago, I sat down with my two children, Andy and Becky, and asked if they had resentful feelings toward me for any wrong I had perpetuated. At the time, they were both in their twenties, and so they felt freer to talk openly and honestly. Andy was the first to respond. He recalled a time when he was thirteen or fourteen and was practicing one part of a song over and over . . . the same melody. I asked him if that was all he knew. Andy recalled that to his adolescent ears, my words sounded like I was saying 'I don't like you or your music.' That damaging impression caused him to decide not to play any music for me again, even though he was a talented musician. Becky had her memory, too. "When I was five years old, we lived in Miami. One day you put me in my room and you wouldn't let me out. I cried and cried, but you wouldn't let me out." (from *The Gift of Forgiveness* by Charles Stanley).

Charles Stanley asked for their forgiveness, which helped the three of them find spiritual healing. In Ephesians 4:31–32, the Apostle Paul wrote that we need to eliminate a *six-headed monster*:

1. **Bitterness.** The internalized, smoldering resentment that keeps a person in perpetual animosity. If bitterness is not resolved by forgiveness, then monsters 2 through 6 kick in.

2. **Rage.** The explosion that leads to revenge.

3. **Anger.** Never-ending internal deterioration.

4. **Brawling.** Public outburst that reveals loss of control.

5. **Slander.** Defamation of character.

6. **Malice.** The root of all vices.

"First go and be reconciled to your brother; then come and offer your gift."
Matthew 5:24

Forgiveness Makes a Difference

At the heart of the matter, forgiveness means setting someone free. When one person has hurt another, a debt needs to be paid. The forgiving person cancels that debt.

The person who refuses to forgive holds a grudge. Some people enjoy this—it can give a certain sense of power. But holding a grudge is like grabbing a rattlesnake by the tail. The holder will get bitten.

Before entering the process of forgiveness, we need to understand three mistaken ideas about forgiveness. First, some assume that understanding an individual's behavior (the reasons for that person's actions) or explaining it away is the same thing as forgiveness. It is not. Knowing that a person lashed out at you in public because he is dealing with frustrations at home does not mean that you have forgiven him.

Another mistaken idea is that time heals all wounds. Many men have grown up without the affection or the affirmation of their fathers. During their twenties and thirties, they may talk about it and think that, in time, it will no longer bother them. Often, however, these men in their late forties or early fifties will face an emotional crisis where they realize that they can't go on without dealing with the rejection. At that point, these men usually need professional help. Time didn't heal the wound—it just temporarily masked it.

The third mistaken idea is that we should confess our bitterness and express forgiveness to someone who had neither solicited it nor wanted it. Actually this will do more harm. Expressing forgiveness with the other person being oblivious to his or her offense will come off as "holier than thou," and the other person may interpret this as one more control issue. It can come off as a feigned forgiveness. And, if the other party is not emotionally ready to deal with it, this can make him feel humiliated for not wanting to respond with his own forgiveness.

Fortunately, it only takes one person to forgive. It takes two to reconcile, but one person can clear the deck of his own bitterness and move on. For those who want to do so, there is a Five Step Process of Forgiveness.

> Before entering the process of forgiveness, we need to understand three mistaken ideas about forgiveness.

Step One: Forgive and Forget the Debt

A story told about Robert E. Lee after the Civil War has him visiting a lady in Kentucky who points to a battered tree outside her home. She says it used to be a beautiful magnolia, but now it's without limbs. The Union Army had blasted it with their artillery and she asked, "What do you think about that?"

Lee looked at her and responded with one sentence. "Cut it down and forget about it."

That is the best advice. *Forgive and forget.* Forgetting an unhappy experience pays a wonderful dividend. It no longer siphons your emotional and spiritual energy and sets you free to use that energy where God has called.

Step Two: Release the Offender

When a debt is cancelled, the debtor is free to go. Sometimes he hangs around until he is invited to leave. That's what happened to John Tolson's father. He left home when John was two years old, never to return again. Like any boy who longs for a father, this left a hole in John's heart. For years, he wondered what it would be like to see his father again, to have him show up for one of his basketball games. John longed for words of affirmation that he would never hear. He would dream about a hug or an *"attaboy,"* but the dream was never fulfilled.

It was difficult to forgive a father he never saw, until a special day at the beach where John had one last conversation with his father. John sat in a chair facing an empty chair just inches away. With carefully selected words, John spoke as though his father were sitting in the chair. John forgave his father and then released him and also years of bitterness and pain. It was a one-sided conversation, but it was enough to bring closure and healing to a middle-aged man.

Step Three: Understand the Growth Process

No one has the big picture of what God is doing, especially with the painful experiences of life. After having been sold into slavery by his brothers, Joseph must have found it difficult to forgive his brothers and release them. But you never find him second-guessing his circumstances. In fact, eventually he became a prince of Egypt and in a position of power where he could save his family from starvation.

Joseph saw the hand of God in the painful and shameful way he was treated. So he told his brothers, "But God sent me ahead of you to preserve for you a remnant on earth and to save your lives by a great deliverance" (Genesis 45:7).

Joseph had the foresight to know that hindsight would explain how God was involved in his life. He was on a journey of growth, and he never wavered from believing God was using all of his life experiences for good. He said, "Don't be afraid. Am I in the place of God? You intended to harm me, but God intended it for good to accomplish what is now being done, the saving of many lives" (Genesis 50:19–20).

> "You intended to harm me, but God intended it for good to accomplish what is now being done, the saving of many lives."
>
> *Genesis 50:20*

Step Four: Make Reconciliation

If you can, make a phone call. That's what Robert did. He's a top officer in a national CPA firm. One day he was challenged to take an intentional step and a first step toward two men in his company that he felt he had wronged. Sometimes you just have to set your emotions on the table and do the right thing without processing it over and over in your mind. An old country preacher used to say, "Get your doer doing, and your feeler will follow."

Robert got his "doer doing." He made the call and all was forgiven and forgotten. That's when the Gospel becomes very attractive—when something tangible happens.

Step Five: Express Kindness

This is the follow-up step. Follow the call with a note, a gift, an *"I thought of you"* event! Lovers used to add a note to the outside of an envelope, SWAK—Sealed With A Kiss. Reconciliation can also use a SWAK or two—Sealed With A Kindness. It is added evidence that you are very serious about what just happened. It also answers the question "I wonder if they feel the same today about the reconciliation as they did yesterday?"

Daily Reflection Questions

Day One

1 What is a "root of bitterness"?

2 Why do people become embittered?

3   What evidence do you see of bitterness in a person's life?

Day Two

1   What physical or mental results of bitterness have you seen?

2   What relational or spiritual results of bitterness have you seen?

3   How does bitterness multiply?

Day Three

1   When have you seen bitterness progress through the other five heads of the "monster"?

2   How does forgiveness set someone free?

3   Why do some people refuse to forgive?

Day Four

I   When have you heard any of the mistaken ideas of forgiveness?

2   What makes it so difficult to forget after we've forgiven?

3   Why is releasing the offender a vital part of true forgiveness?

Day Five

1   Whom do you need to forgive?

2   With whom do you need to be reconciled?

3   What steps will you take to do that, to follow through?

CHAPTER EIGHTEEN

EMOTIONAL ASSETS: DEPRESSION OR JOY

*Suddenly something happened, I can't explain it. I can only
call it a miracle. I felt as if I had been instantly lifted out of the
darkness of a dungeon into a warm, brilliant sunlight. I felt
as if I had been transported from Hell to Paradise.*

J. C. Penney (coming out of depression)

An advertisement for an anti-depressant drug runs like this:
"Depressed mood. Loss of interest. Sleep problems. Difficulty
concentrating. Agitation. Restlessness. Life is too precious to let
another day go by feeling not quite 'yourself.' If you've experienced
some of these symptoms nearly every day, for at least two weeks, a
chemical imbalance could be to blame. And life can feel difficult ALL
DAY."

According to psychiatrist Paul Meier, "About one-fifth of
Christians worldwide experience enough depression to interfere with
their ability to function normally." Every two Christians out of ten that
you meet have deep struggles. They don't all have the same source
but they can cause severe damage if not addressed in a meaningful
way. The Lord was disturbed with the prophets and priests of Israel
because they would not address the wounds of His people seriously
but only superficially, crying, "Peace, peace . . . when there is no peace"
(Jeremiah 6:14). Today's priests or ministers often try to provide a
superficial peace for people's emotional or spiritual pain that is equally
disturbing to the Lord.

In order to deal with the wounds of depression seriously, we must
have more than a superficial understanding of the problem. Such
discernment would include the differences between the experience
of male and female depression, as presented below by Dr. Archibald
Hart in his book *Unmasking Male Depression* (Word Publishing,
2001).

MALE DEPRESSION	FEMALE DEPRESSION
Blames others	Blames herself
Acts out his inner turmoil	Turns her feelings inward
Needs to maintain control at all costs	Has trouble maintaining control
Overtly hostile, irritable	Always tries to be nice
Attacks when hurt	Withdraws when hurt
Tries to fix by problem-solving	Tries to fix by trying harder
Turns to sports, TV, sex, alcohol	Turns to food, friends, emotional needs
Feels shamed	Feels guilty
Becomes a compulsive timekeeper	Procrastinates, delays deadlines
Terrified to confront weakness	Exaggerates, obsesses about weakness
Tries to maintain strong male image	Disintegrates at slightest failure
Tries to act away	Tries to think through
Turns to alcoholism and other addictions	Increased appetite and weight

A classic case study on the symptoms of depression is found in 1 Kings 19—the story of Elijah having fled wicked Queen Jezebel after standing against 450 prophets of Baal (1 Kings 18). It is a classic story of going from the pinnacle to the pit, from a spiritual "high" to the dark night of depression.

Woven into the narrative of 1 Kings 19 is a dialogue between the Lord and Elijah that reveals what depression looks like and how it is expressed. Some of the symptoms would make Elijah a candidate for Paxil® if it had been available at the time.

> "Elijah was afraid and ran for his life."
> *1 Kings 19:3*

1. Fear (1 Kings 19:3)

"Elijah was afraid and ran for his life."

News that 450 prophets of Baal lost their lives made Elijah a marked man. Not only did he not have the time to savor the victory of the Lord over His adversaries, he was now on the run and would soon be trapped by thoughts that he would not have believed possible for a man of God.

Fears can get out of control, which would be one of those "wiles of the devil" to which Paul refers in Ephesians 6. The Enemy knows what deeply bothers us, so he hits us there. The following list contains some of the most common triggers of depression through the years.

✖ Fear your grades aren't good enough for the college you want to attend

✖ Fear you won't find a meaningful relationship with the opposite sex

✖ Fear of being stuck in a dead-end career

✖ Fear that your kids won't turn out well

✖ Fear of a bad medical report

✖ Fear that you won't have enough money for retirement

2. Isolation (1 Kings 19:3–4)

Dr. Philip Zimbardo, Professor of Psychology at Stanford University, wrote, "I know of no more destructive influence on physical and mental health than the isolation of you from me and us from them."

The only thing worse than being fatigued, exhausted, and burned out like Elijah is having to go through it alone. After fleeing from Jezebel, Elijah came to Beersheba. First Kings 19:3 reports, "He left his servant there, while he himself went a day's journey into the desert."

One of the dangers of depression is to turn inward and to hide from those who care the most for us. In an isolated condition, the mind starts playing games, causing you to hear voices that usually say scary things. In that kind of fog, it's difficult to know the difference between truth and a lie.

Isolation is increasingly a problem. Robert Putnam, author of *Bowling Alone*, discovered this after extensive research that involved 500,000 interviews over the last quarter century. He found that Americans have declining social connections where they know their neighbors less, meet with friends less frequently, and belong to fewer organizations. In the last twenty-five years, families spend increasingly less dinnertime together and 45 percent less time having friends over to the house.

This lack of connection is not good for longevity or a state of happiness. One surprising fact offered by Putnam is that joining just one group cuts in half the odds of dying the next year.

> "He left his servant there, while he himself went a day's journey into the desert."
> *1 Kings 19:3*

3. Self-Pity (1 Kings 19:4)

Collapsing in the shade of a broom tree, Elijah declared, "I have had enough." He evaluated his condition based on the reasoning process forged in isolation and fear and succumbed to a *"poor me"* mentality.

Millicent Fenwick said, "Never feel self-pity, the most destructive emotion there is. How awful to be caught up in the terrible squirrel cage of self."

Elijah's mind began going in circles, and when that happens, even God's servant may contemplate suicide.

4. Faded Faith (1 Kings 19:4)

The fear, aloneness, and self-pity were the prime ingredients that caused Elijah to forget God's presence and His past faithfulness. That is typical for someone who is not thinking clearly. If Elijah's servant had been there, he could have reminded Elijah about:

- The famine that he had foretold had come to pass
- His being fed by ravens
- The widow's barrel of flour and jar of oil never running dry
- The widow's son raised to life
- God's fire on Mt. Carmel had consumed the soaked altar sacrifice
- The rains returning at his request
- His ability, with supernatural strength, to outrace the king's chariot

"He came to a broom tree, sat down under it and prayed that he might die."
1 Kings 19:4

Elijah's faith faded not only because of a poor memory, but because he had no one who could loan him faith. That's right—at times we need a loan, we need to borrow from someone else the faith and strength to put everything into perspective. Elijah's spiritual bank account was empty. Before he could return to the old Elijah, he needed emotional and spiritual assets. Eventually they would come.

5. Suicidal (1 Kings 19:4)

"He came to a broom tree, sat down under it and prayed that he might die."

Psychologists say that people take their own lives when the pain of living is no longer bearable. In a physically, emotionally, and spiritually depleted condition, death seems like the way out.

Abraham Lincoln felt that way at one point in his life when he said, "I am the most miserable man living. To remain as I am is impossible. I must die or be better." Lincoln had moved from discouragement to despondency to despair. That's where irrationality sets in and thoughts of death.

The five-year age span that has the highest suicide rate is the group from 80 to 84-year-olds, primarily because so many of them live alone.

No one is exempt from depression regardless of the strength of his or her faith. Those who hit bottom and have suicidal thoughts need help. If a man finds a lump under the armpit, he goes to the doctor and immediately seeks help. And he doesn't feel guilty for doing so. Likewise, we should feel no remorse for seeking the best advice for dealing with the potentially lethal depression that has grown into a major problem for people from all across the globe and in every social stratum.

6. Exhaustion (1 Kings 19:5)

Coach Vince Lombardi said, "Fatigue makes cowards of us all." Psychologists have coined a term called *vital exhaustion* that has three characteristics: (1) Feelings of excessive fatigue and lack of energy, (2) Increasing irritability, and (3) Feelings of demoralization.

Nothing looks right to the exhausted mind, and physical exhaustion has little to do with mental exhaustion. A person who puts in a day of physically taxing work can actually feel mentally refreshed though physically worn out.

Elijah was running—he was physically tired, but his depression came from not understanding what was going on, not being able to see either a good conclusion or rescue on the horizon. His physical state contributed to, but didn't determine, his mental outlook.

7. Feeling Rejected (1 Kings 19:10)

"I have been very zealous for the Lord God Almighty. The Israelites have rejected your covenant, broken down your altars, and put your prophets to death with the sword. I am the only one left, and now they are trying to kill me too."

Elijah's rejection was closely related to his self-pity. Few people have egos strong enough to withstand personal rejection, especially from people who should know better or from people who matter. At this point, their rejection was determining Elijah's sense of well-being.

Elijah is not the only spiritual leader to experience depression; in fact, he is in the company of people like Job, Moses, Jonah, Peter, and Paul. Spiritual giants centuries later also faced the dark night of the soul, including Martin Luther, Charles Spurgeon, and Vance Havener.

> "The Israelites have rejected your covenant, . . . and now they are trying to kill me too."
>
> *1 Kings 19:10*

So the question is what to do when Paxil® is not available. The answer is simple but not simplistic. Let God heal and let the joy return.

Here is how God was able to heal Elijah.

1. He recognized that Elijah's depression was real.

Maybe it was post-adrenalin depression. Often, a significant victory can be followed by a walk through the valley. One day Elijah was exulting over his victory over Baal's prophets; the next day he wants to die. Yet God doesn't scold him for his feelings. He acknowledges that Elijah needs help.

2. He let Elijah rest (1 Kings 19:2–16).

When you are worn out, you need rest. Sometimes the most spiritual thing you can do is eat your favorite meal and then take a nap. It's amazing how some people have the attitude that the only way to prove your spiritual zeal is to burn out. That wasn't the pattern Jesus modeled. He would greatly exert himself meeting human needs and then withdraw for renewal. He understood that physically depleted people have a short cycle of usefulness.

3. He didn't give Elijah counsel for a while.

More beneficial than the power of well-spoken words is the power of presence. Anyone who has grieved deeply will tell you that they remember precious few words spoken to them during their hour of crisis, but they are forever grateful for the silent presence of someone they love and trust.

In 1862, during a difficult period in the Civil War, a Quaker woman and her friend found an audience with Abraham Lincoln for the purpose of prayer and spiritual support. Eliza Gurney, the widow of English Quaker Joseph J. Gurney, did not come to counsel Lincoln. Rather, in the Quaker tradition, she came to spend long moments in silence and prayer for the President of the nation inflamed in the ravages of war. Two years later, Lincoln would write to Elizabeth Gurney, "I have not forgotten . . . probably never shall forget . . . the impressive occasion when yourself and friends visited me on a Sabbath forenoon two years ago."

God was present with Elijah, but He waited for the right time to give insight.

4. He let Elijah explain the problem.

Dr. Paul Meier, co-founder of Meier New-Life Clinics, says that more important than prescription medicine as the antidote for depression is what he calls *"talk therapy."*

> Sometimes the most spiritual thing you can do is eat your favorite meal and then take a nap.

Elijah began to talk after the Lord asked, "What are you doing here?" Elijah rehearsed how faithful he had been for the cause of God only to be isolated, persecuted, and abandoned by other believers.

Elijah may have felt like he was the only faithful one left, but it was not true. Later the Lord would reveal, "I reserve seven thousand in Israel—all whose knees have not bowed down to Baal and all whose mouths have not kissed him" (1 Kings 19:18).

God was giving Elijah time to vent, time to make irrational statements, time to unpack his frustration. God was exploring Elijah's heart, but first Elijah had to understand his heart through the expression of his mouth. This exploration process is essential for anyone who wants to find healing.

5. He dealt with Elijah's false beliefs.

During World War II, the allied forces came across a bombed out building in Europe that had an inscription scrawled on a basement wall:

> I believe in the sun even when it is not shining. I believe in love even when it is not shown, and I believe in God even when He doesn't speak.

God was ready to speak, and Elijah would be reintroduced to the God of Abraham, Isaac, and Jacob. God's awesome display of wind, earthquake, and fire would be impressive but the real power would come to Elijah in profound words whispered in his ear.

At the core of Elijah's problem was an inadequate view of God. It's understandable that he had this view, but it's not permissible to sustain that view. Zig Ziglar likes to say that people's problems are related to *"stinkin' thinkin'!"* When we are refreshed enough to handle truth, God will put us in a place where we can enter "reality therapy," or the healing that comes from dealing realistically with ourselves and realistically with the truth of Scripture.

> "I reserve seven thousand in Israel—all whose knees have not bowed down to Baal and all whose mouths have not kissed him."
>
> *1 Kings 19:18*

6. He gave Elijah something to do.

"Go back the way you came . . . [to] Damascus . . . anoint Hazael King of Aram . . . anoint Jehu son of Nimshi king over Israel . . . anoint Elisha . . . to succeed you as prophet" (1 Kings 19:15–17).

In other words, go back to work. Do something useful. Find someone in need and help that person. Get out of yourself and think about someone else. It's remarkable how your problems can become insignificant when you begin to serve those who need your touch. Ask anyone who has volunteered for a short-term missionary trip. He or she returned spiritually energized though physically exhausted. Dr.

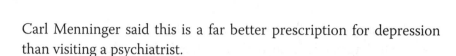

Carl Menninger said this is a far better prescription for depression than visiting a psychiatrist.

7. He gave Elijah a friend.

Entering the story of 1 Kings 19, is Elisha, Elijah's new attendant and friend. Elijah was no longer isolated. Elisha was a gift from God, a brother, a co-laborer, and exactly what Elijah needed.

In the end, one of the greatest weapons to fight depression is perseverance. You may not be able to stop the dark blanket coming over you, but you can choose how to respond to it. You tell the depression that it can come a hundred times, but you will never stop fighting. You will wear depression out. You may get knocked down, but you will always get up.

In October 31, 1974 a great fight took place in Kinshasa, Zaire. Called "The Rumble in the Jungle," this was the championship heavyweight boxing match between Muhammad Ali and George Foreman. Ali was 32 years old and had lost his last two fights, one to Joe Frazier in 1971 and another to Ken Norton in 1973, when Ali's jaw was broken.

George Foreman was the Olympic champion who had defeated both Frazier and Norton, each in just two rounds. He was young, he was strong, and he was eager.

Ali knew he could not beat Foreman by exchanging blows, by matching strength for strength. At the beginning of the second round he started backing up against the ropes and shielding his head with his forearms but occasionally taunting Foreman by waiting for him to come get him. Foreman landed body blow after body blow, pounding as rapidly as he could but also progressively loosing steam. By the seventh round Ali was whispering in his ear, "Is that all you got George?" George knew it was all he had. In the eighth round Ali sprang like a cobra with left-right combinations and knocked Foreman out.

Sometimes the Enemy needs to punch himself out. As you gradually realize this is happening, you know that eventually you will be the victor. This builds confidence in yourself and often shortens the amount of time depression has a grip on you.

> You will wear depression out. You may get knocked down, but you will always get up.

Daily Reflection Questions

Day One

1 Why are so many people depressed these days?

2 What does the world offer as remedies for depression?

3 How effective are these remedies?

Day Two

1 Why do so many Christians struggle with depression?

2 In the chart comparing male and female depression, which statements stand out to you?

3 For which of these statements have you seen examples?

Day Three

1 What caused Elijah, God's powerful prophet, to become depressed?

2 How did Elijah respond to those feelings?

3 In what ways do reactions to depression cause problems in other areas of life?

Day Four

1 With which of Elijah's symptoms of depression could you most identify?

2 In what ways are depression and faith connected?

3 Why are spiritual leaders susceptible to depression?

Day Five

1 At what times do you find yourself getting depressed?

2 What can you do to "let God heal and let the joy return"?

3 How will you change your routine to help you avoid depression and become joyful?

CHAPTER NINETEEN

SOCIAL ASSETS: BARRIERS TO RELATIONSHIPS

You may remember Earl Campbell, the famous running-back for the Houston Oilers, who won the Heisman Trophy in 1977 and led the NFL in rushing three times. Called a "one-man demolition team," Campbell was one of the toughest men on the field to bring down due to tremendous lower body strength and his reputation for plowing through tackles with a jolting stiff arm. The mental image is a powerful runner plowing through defensive players with heads snapping back as they attempt a tackle.

Have you ever been stiff-armed in a relationship? Sometimes relationships can be like that, everyone playing the game, having a great time, until *bam*, it comes to a halt. Sometimes this happens with a sudden jerk—the so-called friend disappears. Sometimes it's more gradual—the person just fades away.

Relationships sour for many reasons but often because one person has a blind spot. The person doesn't see the barrier he or she has erected that prevents the relationship from continuing. Unfortunately, the problem will surface again and again until it is dealt with and eliminated. The list of barriers could be lengthy, but here are a few of the most obvious. As you read them, consider how you are doing in the area of relationships.

Barriers

Hidden Feelings

Holding one's cards close to your vest is a good tactic in poker, but it's a fail-safe way of sending the message "I'll only give you the information I choose and when I choose." People want to know why the person is so guarded. What does he or she have to hide? It's also usually a sign that a person is closed to honest criticism.

Proverbs 9:9 says, "Instruct a wise man and he will be wiser still; teach a righteous man and he will add to his learning." Instructing a person is impossible when we aren't allowed to get close enough for any meaningful two-way exchange. We can treat an acquaintance that way, but not a friend. If we have the time and desire, we can explore the reasons behind the behavior. Maybe that person opened up in a relationship and got burned. Most social inhibitions are the result of fear.

> "Instruct a wise man and he will be wiser still; teach a righteous man and he will add to his learning."
>
> *Proverbs 9:9*

Some individuals fear that once they are truly known—the cards are revealed—they won't be liked. So safety has to be a part of the equation. Jesus worked that way. The woman at the well (John 4) did not open up to Jesus until after He made it safe. Jesus engaged her with questions and soft answers until she was willing to be honest with Him. Jesus had an advantage, of course—He knew what cards she was holding. But anyone who is savvy about human behavior knows the most obvious cards.

Shallow relationships can continue when people are afraid to reveal the hand they are dealt, but they won't move beyond casual encounters and will never be fully satisfying.

Resentments

If something has caused a deep, reflective displeasure toward another person—in other words, someone has been deeply hurt by another—their relationship will be paused until the primary cause is identified and dealt with.

The pain is real, and unfortunately, the more one person loves the other, the more the friendship is desired, the more vulnerable that person is to disappointment. Some might say that his or her expectations for the relationship were too high. Perhaps. More likely, the relationship was poisoned. Here are five ways to *poison the well* and to end a friendship.

1. One-sided commitment

It boils down to feeling a lack of appreciation and being used. Person A puts a lot of thought and energy into the relationship and tries to live out 1 Corinthians 13:5 to not be rude, self-seeking, or easily angered. This individual calls to see how Person B is doing. He or she takes the friend to lunch, plans social events, and is willing to give unselfishly to Person B. And the realization hits—not only does Person B not appreciate all the efforts, he or she is using Person A.

Such one-sided commitments are doomed from the start. Sometimes people hang on for a while, hoping things will change or questioning how they are interpreting the situation. Eventually, the pain is intolerable and the relationship ends.

2. Competition

Maintaining a close relationship with someone perceived as a competitor can be quite difficult. For example, best friends in college can see their friendship unravel when both enter the same competitive environment in the corporate world.

David and Jonathan had a profoundly deep friendship. Their love for each other could stand all tests because David didn't want to be

> Shallow relationships can continue when people are afraid to reveal the hand they are dealt, but they won't move beyond casual encounters and will never be fully satisfying.

Jonathan, and Jonathan didn't want to be David. Their story can be found in 1 Samuel 13–31.

The mutual admiration of either friends or siblings can be sustained for a while under the guise of wanting what is best for each other or the desire for a truly spiritual response. Time, however, has a way of eroding the noble gesture on the part of the one who plays second fiddle.

That's what happened to Miriam. Eventually a root of resentment burrowed into her heart. Miriam, Aaron, and Moses were the children of Amram and Jochebed, a Levite couple during Israel's sojourn in Egypt. Miriam was a faithful daughter, sister, and even prophetess (Exodus 15:20). She saved Moses' life by persuading Pharaoh's daughter to allow his birth mother to nurse him.

She had natural leadership skills and charisma as seen when she led the Israelites in dance and singing after they passed through the Red Sea. But Numbers 12 reveals a heart that had been poisoned gradually by resentment. Both Aaron and Miriam asked, "Has the Lord spoken only through Moses? . . . Hasn't he also spoken through us?" (Numbers 12:2). God was not pleased. "The anger of the Lord burned against them, and he left them" (Numbers 12:9).

It's interesting that Moses had killed a man, and Aaron had made an idol. But Miriam got leprosy because a sense of competition led to heart problems that God wanted to stop in its tracks.

It's tough for people who were once in leadership or in the limelight to be bypassed by others. But each new frame of time requires different gifts or talents, and God gives a new group of people their moment in the sun.

We don't hear anything more about Miriam. She likely subordinated herself to Moses and the plan God had for her for the rest of her life.

> "The unfaithful are destroyed by their duplicity."
>
> *Proverbs 11:3*

3. Verbal Betrayal

"What's spoken in this room, stays in this room." That is the admonition of the small group leader laying the groundwork for the safe expression of deep personal thoughts or life experiences. And it works, that is, until one person shares something outside the group that was intended to be private.

Relationships cannot stand the lack of trust that follows: ". . . the unfaithful are destroyed by their duplicity" (Proverbs 11:3).

Most people don't try to hurt the one about whom they gossip. But titillating news is hard to suppress. The humdrum of life looks for sensations or bits of information that can spice it up. That's why James dedicated a chapter in his book (chapter 3) to explore metaphors for the tongue. He knew that more damage can be inflicted and more lives destroyed by that small instrument of power than by any other weapon. In each illustration, James shows that someone more powerful than human nature or the tongue must be in control. A bit is used in a horse's mouth to turn the animal when in the hands of a competent rider. Its pilot controls the rudder of a ship, or the vessel would be forever off course and tossed around by the waves of circumstance. Because no human being can control the tongue, it must be guarded ferociously and constantly be committed to Christ's control.

4. Mocking and Put-downs

Mocking is another form of verbal abuse. It imitates a person for the purpose of laughter in order to show contempt or ridicule, usually taking words or reactions out of context. When Michael Moore produced his documentary, *Fahrenheit 9/11*, he used selected video clips of President George W. Bush, like the seven minutes he continued to be with elementary students after he was informed that the second plane had hit the World Trade Center. A clock was on the screen to tick away the minutes in a way to denigrate and mock the President.

Mockery not only is a barrier to relationships, it signals that the mocker intends to permanently damage the relationship. "Whoever corrects a mocker invites insult; whoever rebukes a wicked man incurs abuse" (Proverbs 9:7).

Sometimes friends enjoy verbal sparing—the innocent exchange—and matching wits in a *put-down* duel. That can be a sign of health in a relationship until the rules are violated. When the mockery starts to get personal, intending to dig where it hurts, there is an area of sensitivity. Great wisdom needs to be used to know when to back off and then to season the conversation with words that encourage.

> "Whoever corrects a mocker invites insult; whoever rebukes a wicked man incurs abuse."
> *Proverbs 9:7*

5. Smothering

Certain personality types are warm, caring, eager to please. They enjoy being with you, are committed to making you happy, would never do or say anything to hurt you. They can also tend to be overprotective, to take on a *mothering* quality.

In the movie *Planes, Trains & Automobiles,* starring Steve Martin and John Candy, Neil Page (Steve Martin) is trying to get back to Chicago from New York in time for Thanksgiving. As fate would have it, he travels with Del Griffith (John Candy), a shower curtain-ring salesman. Del becomes an annoying, frustrating, and smothering companion as the two of them work at finding any means of transportation to get home.

In one scene, John Candy is sitting in the burned out shell of a car, in freezing weather, abandoned by Steve Martin and says woefully,

"I'm the most annoying person to come down the pike. I finally find someone whose company I really enjoy, and what do I do? I smother the poor soul!"

A fine line stands between being concerned and being nosy—between caring and smothering. Attempts to get too close feel threatening to the other person because he or she wants space, to be able to breathe and live without every thought and action being observed and critiqued by another.

The danger is that the smothered individual can develop physical problems if he or she internalizes the stress and refuses to set boundaries with those who do more harm than good. Research shows that smothering relationships take away a person's sense of control, which can lead to a negative impact on physical health.

Another form of smothering is when one person is always right and the other is always assumed to be wrong. No matter what is said, how much there is a desire for shared responsibility in conflict, the smothering one sees absolutely no reason to confess his or her share of responsibility. This can lead to a personality disorder that will eventually destroy both the one who smothers and the smothered.

> A fine line stands between being concerned and being nosy— between caring and smothering.

Risky Behavior

Normally, risky behavior is equated with adolescence; however, adults can also sabotage a relationship by engaging in addictions or illegal behavior.

Excessive drinking is risky behavior, and most of the reasons are obvious. Not only are health, job, and other drivers at risk but also those closest to the drinker. A spouse, child, or friend will flee if threatened. Alcoholics Anonymous and other 12-step programs have saved millions who were in the process of destroying their lives. Alcoholics Anonymous claims to have 2 million members in over 150 countries. Imagine how many friends and family members are affected, both those who were forever scarred by the drunk and those who were restored because help was found.

Physicians who treat alcoholics say that at some point a "psychic change" takes place when people submit to an unquenchable craving for alcohol and, though remorseful and after having made a firm resolve to never drink again, slide down the same slope. At first they think that they can drink in moderation but not be controlled by it. But alcohol is a demon they cannot control on their own; thus, part of the psychic change is feeling doomed and utterly without hope.

At that point, it is as much a spiritual issue as it is physical. At the point when we are in over our head, we cry out for help. George W. Bush came to that point when he risked his marriage to Laura, his relationship to his two daughters, and his career. He cried out, as David did in Psalm 51:1, "Have mercy on me, O God!"

The Lord was merciful to George Bush, and he faced the next "psychic change." He was forgiven, he was clean, and he could never drink again. His next challenge was having the world's social elite ridicule him because he would have water instead of wine with his meal. But he was determined. He had nearly destroyed his most important relationships once before, and he would not do it again.

If your life is unraveling because of alcohol or any other addiction, *get help*. Call a counselor, a pastor, or a friend who has been there. Millions have seen the fortune of family and friends restored—*you can too*.

Changes in Life

Life is never static, even though it is changing at an imperceptible pace. Sometimes the change is more apparent and drastic, especially when a person comes to Christ, and the old values and way of life fall off like an old garment. Paul told the Corinthians, "Therefore, if anyone is in Christ, he is a new creation; the old has gone, the new has come!" (2 Corinthians 5:17).

> "Therefore, if anyone is in Christ, he is a new creation; the old has gone, the new has come!"
>
> *2 Corinthians 5:17*

Not everyone is thrilled with the new values embraced by a friend or spouse, especially if those values threaten the person's worldview or lifestyle. Many relationships have not survived someone's spiritual transformation. The two come to a fork in the road and never will be on the same path again.

Other changes allow relationships to slip away. You have heard the old adage, "out of sight—out of mind." A person may move away and then try to maintain the bond that was once there, but it's nearly impossible.

Aging, adversity, health issues, and other life changes have a way of changing the dynamics of a relationship. This is a natural process that we should permit to happen without remorse. But all changes bring a certain sadness. Those who don't want the changes to be a barrier to a relationship need a strong, mutual commitment to work against the gravitational pull with an equal determination to stay connected. This must be intentional—no relationships survive passivity, no matter whether it is marriage or friendship.

Daily Reflection Questions

Day One

1   Why are relationships so important to us?

2   How did you feel about the discussion of relationship barriers?

3   Why do we hide our true feelings from others?

Day Two

1   When have you felt deep resentment toward another person?

2   What was the cause?

3 How did you handle those feelings?

Day Three

1 When have you felt betrayed by a family member, friend, or co-worker?

2 Why does so much of today's humor include sarcasm and mocking?

3 When does this kind of joking hurt?

Day Four

1 Why does one spouse "smother" his or her mate?

2 Why do parents "smother" their children?

3 How do those being smothered typically react?

Day Five

1 In what ways has Christ changed your life?

2 How have those changes affected your relationships?

3 What can you do to remove the relationship barriers that you have erected?

CHAPTER TWENTY

SOCIAL ASSETS: YOU AND YOUR NETWORK

Humans don't survive well being alone. In fact, solitary confinement as a means of punishment is called "psychological death." Prisoners suffer memory loss, severe anxiety, and hallucinations. In other words, they go crazy.

At creation, God said, "It is not good for the man to be alone. I will make a helper suitable for him" (Genesis 2:18). He was referring to Adam's need for a wife. The Genesis passage starts with a social network, and two people qualify. If not a husband and wife, it can be two friends. (Chapters 27 and 28 will discuss the need for and the quality of friendship.) And adding a third party provides the strength of a cord. "Though one may be overpowered, two can defend themselves. A cord of three strands is not quickly broken" (Ecclesiastes 4:12).

Adding numbers to the social equation can add strength. Without an understanding of roles and purposes for the added strands, however, the result will be a knot. A person may have many friends and numerous acquaintances, but the destination of those relationships can be confusing or guarded, leading to problems.

Jesus developed relationship networks. His largest one was twelve, and the smallest was three (Peter, James, and John). While spending time with Jesus, these three disciples probably had little understanding of the role each of them would play. They followed Jesus, not to play a role, but because He had "the words of eternal life" (John 6:68).

Networking has become an important word in the business community. Making the right connection is critical to building a path to promote or to launch a product. This is also seen as a way to jump-start and sustain a career. It is also important in other areas of life.

Those who study social networks point to at least four critical links in the network chain. Dr. David Krakchardt, a leading researcher in social networks, uses the metaphor of a "Kite Network" to describe the way people are connected to one another. It is a good illustration and more understandable if we assign the letters A, B, C, and D to the four key links for a kite.

This diagram assigns these roles.

> "Though one may be overpowered, two can defend themselves. A cord of three strands is not quickly broken."
> *Ecclesiastes 4:12*

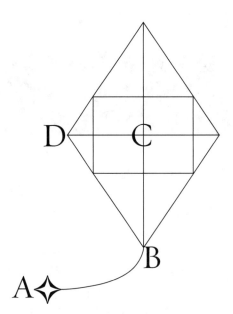

A. The A stands for **ANCHOR**. This is the person who steers you in the right direction and is a stabilizing influence during turbulence. This can be your mother or father, an uncle, a sibling, or a friend. For the sake of memory, we will assign four characteristics that make an anchor an anchor by using the acronym "WISE."

Wisdom
Unfortunately, this is not in ample supply. A person's life anchor needs solid ideas and a Solomon-like quality of providing understanding about how the world works—what product does the world need, even if the world doesn't know it? They have a strong foundation of faith that connects both Biblical wisdom and the wisdom of the world.

> A person's life anchor needs solid ideas and a Solomon-like quality of providing understanding about how the world works...

Insight
Knowing how to apply wisdom takes insight. Sometimes this involves timing. That is, when is the best time to roll out a product or to tackle a major project? Who are the key players? What other products are on the market that may become a potential competition or a barrier? It is also the ability to verbalize or express knowledge. Some people have wisdom but are unable to express it.

Savvy
A person can have the wisdom to understand what products or programs are needed and the insight of when to roll them out, but he or she also needs the practical know-how or common sense of how to get the job done. This doesn't happen by just thinking wise thoughts. It takes appropriate action at the appropriate time. It also takes the persistence that is required to overcome inertia.

Experience

Nothing gives clarity to life like experience. The experienced person knows where the land mines are located. This person knows how people respond. He or she knows that good ideas often run out of steam or are undercapitalized. To have credibility, the anchor must speak from experience and not from prejudice. This person can be trusted, for experience has taught him or her that only those who are faithful can have a deep impact on another human and on the goals they seek to accomplish.

An ANCHOR may not have all four of these characteristics in equal proportion, but we know one thing for certain: We trust his or her judgment. We know that this person is willing to give us his or her time and serious thought. To change the metaphor, this person is like the North Star, always there, always in the same place, always helping us to get our bearings for the journey.

B. The next link in the social network is the **BROKER**. A broker takes another person's wisdom, adds his or her own, and then unlocks the door of opportunity. The broker is the most critical person in the action/connection structure of the kite. We will use the word "KEY" to describe this person's role.

Knowledge

The broker's knowledge is in the area of what you need to do to get the job done and the people it will take to get moving. This person is not just a well-connected person with multiple friends; he or she is connected in the right places with the right people. Some have called this person a "deal maker" or a "rain maker" because things get done when he or she goes into action. The wheels spin very little; this person can make a couple of phone calls and connect us to people who can change our horizon.

Equity

This is *relationship* equity. The broker not only knows whom to call; he or she knows that the people called will answer the phone or return the call. That kind of trust is built over time. Brokers have earned the right to have access, and that makes them very special people.

The Apostle Paul was a world-class broker. His spiritual office was "apostle," but his skills were as an anchor and a broker. His wisdom flowed through his pen to the churches of Rome, Corinth, Galatia, Ephesus, Colosse, and Thessalonica. He took the time to provide guidance for Silas, Barnabas, Titus, Timothy, and others.

With Onesimus, he became a broker. Onesimus, a runaway slave

> Nothing gives clarity to life like experience.

from the household of Philemon, had somehow met Paul in Rome. Then he became a Christian and an encouragement to Paul while Paul was in chains in a Roman prison. Paul wrote a letter to ask Philemon to receive Onesimus now as a brother in Christ, not as a slave.

Paul's plea for Onesimus is based upon Onesimus's spiritual transformation but also on the friendship equity that Paul had with Philemon. Paul used some of that equity when he wrote, "So if you consider me a partner, welcome him as you would welcome me" (Philemon 1:17). Philemon could not resist. The right person made the appeal. Onesimus was restored to favor and his place in Philemon's household.

Yearning help

Paul was not reluctantly approaching Philemon. He loved Onesimus and made this a part of his appeal, "Yet I appeal to you on the basis of love. I then, as Paul—an old man and now also a prisoner of Christ Jesus" (Philemon 1:9).

A broker won't use his friendship equity without a driving desire to do so. So a good case has to be developed for the course of action. We should remember, however, that not every contact made by a broker will be productive. The contact may have other pressing issues or may not be ready to respond to a specific need. But the contact respects the broker, will respond if possible, and is not put-off by the request. Just the opposite is true—the contact is honored to be in the broker's network.

C. The third link is a **CONNECTOR**. The connector is at the center of contact cross sections. We will use the metaphor "LINK" to describe the characteristics of this person's position.

Lots of friends

Some people are like that—they are everyone's friends. They have been in social circulation for a long time, and people enjoy being around them. Like the broker, they have no problem having people return their phone calls or getting a foursome for a round of golf. If they receive a call from a broker and decide to spring into action, they have no difficulty in coming up with names.

In some ways, Peter was a connector. His personality and position within the Galilean fishing community gave him access to everyone associated with his trade. Eventually, the church would meet at his house—typical for someone well connected.

> "So if you consider me a partner, welcome him as you would welcome me."
> *Philemon 1:17*

Ideas

Connectors are also idea people. They may not have every connection needed, but they make good suggestions about social paths not yet traveled.

New networks

One of the greatest assets of a connector is to introduce us to new networks. If our social, business, and church life all involve the same people, we will soon run thin on contacts. Life consists of a variety of communities. We have a family support community, a career community, a faith community, an investment community, a recreation community, and, perhaps, a personal growth community. If the connectors from each of these communities get to know each other, it multiplies the breadth, depth, and speed in which the word gets out about our idea, need, or project.

Knowledge

Connectors are not just social butterflies; they are also people of depth, or they won't prove to be much use in disseminating thoughtful ideas. The best connectors are known to be people of substance, not panhandlers. This whole process is not about hype and shortcuts to meet unworthy goals. If that becomes the perceived agenda, the network will quickly collapse.

D. The final link is the **DOERS.** The connectors launch them into action. They are the worker bees who get the job done. The metaphor of their characteristics is "TAP."

> The best connectors are known to be people of substance, not panhandlers.

Talented

Depending on the size and scope of the project, unique talents will be required. Almost every situation needs graphic arts and marketing. There can be a great buzz about an idea and high voltage synapses firing from connectors to the connected, but if no one has the skill to capture the public's attention, it will be dead in the water. Part of the wisdom employed by the connector is knowing what talent resources are needed and then who to call.

Available

You might find the person with the right talent, and he or she may even seem interested in the project. But availability is essential. Many projects have been brought to a halt because a "doer" with a specific talent volunteered to help but, in reality, didn't have the time. It really becomes frustrating when they won't admit this and continue to make everyone feel they are still on track to make it happen.

Productive

All projects have timelines and deadlines. A talented person who has made the commitment to be available can still create problems by delays in productivity. When a target is met, something is produced or energy is unleashed that is invigorating to all who are involved. That is absolutely necessary, especially when the project is long term, taking months and maybe years to be accomplished. In that case, periodic bursts of adrenaline are needed to keep the momentum going. The production of a talented person can provide that energy.

Get Going

One social network does not meet all needs; a look over your shoulder will tell you that. Take a sheet of paper and list across the bottom the five categories where social networks played a role in your development:

Family Support — Career — Faith Investment — Personal Growth

Create a kite for each of these categories, by actually drawing the kite and assigning names or resources for each of the links. Here is an example for FAITH.

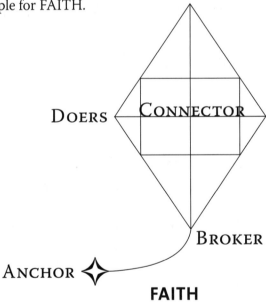

DOERS—Who provided a talent that helped produce fruit (teachers, preachers, books, people who met a special need)?

CONNECTORS—What people or resources (books, etc.) within different religious networks gave you the greatest number of contacts?

BROKER—Who introduced you to the network of people and ideas that made your faith grow?

ANCHOR—Who was your spiritual father, mother, mentor, or friend?

> One social network does not meet all needs; a look over your shoulder will tell you that.

As you do this for the essential areas of your life, you'll not only see that the social network was engaged without your being aware of what to call it, but now have the creativity to think about the next area that needs a network.

This chapter has been about you, your network, meeting your needs. Jesus said that the greatest among you is a servant, so now you know more intelligently what others need. Identify the role that you can play. For whom can you become an anchor, broker, connector, or doer? If you don't ask that question, then in the final analysis, this chapter is about selfishness.

Daily Reflection Questions

Day One

1 Why is solitary confinement such a horrible punishment?

2 What is "networking"?

3 In what ways is your relationship network important . . .

At home?

In your community?

At church?

In your career?

Day Two

1　Who are your network "anchors"?

2　What "brokers" do you know?

3　What builds relationship "equity"?

Day Three

1   Who have served as your network "connectors"?

2   Why is knowledge important for a "connector"?

3   Why do relationship networks need "doers"?

Day Four

1   Which one of the four network roles most describes you?

2   Which role(s) would you like to fill for others?

3   Which role(s) do you most need others to fill for you?

Day Five

1   What area of your life most needs a network?

2   For whom can you be an "anchor"?

A "broker"?

A "connector"?

A "doer"?

3   What will you do to strengthen your networks?

PRIORITY
THREE

A Personal, Progressive Commitment to Relationships

A notable Christian leader in the U.S. once said, "I just hope I can find eight men who want to carry the casket at my funeral." Of course he was joking—he was a man of many friends. But the point he made was poignant. Life can be made up of the fast pursuit of getting ahead and strengthening the financial bottom line, and neglect the most valuable asset of all—personal relationships.

When you are in the pursuit of strengthening the bond with the people God has given you, you are strengthening the body of Christ. Yet few people study the skills necessary to be a better spouse, better parent, better friend, or better member of the local or universal church. We think we have the innate ability to figure relationships out or just 'wing it' until there is a crisis and then seek help.

A man who had a profound impact on John Tolson and Larry Kreider was Jim Smith. Jim's last years were invested at Highland Park Presbyterian Church as the head of the counseling ministry. All relationships were important to Jim, and he succeeded at all of them. His influence was so pervasive that he was the subject of a lead article in *Texas Monthly Magazine*. Unfortunately, pancreatic cancer took him when he was at mid-life.

Jim's legacy lives on in the words penned by Curtis Meadows, words now framed and hung on a wall in one of the Highland Park Presbyterian offices. As you read this tribute, reflect on what can happen when a person lives out **Priority Three.**

I Have a Friend Called Jim Smith

I had a friend called Jim Smith. He greeted me as "Brother" and waved good-bye as Friend. He listened with his heart but spoke with his head. God gifted him with wisdom, yet tempered it with love. I had a friend called Jim Smith.

As Teacher, Mentor, Counselor, or Coach, he was there beside me. He was there for my family, for my colleagues, and for those I did not know. He was there for his family, for his Church, and for all who cried out. He was there because he cared and because his Master needed him there. I had a friend called Jim Smith.

His name was common but the man was not. From rough and rocky soil came this man of compassion, forgiveness, and learning. His mind always seeking, the hands always busy, the love always there, he was alive in God's service. I had a friend called Jim Smith.

"What can I do for you?" he asked. *"Do you need help?"* he called. Oh yes, we replied, oh, yes, yes, yes. And he came to us and we cried with him and he loved us to life again. Oh yes, yes, yes, we called, and he held us and laughed with us and lifted our burdens. He was God's love alive on this earth. It really was there and it was brought even to us by this humble man. Oh my yes, I had a friend called Jim Smith.

He gave us his time, the one unique gift we can give to another. He spent his life serving others, and I was one of the others. In this hurried world of false importance, he paused to touch me, to focus his precious moments of life upon me, bringing messages of encouragement, weaving strands of hope and understanding. At those moments, he was the vessel of my Savior, pouring forth from the pages of Scripture, he was authenticating the promises, we were not alone to face our terrors. I had *more* than a friend in Jim Smith.

Now, how do we deal with his parting. How we shall miss him! So many fears yet ahead, so many hills yet to climb, so many like me, yet afraid. *"Be still,"* he calls at Christ's side. *"I'm yet with you. I'm alive in your heart; I'm alive in your mind. I'm alive in my books; I'm alive in my tapes. I've left you my wisdom; I've left you my thoughts; I've left you my love. You were my friend. I witnessed God's love for you . . . go and do the same for others. Share His love and teachings, continue the ministry and God will use you instead of me."*

Even now he is teaching, even now he is caring, even now he's alive in my life. What a friend is my living friend, Jim Smith! All thanks be to You, Lord Jesus! Amen! (Curtis W. Meadows, Jr., February 26, 1993)

CHAPTER TWENTY-ONE

UNDERSTANDING YOUR SPOUSE

In one of the Peanuts cartoons, Lucy is frustrated over the communication differences between her and Charlie Brown. As she walks along the street, she bemoans, "That Chuck . . . he's something else. I don't even know why I think about him. He doesn't seem to understand girls' emotions. In fact, Chuck doesn't seem to understand girls at all. Chuck's hard to talk to. He doesn't understand life. He doesn't understand laughing and crying. He doesn't understand love and silly talk and touching hands and things like that. He plays a lot of baseball, but I doubt if he even understands baseball."

Then she reaches Charlie Brown's house and knocks on his door. "I don't think you understand anything, Chuck," she hollers. As Charlie sticks his head out to see who is at the door, Lucy walks away, and he says, "I don't even understand what it is that I don't understand."

A lot of men and women don't understand what they're supposed to understand because of the inherent differences between the sexes. Here are **eight major differences** that are worth looking at.

The Way We Communicate

Someone said, "Before the wedding, we didn't have enough time to say it all. After the wedding we don't even speak the same language."

Another said, "When I got married, we had an ideal . . . it's turned into an ordeal, and now I'm looking for a new deal."

Generally speaking, women tend to talk in specifics and men tend to talk in generalities. There are exceptions. Some men are very specific and are the more verbal of the pair; however, listen to the differences in the conversations at a party. Men will talk in generalities, telling jokes, talking about work or recreation. Women, on the other hand, will talk with greater detail about their feelings and attitudes.

If a man goes on a trip, he returns home to a series of questions from his wife: "Where did you stay? What kind of room was it? Where did you eat? What did you eat?" She wants details. Usually the man is either forgetful or unobservant. He may see her questioning as nagging and fishing for useless information. She sees her questions as a sign of interest in what's happening in her husband's life. They are also a way to communicate, to go beyond the Cliffs Notes version, to spend more time connecting with each other.

The problem is timing. If a wife hits her husband with thirty questions the minute he walks in the door when he is tired and ready

> A lot of men and women don't understand what they're supposed to understand because of the inherent differences between the sexes.

to unpack and unwind from the trip, he may appear agitated when all he needs is a little space.

So they go after each other like two trial attorneys, each pleading his or her case. The next day, the husband has forgotten about the incident. He backs his car out of the garage and heads to work ready to take on the world. She, on the other hand, has filed the emotions and the details of their conversation and is ready to start where they left off as soon as they're together again.

At some point, they will have to understand what the other person needs and begin to work on it. The wife will have to wait for the right time to ask her questions, and the husband will have to intentionally spell out in detail the things she wants to know.

These are gifts that the husband and wife can give each other. Another way of saying it is that these are deposits each can contribute to each other's emotional bank account. Couples can go for a long time without connecting—like two ships passing in the night—and one day, one of the partners erupts, collapses, or leaves. They may not be able to describe what has happened, but they are depleted. Their emotional account is empty. Before long, the marriage is in crisis.

> Couples can go for a long time without connecting . . . and one day, one of the partners erupts, collapses, or leaves.

The Way We Deal with Our Feelings

Women tend to be in touch with their feelings first and then their thoughts. This has nothing to do with their intellectual capacity but the sequence of how they process things.

On the other hand, men tend to be in touch first with their thoughts and then, maybe, their feelings. They are shaped (as are women) by cultural expectations of masculinity and femininity. The culture seems to have a prescribed formula for men that is summed up as follows.

The Creed of the Real Man

"The real man, he shall not cry, he shall not display weakness, he shall not need affection, gentleness, or warmth. He shall comfort but not desire comforting. He shall be needed but not need. He shall touch but not be touched. He shall be steel, not flesh. He shall be inviolate in his manhood; he shall stand alone" (from *The Friendless American Male* by David W. Smith). With this cultural voice speaking in his ear, the man stoically goes through life responding to a woman's expressed feelings as though they were thoughts and saying something like, "You shouldn't feel that way." That's not a wise comment because it doesn't help—it just aggravates the situation. Feelings are spontaneous emotional reactions that often are impossible to control and, sometimes, even surprise the one who experiences them.

A man who expresses his thoughts but either cannot, or chooses not to, express his feelings often makes his wife feel as though there is no hope for a close, warm connection. A man often sees danger, however, in getting too close because he has things he really doesn't want to share, whether because of guilt or fear that he might be rejected if all were known. After all, no man is as strong and self-assured as he appears. He needs to remember that the Lord told Paul, "My grace is sufficient for you, for my power is made perfect in weakness" (2 Corinthians 12:9). The road to strength and to endearing relationships begins by acknowledging our weaknesses and allowing the Lord to do His creative work in the areas that give us the most trouble.

> "My grace is sufficient for you, for my power is made perfect in weakness."
> *2 Corinthians 12:9*

The Way We Desire to Fix Things

Women are great at caring for children and the needs of others because they have a built-in need to fix things, especially the problems in their families. The husband may be a fixer as well, but he is fixing things all day in his business. By the time he comes home, he is tired and doesn't want to be fixed by his wife or take the time to fix his kids.

The woman also tends to be more emotionally involved with the children, nurturing them along, making sure they are doing well, and wanting to talk about it if there is a problem. When the kids grow up and become teenagers, the mother wants to continue this process, and this creates conflict. The kids don't want to be fixed, and the natural process of detachment takes place. They still want their parents around and involved but not in the same way as when they were 5 years old.

The husband usually does better with his teenage children because he gives them more space. He believes that if there is a problem, it will work out. He is not threatened by their need to move from dependence to independence. It's just a natural part of growing up.

That's why there are no father-in-law jokes. The jokes are about the parent who won't stop parenting and that's where mothers find themselves.

The best thing a husband can do when he recognizes that his wife is stressed-out over the affairs of her children is to acknowledge how she is feeling and, together with his wife, search for solutions to the dilemmas they face. The process of talking together, thinking out loud together, praying together, and planning together creates not only unity but also feelings of warmth and caring for one another.

The Way We Spend Time Together

This is determined by our age and stage of life, but it also reflects how each partner views the home. The man sees his home as his castle. After a hard day at the office, he crosses the drawbridge, pulls it up, goes into the living room, and proceeds to his favorite chair.

If he has smaller children, he doesn't realize that the alligators are in the house, not in the moat. The mother has either been caring for the children all day or facing her own dragons in the work world, and the two of them face 5:30 p.m. as a descent into the valley of the shadow of death. At this point, it really takes teamwork to prepare supper, go over homework, get the kids ready for bed, and break up fights. The temptation is for one of the parents to escape—to get home from work later, find meetings to attend after the dinner hour, or something similar. That is a sure scenario for a meltdown.

On the other hand, most women see their home as a nest, where everything is tidy and in order. There everyone loves and respects one another, uses his or her best manners, and never utters a harsh word. During or after dinner everyone shares in detail all that has gone on during the course of the day whether at school or at work.

Life at home never turns out the way either the husband *or* the wife imagined. It doesn't have to be a total disaster, but salvaging the situation takes commitment. Facing difficulties together and setting boundaries for the kids' bedtime are critical steps for allowing downtime and quiet-time for the husband and wife to do whatever they enjoy together. Those few hours have the power to restore their energy and their feelings of connectedness to one another.

The Way We Approach Sex

A couple had been fighting with each other, and the woman was overheard to say indignantly, "How can you think of having sex when we're not even speaking?" The man replied, "I thought we could do it without talking."

Both comments reflect the difference in the ways a man and a woman approach sex. Social scientists say that men tend to give emotional warmth so they can have sex, while women will have sex in order to have a shared relational encounter. For all the hype about whether women experience an earth-moving physical experience during the sexual act, the response to an Ann Landers question on the subject puts it in perspective. Out of 100,000 responses, 70,000 women said that what they were really looking for was to feel close, nurtured, safe, warm, and connected.

Some Christians wonder if the Bible says anything regarding the

> Facing difficulties together and setting boundaries for the kids' bedtime are critical steps for allowing downtime and quiet-time for the husband and wife to do whatever they enjoy together.

purpose of sex. They may have been led to believe that believers who are really spiritual don't think about such things or have a jaded, puritanical view that treats sex as either a taboo subject or something removed from God's radar screen of allowable and enjoyable experiences.

Scripture is clear that the physical relationship is for the expression of love, commitment, and unity. It exists because of the need for a partner (Genesis 2:18), the need to multiply and be fruitful (Genesis 1:28), and the need for sexual fulfillment (1 Corinthians 7:3–5).

The Way We Build Friendships

Men build friendships around activities. They fish, hunt, play golf, and go to sporting events together. Sometimes they center their friendship around projects, like working together on a home, rebuilding a car, or, if they live near a ranch, helping build a barn or branding cattle. Women, however, build relationships by sharing with one another. They talk, compare stories about the kids, and share their feelings. If they need to plan an event together like a women's retreat, they will require three times as many meetings as men. A planning meeting is a social event.

A man often has a difficult time building long-lasting, meaningful relationships because he sees another man as a competitor. He may have a business friend or a recreational buddy but few close confidants.

Former chaplain of the U.S. Senate, the late Dick Halverson, told the story of having lunch one time with a man who owned one of the largest construction companies in Los Angeles. After spending time in conversation over a wonderful meal, the man finally looked at his watch and asked Dick, "What is it that you want?" In other words, "What is the purpose of our getting together?" Dick responded, "I don't want anything. I just want to be with you." Dick knew that relational dynamics change when you don't have an agenda but want to get to know people on a deeper level.

> Scripture is clear that the physical relationship is for the expression of love, commitment, and unity.

The Way We Get Our Egos Stroked

For a man, work is an extension of his personality. He feels fulfilled when he is doing well in his career and has a network that can keep that career moving forward (see Chapter 20).

A woman sees her family and home as the primary extension of herself. She is constantly thinking about her nest. A woman is often the first to seek counseling because she can sense when things are not right at home.

Ego is not a bad word. It is self-awareness, and a person's identity can either be damaged over the years or encouraged and nurtured.

One of the worst things that can happen is when a man is struggling with his job and comes home to a wife who piles on him a barrage of degrading comments, or when a woman has worked at her job all day and then comes home to a husband who is critical of the way she lets the house fall apart.

The Way We Approach Intimacy

Here are three ways to describe the way relationships work between a husband and wife.

1. Functional

Two people live under the same roof—they pay the bills and take care of the kids, but they don't really connect—each does his or her own thing.

2. Enmeshed

In this relationship, the two people are so intertwined that each one loses his or her identity. They can't make individual decisions and find it difficult to have separate interests or activities.

3. Relational

The most healthy model of interaction is the relational, where each person of the couple is committed to the other, where connecting is important and sharing is critical, but where the two individuals don't smother one another. These people have autonomy, but they choose to come together in unity to add strength to one another in the bond of love.

A great marriage is when the partners encourage one another to flourish in their personality and gifts. They are totally committed to one another in what Paul calls a "mystery" (Ephesians 5:32), just as Christ is committed to and united with His bride, the Church.

Daily Reflection Questions

Day One

1 What is most difficult to understand about your spouse?

2 With which communication issue do you most identify?

Why?

3 What makes communication such a challenge?

Day Two

1 In what ways are men and women different emotionally?

2 What issues have these differences raised in your marriage?

3 Why is it important to be sensitive to the way a spouse deals with his or her emotions?

Day Three

1 What are some cultural myths about sex?

2 What evidence do you see of the differences in how men and women approach sex?

3 What problems can these differences cause in marriage?

Day Four

1 Besides your spouse, who is your closest friend?

What forms the basis for that friendship?

2 What friends do you have as a couple?

3 What can you do to build more friendships as an individual and as a couple?

Day Five

1 Which of the three descriptions of relationships best describes your marriage?

How do you feel about that?

2 What can you do to move toward the "relational" model?

What's stopping you?

CHAPTER TWENTY-TWO ========

{ MAKING YOUR MARRIAGE SIZZLE }

(PART 1)

A man was once asked how his marriage was doing, and he said it was like a three-ring circus. "First came the engagement ring, followed by the wedding ring, and now there is the suffer-ring."

The years and decades of a couple's married life have many challenges, but is the suffer-ring inevitable? One woman added, "What if our marriage has already sizzled but now it's fizzled? What if I sizzle but he doesn't?"

It really boils down to two issues—figuring out what it takes to make a relationship work for the long haul *and* then working at it every day for the rest of your life. Maintaining the sizzle in marriage is not easy because of three factors: baggage, models, and stress.

> "Come to me, all you who are weary and burdened, and I will give you rest."
> *Matthew 11:28*

Baggage

When two individuals come together, they bring with them a lifetime of expectations of what the marriage will look like. They each have desires and dreams that may or may not be realistic. Some of the desires may come out of a bad experience where they were hurt deeply during dating, or they may carry the scars from the way they were parented or treated by their siblings. No partner can heal all the wounds of the other or be the source of fulfillment with excessive expectations. Jesus said, "Come to me, all you who are weary and burdened, and I will give you rest" (Matthew 11:28). He didn't say, "Go to your spouse." No husband or wife can walk on water, but the One who did is the One who can handle all our baggage.

Models

Where does a person go to find how a marriage should look? If the individual's parents had a great relationship, he or she has a model, which becomes the goal of the new relationship. But it can also be used as a weapon to use on the spouse for not providing the same type of marriage.

If an individual's parents were divorced, or remained married and miserable, this person may assume that all relationships end up in a wreck and, thus, become almost paranoid. Or this may become an incentive to not make the same mistakes.

Television and movies provide a negative or a glamorized view of marriage. For example, some couples are portrayed as deeply in love (forever) because they are each other's soul mate. This can cause regular folks (not those acting roles) to feel dissatisfied because, by comparison, their marriages seem soulless. They may, then, be tempted to discard the mate for someone who seems more like that ideal.

Stress

A hundred years ago, finding enough food and shelter was difficult, and this, combined with health and other challenges brought stress to a marriage. Today the pressure at work, both in time away from the family and the intensity of the competitive environment, creates a double bind. The pressure now is on both the career and the home fronts.

When the kids are not getting the attention they need or are acting-out in disobedience, the problem is aggravated because the parents don't have the time to deal with it before heading back to work. Stress is not related to the exhaustion of the work itself. It is the by-product of unreasonable situations. If this continues unabated, it will lead to despair or depression—another layer of stress.

The Sizzle

Four actions can make a marriage sizzle, but first we need to make several observations.

1. *We change as we get older.* The person you married is not the same today as he or she was at the altar. We find that difficult to believe and refuse to become pro-active in helping our partners and ourselves recognize the changes and deal with them. It may be true that we can't teach an old dog a new trick, but you aren't an old dog. God gave you the capacity to change by allowing Him to change your attitude or your heart.

2. *Two people living together do not automatically grow together.* We are like emotional bank accounts in which we are either making deposits or withdrawals by the way we speak to, and treat, one another. All of life's experiences either add or subtract until one day we realize how satisfied and fulfilled we are, or sadly, that our account is nearly depleted.

3. *No matter how challenging or poor a marriage becomes, it can change.* God has given us a reset button for relationships— it's called repentance, learning how to say, "I'm sorry." These two words are difficult to say, especially as the first one to say them, but they are powerful. If you refuse to say, "I'm sorry," you will add

God gave you the capacity to change by allowing Him to change your attitude or your heart.

layer upon layer of resentment and wake up one day wondering what happened.

4. *Any relationship, even a good one, can be improved.* A special touch, an encouraging word, an engaging conversation, a timely gift, time to be away alone—just the two of you—can keep the bloom on the rose.

5. *We can't avoid the importance that God plays in marriage.* Marriage is an instrument to shape and direct our lives. A faulty relationship with your partner will affect your relationship with God, and a faulty relationship with God will always affect your relationship with your partner.

It looks like this:

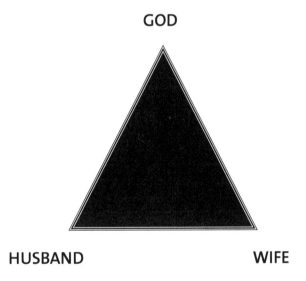

The closer a man or woman comes to God, the closer they come to each other because it creates depth in their relationship. In shallow marriages, each is concerned with having the *stuff of life* without going to the *source of life.*

Marriage, then, is like a megaphone to get your attention that God wants you to grow together and to become all He has in mind for you as you come closer to Him.

So now we look at *four actions* that will make a marriage sizzle—two in this chapter and two in Chapter 23.

Commitment

When it's all said and done, neither warm and fuzzy feelings nor wealth or social status make a marriage work. Instead, the key is *commitment,* a word that seems slightly out of date these days.

In the last book of the Old Testament, God's messenger, Malachi, tells Israel why God is displeased, why he no longer pays attention to their prayers: "The Lord is acting as the witness between you and the wife of your youth, because you have broken faith with her, though she is your partner, the wife of your marriage covenant" (Malachi 2:14).

God views marriage as a life-long commitment. You stood at an altar before your partner, your family, friends, and God and said, *"As long as we both shall live."*

God gave instructions to Moses regarding divorce primarily as a means of protecting the woman (Deuteronomy 24:1–4). During that period, a man could kick his wife out of the house for almost any reason—because he found something "indecent" about her. Indecency could mean because of sexual unfaithfulness (the only reason Jesus allowed divorce—Matthew 5:31–32), or it could be for something trivial (the husband didn't like his wife's cooking). The bill of divorcement protected women from being discarded without any opportunity of being married to another man and having no ability to provide a living for herself.

> "The Lord is acting as the witness between you and the wife of your youth, because you have broken faith with her."
>
> *Malachi 2:14*

God "hates divorce" (Malachi 2:16) because of the havoc it brings to the family and because it cheapens a covenant made before God. Make no mistake, however; God doesn't hate the people who get divorced. He also deals with us at whatever point we are. If the marriage fails beyond restoration, God is ready to forgive and move on with us if we are ready to repent and not try to rationalize away our poor choices.

Commitment to the marriage is more important than the feelings of love. If you are committed to a person, you will work at making the relationship work when things get tough. Family Counseling Director at Highland Park Presbyterian Church in Dallas, Texas, Jim Smith said, "Love is constructive behavior, doing what is best for your partner regardless of how you feel toward him or her at the moment." It's learning to love the one to whom you are married. Remember that old country preacher who said, "Get your doer doing, and your feeler will follow." In other words, make an unconditional commitment to do the right thing to build your marriage and eventually, the feelings of romance will return.

Remember also that all marriages have problems, even those that seem "perfect." Even when facing what seem to be insurmountable odds, they survive. Why? Because divorce was never an option. One woman said, "I will never divorce my husband. I may kill him, but I will never divorce him." In that relationship, if the man lives, the marriage will survive.

Communication

Marriage counselors say that these are the most prevalent problems: (1) expectations are not met; (2) lines of communication have broken down. Charlie Shedd once told about a woman who said, "You heard of the sphinx? I married it! I feel like I'm living with a total stranger. Our marriage has never been very good, but lately it's been getting worse. Do you know how barren it is to exist with someone who makes guttural sounds and that's only when he wants something like sex or food, or to change the channel?"

God refers to your spouse as a "partner" (Malachi 2:14). It's difficult to be a partner with no communication. One man said, "I know we don't communicate, but it's one of my few pleasures." That marriage will have a difficult time surviving. This is especially true if that husband is having financial difficulty, and his wife doesn't know it. Call it pride or stubbornness or just plain fear, failing to tell a spouse that spending needs to be curtailed can wreck both a marriage and a life.

George, a man in his late 50's, was about to be laid off from work, which would mean personal bankruptcy if he didn't have another job on the horizon. His wife had no clue of the pressure he was facing because he refused to talk about it. One weekend, she decided to fly to Texas to spend time with her daughter and family. It had *perfect* written all over it—go shopping, go out to eat, lavish attention on her grandkids. Little did she know she would receive the most horrifying phone call of her life from her son back home.

George had cleaned the house, typed a note, and taped the note to the windshield of the car. There he took his own life with a borrowed shotgun. George was bankrupt, and he couldn't bear the thought of telling his wife. He was unable to communicate and, therefore, unable to jointly find a solution to their crisis.

It's impossible for a couple to not communicate at some level, even if it's just barking out instructions or arguing over some trivial matter. John Powell in his classic book, *Why Am I Afraid To Tell You Who I Am*, identifies five levels of communication. The degree a couple goes in this process, the more meaning their relationship enjoys.

Level 5

Cliché conversation (shallow conversation, for example, what the weather is like, how the food tastes, and so forth)

Level 4

Reporting facts

Level 3
Sharing ideas and judgments

Level 2
Sharing feelings and emotions

Level 1
Personal disclosure of fears and struggles—gut level—life-changing communication

If George had been able to work through these levels with his wife, she would probably have done everything in her power to encourage him and to help him find a solution. After all, women have a God-given gift of intuition and knowing what to do during times like that.

Communication is not always as straightforward as it seems. First of all, words can be interpreted more for their tone than their actual meaning. You may think you are communicating a message of concern and compassion, but your fidgety body language indicates you want out of there. Tone of voice makes up 38 percent of communication, nonverbal body language makes up 55 percent (eye contact, posture, etc.), and the actual words are responsible for 7 percent.

But even the actual words get lost in the fog. Every time you talk, there are six possible messages:

> 1. **What you mean to say**
>
> 2. **What you actually say**
>
> 3. **What the other person hears**
>
> 4. **What the other person thinks he hears**
>
> 5. **What the other person says about what you said**
>
> 6. **What you think the other person said about what you said**

"The tongue of the righteous is choice silver."
Proverbs 10:20

It's tempting to give up with all of this complexity. But that is no solution. The temptation is in two extremes—either to clam up and not talk at all or to become a chattering fool. Solomon, in Proverbs 10:8 and 10, tells about how a chattering fool comes to ruin, but "the tongue of the righteous is choice silver" (Proverbs 10:20). The silver will come if the couple makes a commitment to one another that they will never give up on thinking together, talking together, praying together, and working for God together.

Daily Reflection Questions

Day One

1   What "baggage" did you bring to your marriage?

2   In what ways did your parents' marriage affect your view of marriage?

3   What causes the most stress in your marriage?

Day Two

1   How has your spouse changed since the wedding?

Why, do you think?

2 In what ways have you changed?

Why?

3 How have these changes affected your marriage?

Day Three

1 Why is God so important to a successful marriage?

2 What role does God play in your marriage?

3 How has this changed during the years of your marriage?

Day Four

1 What do you see to indicate that "commitment" is out of date in society these days?

2 Why do some people give up so quickly on their marriage?

3 What can you do to renew your marriage commitment?

Day Five

1 Which of the levels of communication best describes your marriage?

2 What makes communication so difficult in marriage?

3 What can you do to communicate more effectively with your spouse?

CHAPTER TWENTY-THREE

Making Your Marriage Sizzle

(PART 2)

In the last chapter, we saw that two of the four actions to make a marriage sizzle were commitment and communication. The two actions that we will discuss in this chapter are *caring* and *courtship*.

Caring

Malachi 2:13–16 reminds us that God can be impossible to reach because of how a man treats his wife. God no longer pays attention because the husband has broken faith with his "partner" (Malachi 2:14).

Our culture overemphasizes the romantic attraction between women and men and fails to build a case for how two people who have the potential of living together for fifty years need to build an enduring friendship. A spouse is a partner. Another way of saying it is a spouse is a friend and hopefully, the best friend.

Every day we should think, "What kind of friend am I going to be today?" rather than, "How is he (or she) going to meet my needs today?" Being friendly must be intentional—it takes a deliberate act of the will. If friendship is not on your radar screen, your spouse will either be hurt or never edified in the way God intended.

So what are the characteristics of a friend that need to be understood and embraced? There are at least four.

1. Mutual Acceptance and Respect

When a man and woman commit themselves to each other in marriage, they are forsaking all others to establish this relationship. They are leaving their fathers and mothers (Ephesians 5:31) and all other crucial relationships to focus on their primary relationship. They are then to remain faithful to each other for the rest of their lives (1 Corinthians 7:10–11). Faithfulness will not be a problem when mutual understanding and respect are present. Respect comes when the spouse is patient and understanding (Colossians 3:19) and when each honors the other (1 Peter 3:7). Notice the key words in Peter's admonition to the husband—consideration and respect.

We should be considerate and respectful at two times—when we feel like it and when we don't.

A high profile TV actor married a woman he deeply loved and adored. She was a professional woman who had established a reputation as a rising star in the marketing department of her corporation. The wedding had all the glamour expected when two people of this stature

> Every day we should think, "What kind of friend am I going to be today?"

joined together in marriage. And the setting was the lawn of a resort overlooking the Pacific Ocean as the sun was setting—a beautiful day in paradise.

Prior to the wedding, the couple met with the minister for counseling and to talk about their dreams, expectations, and eventual challenges. When asked why they were attracted to each other, they didn't answer with typical superficial responses because they had become good friends, despite their position, wealth, fame, and physical qualities. They liked each other as much as they loved each other. Their commitment seemed unshakable and their communication constant, meaningful, and fun. So they declared their intention to do whatever was necessary to both prove and maintain their respect for one another.

Then the first test arrived. The wife realized that even though her husband wanted her to continue her career (if that is what she desired), she could not be a super executive and a super wife at the same time, especially at the beginning of their marriage. Out of consideration for him, she took the initiative and submitted a letter of resignation to the corporation. Together they agreed to try starting a similar business that could be run from their home. That marriage started on a solid foundation of mutual respect. Many storms will come and threaten the foundation, so marriages that don't begin right have little chance of surviving.

> Many storms will come and threaten the foundation, so marriages that don't begin right don't have little chance of surviving.

2. Assume Responsibility for One Another

At times a partner can see the other struggling. A person who cares is aware, sensitive, and ready to help.

A wife can feel overwhelmed when the children are young and require nearly twenty-four hour supervision, especially when she is working and the pressures of work and home are taking a physical and emotional toll. These situations can end in a meltdown. The last thing the wife needs is a lecture and the first thing she needs is a husband who is willing to step in. That leads to a third characteristic.

3. Concerted Initiative

The word "concerted" is very important. It brings an image of a concert with the brass, percussion, woodwinds, and string instruments blending together to create a moving piece of music. "Concerted" means to draw on all available energies and resources to get the job done.

A very faithful and talented man in the ministry was at a low spot in his career. He was out of gas, and he felt unappreciated and even used by those he thought were his friends. His wife sensed this and picked up the conductor's baton. She planned a party. She called friends from out of town to put it on their schedule, and she arranged a location, catering services, and entertainment. She had committees organized to divide the load and double the output. People jumped on the bandwagon and each contributed what they could to the cause. After this concerted initiative, that man went home singing another tune. Not only was she his wife, she was also a faithful friend.

4. Unconditional Love

At some point, every married person acts unlovable toward his or her spouse. We will mess up, foul our nests, and behave like total jerks. Some will even break the hearts of their partners. We live in an age of seduction and exhaustion, two volatile ingredients that lead to one partner dishonoring the other. When this happens, divorce may follow, but it doesn't have to. Unconditional love says, "I will never leave you. You can hurt me, kick me in the teeth and drop me to my knees. I may die of a broken heart but I will not be the one to leave."

Knowing that your spouse is steadfast in love doesn't make you want to take advantage of him or her; it makes you want to never disappoint your spouse, to never have to look in the eyes of one who wells up with tears and seems to ask, "How could you do this?"

Husbands need to understand the factors that cause depression among women. According to James Dobson in *What Wives Wish Their Husbands Knew About Women*, these include:

- Low self-esteem
- Fatigue and time pressure
- Loneliness, isolation, and boredom
- Lack of romantic love
- Financial difficulties

Every man needs to turn on his awareness radar and scan the horizon for these blips on the screen. To do so shouts loudly and clearly to the wife, "I care about you!" When you find a need and fill it, the Lord listens intently to your prayers.

> When you find a need and fill it, the Lord listens intently to your prayers.

Courtship

Usually the courtship process lasts a very short time, during which the man and woman are on their best behavior: kind, courteous, generous, fun, entertaining, spontaneous, creative, and understanding. After the wedding, the challenge is gone; so two people often drift away from what they were. This may take decades.

At some point, the couple needs to make a conscious decision to re-energize the courtship process. This means etching into the schedule specials night out and weekends away.

It means an occasional call to home or the office to "just check in" with the spouse and to say, "I love you." It means bringing unexpected gifts, just to say, "You were on my mind."

You can't make a marriage sizzle unless you turn up the fire. If for no other reason, do it for the sake of your kids or grandkids. Give them a model of what a good marriage looks like. Give them a reason to marry only that person who will treat them the same way.

Brenda came from a healthy, not perfect, but loving family. She went away to college, and during her freshman year, started dating a young man who met the approval of both her parents. They were actually quite fond of him. One long weekend, the couple went to meet the boy's parents.

The next week, Brenda called home, in tears and confused. She thought her affections for her boyfriend were real, but when she saw how his father treated his mother, she was frightened. "Is this the way Kyle could end up treating me?" she wondered. She would never find out because the thought blocked her emotions, causing her to back away from the relationship.

That doesn't seem fair. Should every young man who comes from a dysfunctional home be penalized for what "may happen" because of a family history? Certainly not, but in this case Brenda may have seen the seeds of abusive behavior in Kyle's mannerisms. Maybe it was a woman's intuition or, perhaps, just paranoia. But the fact remains: Kyle's parents had an unattractive marriage. The only sizzle they knew was the heat of argument, and to this day, they don't know how it shaped their son's future.

Finally, realize that all breakdowns in relationships happen when selfishness enters in. When two people are married and live together, they automatically have what Paul called "divided interests" (1 Corinthians 7:34). That means there are distractions—you will be distracted from one another and sometimes distracted from what God has in mind for your life. Expect it. Then plan on times for undivided attention, put your marriage back on the front burner, and create an aroma that you, your family, and your friends can enjoy.

> You can't make a marriage sizzle unless you turn up the fire.

Daily Reflection Questions

Day One

1 Why is friendship important in marriage?

2 Why is respect so important in any relationship?

3 What can you do to be more respectful to your spouse?

4 Read Ephesians 5:31. In what ways do husbands and wives "leave" their fathers and mothers when they get married?

Why is this leaving so important?

Day Two

1 When has your spouse been especially sensitive to you and your needs?

2 What can you do to take the initiative in your marriage to strengthen your relationship?

3 In what areas should you be more sensitive to him or her?

Day Three

1 The old song says, "You always hurt the one you love." Why is this so?

Why do people in love act so unloving toward each other?

2 When have you experienced unconditional love (besides in your family)?

3 What makes loving that way so difficult?

Day Four

1 What's good about the dating process?

What's not so good?

2 Why do couples stop "dating" after the wedding?

3 What can you do to "court" your spouse again?

Day Five

1   Why is it important to put the sizzle back in your marriage?

2   What steps can you take to add the sizzle?

3   What will you do first?

CHAPTER TWENTY-FOUR

PARENTING: PROTECTION

Much has been written on the subject of parenting. Most of the information is valuable but usually more than a parent can remember, especially the next time the child throws a fit and Mom or Dad is trying to remember what principle to apply. But we cannot escape this issue if we have a commitment to **Priority 3: A Personal, Progressive Commitment to Relationships**. So we have boiled down the most important issues to three gifts that every parent can give to his or her children.

This concept is not original and is shared through the permission of Dave Veerman and Chuck Aycock who presented the material in their book, *From Dad With Love*—later reprinted by The Gathering/USA, Inc. under the title, *Dads That Make A Difference*.

Before we look at the first gift, *protection*, we need understand the critical role our fathers played in our development. For good or bad, our fathers had a tremendous influence in shaping us. According to Eddie Staub, the founder of Eagle Ranch near Gainesville, Georgia, who has provided group homes for troubled children for many years, "The impact of mothers on a child is essential, but the impact of fathers is magical." When the father is not around, all kinds of problems stack up. One shocking yet revealing statistic is that 85 percent of men in prison grew up in fatherless homes.

Most men and women carry the imprint of an absentee father into their own parenting arena. This imprint was created by a dad who was either present or absent; engaged or detached; loving, abusive or indifferent; accommodating or domineering. Like it or not, parents cannot be ultimately effective if they do not come to terms with the expressed or unexpressed feelings toward their fathers. The pain can run deep and the scars are forever obvious.

No dad is perfect, but if he hurt you, healing will not take place unless you have the courage to live with the loss of an "idealized" father, and grieving may be a natural part of the process.

One cold January morning, a video production crew flew to Atlanta and then traveled to Gainesville to interview some children who were living in a group home at the Eagle Ranch. All of them had riveting stories about their past and gripping ways of expressing how they felt about their fathers.

One boy, his blond hair shining with all the production lighting, looked like a poster child for white suburban America. The interviewer

> One shocking yet revealing statistic is that 85 percent of men in prison grew up in fatherless homes.

posed a question that caused the child's countenance to drop. "If you could tell your father anything, what would it be?" asked the host. The boy's eyes gazed at the floor, and for six or seven seconds he said nothing. Then he looked up with a blank stare and responded, "I'd tell him . . . (he paused again) . . . I'd tell him never to come back."

His father would come and go in his life and tease him with *what could be*, but break his heart with *what was*. So how does the child who has grown up deal with this reality? It's not easy, but four steps can help.

Step 1: Express Your Feelings

If your father is no longer available, then this conversation still needs to take place—you and an empty chair, visualizing that he is sitting across from you.

You might start with a question that shows interest in his childhood: "What was life like when you were a kid, Dad?" You don't want to make accusations about how you were raised, but how you felt when he behaved in certain ways. No matter how bad the relationship, find something good that he did that is worth a compliment.

Step 2: Confess Your Faults

Everyone is guilty of hurting his or her dad, so admit it—and be specific, if possible. Even if he does not remember the occasion, the lines of communication will be opened, and he will not feel as threatened to recognize his own failures.

Step 3: Forgive Your Father

This does not mean to condone his behavior or lack of involvement in your life, but forgiveness will help free you from the chains of resentment. It may take several meetings before all the cards are on the table, but it can be liberating to finally deal with it and to get on with life.

Step 4: Commit to the Relationship Going Forward

Over time, both of you have changed. As a son or daughter you can honor your father by forgetting the past and charting a new course for your relationship. In doing so, you also will be saying that you will not carry these feelings into your parenting role because they are now resolved.

A relationship will have no focus without an intentional effort.

> Everyone is guilty of hurting his or her dad, so admit it— and be specific, if possible.

Once you have made the necessary steps to settle unresolved issues with your father, you can make a commitment to your own children and the priority they play in your life.

No one expressed this commitment better than astronaut Rick Husband in a recorded video he made the night before his fatal flight on the space shuttle Colombia. It was played during the February 2nd, 2002 service at Grace Community Church in Houston. "If I ended up at the end of my life having been an astronaut, but having sacrificed my family along the way, or living my life in a way that didn't glorify God, then I would look back on it with great regret . . . What really meant the most to me was to try and live my life the way God wanted me to, and to try and be a good husband to Evelyn, and to be a good father to my children."

With that kind of commitment in mind, we proceed to the first gift that all parents can give their children, *protection*. Protection usually implies keeping children from playing in the street, sticking fingers in electrical outlets, or having access to porn sites on the Internet. There are obvious ways to protect a child physically and morally, but protection emotionally and spiritually is also important. To protect means to create an environment in which the child can thrive without external threats. This occurs most productively in a home that is open, loving, communicative, fun, interesting, and that emphasizes personal growth and redemption. Such an environment provides protection in four ways.

Provide a Feeling of Belonging

Every child develops a sense of home. You did. Think of the memories that come flooding back into your mind as you describe the sounds and aromas. Hopefully, there are good memories: the smell of cookies baking in the oven when you came home from school, the squeak and creak of a rocking chair, the laughter over a child's sharp wit, or a shared joke.

The feeling of belonging also comes when there is a sense of family heritage. This could include telling family stories, creating traditions and rituals by taking family vacations, or having special meals at different points on the calendar. For some, it might have been Mom's egg casserole on Christmas morning or a predictable snack food during the Super Bowl. This heritage might include family projects like delivering food to the underprivileged during the holidays, going on a mission trip, or creating a family video.

This protects the child from the agony of being unimportant, feeling unloved, and not developing a healthy sense of worth.

It protects the child from the fear that they are without a solid

Every child develops a sense of home. You did.

core of people who will be there for them and will do whatever they can to prove their love.

Provide Appropriate Boundaries

Paul told the Ephesians, "Fathers, do not exasperate your children; instead, bring them up in the training and instruction of the Lord" (Ephesians 6:4).

A child without boundaries is a frustrated child. Some parents don't want to stifle their children's creativity by having a bunch of rules that need to be obeyed. What they don't realize is that those rules are like fences, and there is no freedom without fences. Many years ago, a young man walked with his family across a bridge over the Royal Gorge in Colorado. The boy was frightened by the height of the canyon and his perception that no barrier stood on either side of the road sufficient to protect him from a fall. Had the barrier been there, he could have enjoyed the walk and the view, instead of staying safely in the center of the bridge.

Boundaries provide reasonable discipline and rules. These rules deal with chores, homework, manners, curfews, and respect. Though a child may not admit it, he or she wants those boundaries, and deep inside, the child feels special that his or her parents care enough to have expectations.

Parents must, however, distinguish between a careless act and an act of defiance. Not every wrong behavior is a deliberate act of disobedience. A kid needs to be able to breathe without fear that every step he takes will merit punishment. The parents also will realize that they have to pick the right battles to fight and when to fight them. Children entering adolescence will test the boundaries, probing to see where they can find gaps with things like hairstyle, language, music, lies, body piercing, alcohol or drugs, messy room, TV use, Internet use, household chores, spending habits, friends, curfews, church attendance, clothes, R-rated movies, car use, telephone use, sibling relationships, homework, grades, and so forth. At some point, a parent will have to draw a line in the sand for those non-negotiable issues and say, "Beyond here you do not go."

Wise parents will also let their children experience the natural consequences of some of their actions. Linda, a 14-year-old with an attitude, was upset with her father one day and stormed into her room, slammed the door, and locked it. Her father went to the garage, picked up a hammer and screwdriver, walked back in the home, released the lock, took the door off its hinges, and took it to the basement. The mortified teenager now had no privacy. Having suffered the consequences of her indiscretion, she learned her lesson. The good

> "Fathers, do not exasperate your children; instead, bring them up in the training and instruction of the Lord."
> *Ephesians 6:4*

thing about this approach is that the punishment fit the "crime." It was appropriate, had a certain humor to it, and didn't involve an outburst that could be regretted later. Counselors report that as many as 30 percent of 20-year-old adults are estranged from their parents because of excessive punishment during their childhood. They are the exasperated ones, who don't want to hear anything of the Lord's instruction from their parents.

Though traditionally we think of boundaries or rules in a negative sense, there can also be positive boundaries or guidelines for kids. Parents may have books they want their children to read, camps to attend, and journeys they will take together. Parents know that these experiences will shape the minds and hearts of their children and point them in a direction that will guide the rest of their lives.

Provide a Moral Framework

Famous UCLA basketball coach, John Wooden says, "Be more concerned with your character than your reputation . . . because your character is what you really are, while your reputation is merely what others think you are."

Children who grow up without character or a moral framework will be victimized. They will become the victims of any guiding principles that appeal to their self-interests or prurient interests. Without a moral framework, how do they decide what priorities are essential for living? Parents know that these don't just fall in one's lap but come through constant emphasis and reinforcement. Parents who abdicate their role in the moral area release to the world more lost souls to wreak havoc on others.

In Deltona, Florida, four young men decided that they wanted revenge because some students refused to return an Xbox console. When the police arrived the next day, they found the bodies of four men and two women, along with a family dog, beaten beyond recognition.

How does someone murder another person so brutally that it takes dental records to determine the victim's identity? The reasons are complex, but how things would have been different if, as children, the murderers would have received the protection of a moral and spiritual framework. How things would have been different if their parents had read, believed, and embraced the truth of Psalm 78:

> *O my people, hear my teaching;*
> *listen to the words of my mouth.*
> *I will open my mouth in parables,*
> *I will utter hidden things, things from of old—*

> "We will tell the next generation the praiseworthy deeds of the Lord."
>
> *Psalm 78:4*

what we have heard and known,
*   what our fathers have told us.*
We will not hide them from their children;
*   we will tell the next generation*
the praiseworthy deeds of the Lord,
*   his power, and the wonders he has done.*

He decreed statutes for Jacob
*   and established the law in Israel,*
which he commanded our forefathers
*   to teach their children,*
so the next generation would know them,
*   even the children yet to be born,*
and they in turn would tell their children.
*   Then they would put their trust in God*
and would not forget his deeds
*   but would keep his commands.*
They would not be like their forefathers—
*   a stubborn and rebellious generation,*
whose hearts were not loyal to God,
*   whose spirits were not faithful to him.*

This passage predicts generational spiritual health. You are a part of a five-generation pattern of thought, lifestyle, habits, values, and spirituality. You were directly influenced by your grandparents through your parents, and you will impact your grandkids by the way you raise your children. That totals five generations.

The moral framework also determines attitudes about money, how to treat people, and what is ultimately spiritually important. Morality is more than just a casual thought about what is appropriate or inappropriate. It is often the difference between life and death.

Provide an Emotional Connection

In the research done by psychologists after the mass murders on high school campuses, one common denominator appeared. Neither of the parents or a meaningful adult ever bonded with the kids who performed those horrendous acts. They had no emotional connection. The children often grew up in middle to upper middle class neighborhoods. They had the good "stuff" of life but not the really important stuff.

So what does a parent do, especially in the earliest and most formative years, to create this emotional connection? You start by being available.

> You are a part of a five-generation pattern of thought, lifestyle, habits, values, and spirituality.

1. Be there at bedtime. Tell stories, pray together, read together, and laugh together. Let the children go to sleep with the emotional warmth of the last fifteen minutes of the day.

2. Be there when they hurt. When they are sad, be aware of their countenance and take them aside for a conversation. Your genuine concern will speak volumes about their importance to you.

3. Be there when they make mistakes. Don't cover for them when they blow it, but let them know that we are all flawed and that we can all recover from our stupidity and our sin.

4. Be there when they have special activities. Dad and Mom on the sidelines, in the grandstand, in the audience, is a nutrient to emotional health.

5. And finally, listen with understanding to either their pain, their joys, or their overly long narrative about some mundane subject that is important to them but is boring to you. And do so while resisting the temptation to yawn, look away, or glance at your watch.

And what is to be gained by providing this kind of protection for your kids? How about **ROI**—Return On Investment. Maybe, one day, you will enjoy the emotional and spiritual health of your grandchildren and will reflect back on how you arrived where you are, and the truth of Psalm 78 will come home with new and satisfying clarity.

> Your genuine concern will speak volumes about their importance to you.

Daily Reflection Questions

Day One

1   Why do fathers make such an impact on their children?

2   How do you think your father's model of a parent has affected (or will affect) your parenting?

3   How about your spouse?

Day Two

1   If you could talk with your father and tell him anything, what would you tell him?

2   In what ways has your father hurt you?

How have you hurt him?

3   What steps can you take to help heal those hurts?

Day Three

1   What do you need to forgive your father?

What will it take for you to forgive your father?

2   What can you do to make sure not to repeat, with your children, your father's mistakes with you?

3   What are you doing to protect your children emotionally?

Day Four

I   What boundaries did you have growing up?

2   How do you set appropriate boundaries for your children?

Why do boundaries provide security?

3 When you were a child, did you feel secure or insecure?

Why?

Day Five

1 Looking back through the past few generations, what patterns do you see in your family?

2 What emotional connection do you have with your parents?

How was it formed?

3 What can you do to bond emotionally with your children?

CHAPTER TWENTY-FIVE

PARENTING: IDENTITY

Nearly every person has looked in the mirror and thought, "If only my nose weren't so big . . ." or "If only I could lose weight . . ." or "If only I didn't have bags under my eyes . . ."

This discussion begins in early childhood and continues for the rest of life. Voices from the past shaped the image in the mirror. Parents, whether they realized it or not, shaped their children's futures by accepting, affirming, acknowledging, and appreciating their uniqueness. They played the most important role in helping children feel good about themselves or creating fragile identities through negative talk and criticism. The culture also played a big role. The message constantly hammered through movies, TV, radio, and commercials is that you are OK if you have beauty, brains, bucks (or things), and brawn. It is a constant barrage of messages that screams out, "You don't measure up!"

During the middle school years, students are the most vulnerable. If their identity is not greatly strengthened through affirmation at home, they may look all right on the outside, but on the inside they are crushed.

> During the middle school years, students are the most vulnerable.

Peretti's Burden

That's what happened to Frank Peretti, best-selling novelist. For more than thirty years, no one knew that a wounded spirit had nearly crushed him during his junior high school days. He probably wouldn't have told his story if not for the Columbine High School killing spree perpetrated by Dylan Klebold and Eric Harris.

In comparing himself to Klebold and Harris, Peretti makes no excuses for the killers' behavior, but he also explains the anger that festers when someone is bullied and his or her identity lies in ruins. He came forward to tell his story because he believes that those who are made to feel inferior carry great psychological wounds. He thought that he might be able to prevent another Columbine.

As an infant, Frank had been rushed to the hospital because of a growth on the side of his neck that was beginning to strangle him. He had cystic hygroma, which led to an accompanying malady of a swollen tongue. With black oozing scabs, his tongue would stick out of his mouth and would cause painful embarrassment.

His junior high locker room was terrifying. As skinny as a rail and with this grotesque facial problem, Frank was the victim of physical and mental tormenting. The stronger boys would slam him up against the lockers, snap him with wet towels, and humiliate him with name-calling. In fact, Peretti says he can still hear their voices, recall their names, and remember how desperately he wanted to get even.

Two things prevented him from exacting his revenge. One was his parents who loved and supported him unconditionally, and the other was a teacher who found out what was going on and wouldn't just shrug it off—a teacher who was willing to ask a downcast boy, "How are you doing?" As a result, he saw the school counselor and was spared further harassment.

How Can Parents Help?

So what can parents do to help their children have healthy identities? They know their kids aren't perfect and act like hellish imps at times. They also realize that their kids are fragile and need a steady stream of encouragement. Over time, each child needs to understand two facts: first, he or she is a sinful creature living in a fallen world (Romans 3:23); second, he or she is the apex of God's creation (Psalm 139). Children soon learn, without any effort, that they must deal with their corrupt nature. Because of that, the Evil One constantly pummels them with depreciating phrases such as, "You're no good," "You'll always be a disappointment," "How disgusting," and "You will never be anything but a loser."

> "I praise you for I am fearfully and wonderfully made."
> *Psalm 139:14*

Here is where parents can come to the rescue, not to rescue kids from the reality of their sinfulness but from an identity that is marred by lies. So is there anything parents can do? Absolutely! They can take at least four actions.

Love Them Unconditionally

The psalmist says with delight, "I praise you for I am fearfully and wonderfully made" (Psalm 139:14), and again "What is man that you are mindful of him, and the son of man that you care for him? You have made him a little lower than the heavenly beings and crowned him with glory and honor" (Psalm 8:4–5). God loves His creation unconditionally. That's how parents should love their children.

Each child is unique—one of a kind. God has given each one a unique fingerprint and a special touch. No child should be compared with brothers and sisters and expected to develop at anyone's pace except his or her own.

Just like adults, each child has a love language and needs to be loved in that language. Children reveal their love languages by the way they treat their parents or their siblings. According to Gary Chapman, the five love languages are as follows: physical touch, gifts, acts of service, words, and quality time.

At age two and a half, Gabriel revealed two of these languages. He's all boy, loves to wrestle and tumble, knows no fear, and is in perpetual motion every waking moment. When his dad is taking out the garbage, Gabe wants to carry a bag. When the lawn is being mowed, he has to serve by sweeping the grass into piles. When his mother comes home with groceries, he insists on carrying a bag inside. Sounds like Gabriel's love language is *acts of service*. Yes, but he also is affectionate—wants to hug and kiss (*physical touch*). Eventually, one of these will become more dominant. So how do Gabriel's parents show love to him? In whatever way works, but returning affection or doing things for him are sure winners.

Parenting requires a lot of experimentation. What works with one child doesn't necessarily work with another. In fact, what works one week may fail the next week. This process can be both encouraging and exasperating. With young children, we have ample opportunity to find the right formula for capturing their hearts and directing their growth. We also have time to recover from a failed mission.

So don't panic. Making mistakes is part of the journey, and kids recover quickly, especially when they know they are loved unconditionally.

> Parenting requires a lot of experimentation. What works with one child doesn't necessarily work with another.

Affirm Their Worth

We know that our children are extremely valuable, *but do they*? Every child, at periodic times in his or her development, needs to feel special.

David, a man in his mid-fifties, was walking down a church hall one day and stopped to make way for a line of eight or nine children who were going from recess in their day care routine back to their home room. At the end of the queue was a three-year-old girl who looked up at David and began to hit his leg. David knelt down in an attempt to make a connection, but the girl continued to hit him with her little fists. The day care leader looked back and noticed what was going on, stepped in to pick up the child, and followed up with an apology. "I'm sorry, but Shannon has no father or any other man in her life, and from time to time, she acts out in this way."

Little Shannon had a spontaneous reaction of frustration that stemmed from a hole in her heart with no meaningful male to fill it. So what does every child craves? We can sum it up in four basic desires.

1. Children crave affection.

Counselors will explain that adults can damage a child's identity as much by withholding praise as by verbal outbursts. Children need to hear adults repeat, "I love you" or "I'm proud of you."

You may respond, "What if they have been messing up? What if I'm not feeling love toward them? What if I'm not proud of them?" Surely you don't feel this way all the time. Compliments need to be timed correctly to be effective. Look for the little things they do well and acknowledge those. Tell them you love them when you tuck them in to bed at night.

2. Children want to be wanted.

Children know when adults enjoy hanging around in their world, when they get down on their level to wrestle, play, or just have a talk. One of the most positive things a parent can do is to invite the child's comments and conversation at a table of adults. A child feels wanted and significant when a parent takes him or her seriously. When a child tells silly stories, the parent goes along with it and asks questions to allow him or her to elaborate. When you participate in their world, they want to participate in yours.

You can tell when a child feels wanted and significant—they feel comfortable in the presence of adults. They are comfortable in their own skin, no matter what age. They also feel comfortable in the presence of adult strangers. This carries its own dangers, but children can be taught to look for threatening signals or how to stay away from unsafe situations.

> One of the most positive things a parent can do is to invite the child's comments and conversation at a table of adults.

3. Children want to be hugged.

Several years ago a disturbing book was published. *Love at Goon Park*, written by Deborah Blum, illustrates the tragic consequences when children are deprived the most basic human emotion of love.

The book featured stories from orphanages. In the middle of the 18th century, the Hospital of the Innocents in Florence, Italy, received more than 15,000 babies over two decades. Ten thousand of those children died before they reached their first birthdays.

A 1915 study stated that of the nine in ten orphanages surveyed, no child survived past the age of two. The prevailing wisdom of the time was that infections were spread by touch. In order to prevent the opportunity for a baby to be exposed to germs, special boxes with inlet sleeves were used to allow a nurse or staff person to change a diaper without having a skin-on-skin encounter with the child. In addition, popular psychology publications warned the public about giving too much love out of the fear of spreading disease. All of this nonsense was called to intellectual accountability when psychologist Harry Harlow revealed the terrible results for those deprived of physical affection.

Touching is not just important; it is essential for human health. Hugging and loving on babies changes over the years, to horsing around, especially with boys. But whether it's sons or daughters, both need to feel the touch of both parents and to let the emotional strength empower them for the rest of their lives.

4. Children want to be appreciated.

This comes when a child feels they are making a contribution to the family. That's why enlisting their help with household chores or work projects is important. It teaches them discipline and gives them a sense of self worth. The happiest adolescents on the planet are those who have grown up playing on a team—the family team. They learned what hard work and expected results were all about; consequently, they could celebrate as a family over the tasks they completed together. Every home has needed yard work, repairs, or some other face-lift, and an "*attaboy*" is a wonderful payment to those who pitch in and work hard.

Acknowledge Each One's Uniqueness

In the last point, we talked about how important it is for a child to feel special. This also happens when the parent understands how each child is unique and how different children are from one another. Finding and celebrating each one's uniqueness is critical because if the parents don't identify it, the child will look for it the rest of his or her life.

It's easier for parents to give attention and point out the uniquenesses of children who are the first child, the funny child, the beautiful child, the smart child, or the talented child. But what about the one who doesn't seem to be exceptional?

The parent can start by looking for this child's motivated pattern. What are they motivated to do? What do they do well? A child who spends hours working with Legos or creates a complex design with other materials is sending a message. This child's unique motivated pattern may be toward design or engineering. Children also display behavioral patterns. Some are extremely loyal; some are courageous and some compassionate. Some play the role of peacemaker.

A parent who is trying to shape the children's identity can help them identify, celebrate, and develop a latent talent. This means that the parents' dream for their son playing outfield for the Red Sox may need to be shelved, exchanging the baseball mitt for a violin. Kids will gravitate toward their patterns, with or without their parents' encouragement.

> Finding and celebrating each one's uniqueness is critical because if the parents don't identify it, the child will look for it the rest of his or her life.

Appreciate Their Presence

A public school survey in Maryland revealed that parents spend an average of 15 minutes a week in meaningful dialogue with their children—not much time for either bonding or molding. Time pressures in the twenty-first century are intense. Most parents do not intentionally spend time away from their kids but rather drift into lifestyles with little connection.

At some point in time, every parent wakes up and wonders either where the time went or where it is going. Yes, children do grow up fast. So we need to slow down long enough to enjoy each day we have with them. We should observe their world. What pictures do they have on their walls? Who are their friends? What is their favorite music? What gets them excited?

Make eating dinner together as a family a high priority. And make it fun. For example, you could play the "what if" game. "What if you had $1,000—what would you spend it on?" or "What if you could go anywhere—where would you go?" or "What if you could have a conversation with someone from history—who would that be?" Adding fun to the equation is a way to make children feel wanted and appreciated. You can even have fun with spiritual questions. The father could state: "Tonight we are going to have a family discussion on whether we really believe the story about Jonah and the big fish is true." Everyone is allowed to chime in, give his or her opinion, and then defend it.

Putting your own beliefs up for debate is a way of saying, "I'm not holding on to them just because it's the thing to do, but I appreciate your view and we ought to search for a conclusion together." This is another way of implementing Psalm 78:1–4. If handled right, you are also creating an appetite for the things of God and you can enjoy the flavor together.

> Make eating dinner together as a family a high priority. And make it fun.

Daily Reflection Questions

Day One

I Why do children struggle with low self-esteem?

2 What were you like in junior high?

How did teachers and other kids treat you?

3 How can the way parents love their children affect their identity?

Day Two

1 Why is it so difficult for parents to love their children unconditionally?

2 What's your dominant love language?

How do you know?

3 What's the dominant love language(s) of your child(ren)?

How do you know?

Day Three

1 Why do you think children crave affection?

2 What can parents do to let their children know that they're wanted?

3 What happens to children who don't receive affection?

Day Four

1 Does hugging come naturally to you?

Why or why not?

2 How do you know when you are appreciated?

3 To whom do you need to give an "attaboy"?

Day Five

1 What unique abilities, traits, and talents do each of your children possess?

2 What can you do to make each child feel special and unique?

3 Read Psalm 78:1–4. What can you do to repeat this pattern in your family?

Why would that be good to do?

CHAPTER TWENTY-SIX

PARENTING: CONFIDENCE

Monty Roberts knows something about the important role confidence plays in the development of a happy child. His book, *Horsesense for People*, is an insightful revelation of how shy, skittish horses can be broken in around thirty minutes with a technique that is equally effective in developing a healthy confidence with children. He knows what he is talking about—he has raised 47 foster children.

The kind of confidence we are talking about is where a child has a firm enough foundation to test his or her ideas, values, and relationships in a nurturing environment. The child feels the freedom to both accept responsibilities and to fly.

Confidence doesn't just happen. It is the result of someone taking the time to release a child from fears or insecurities and be given the opportunity to reach his or her potential.

Not all children begin that way—neither do horses; in fact, neither do dogs. In his book, *Lessons From A Sheep Dog*, Phillip Keller describes how he rescued a chained-up border collie, Lass, who would chase kids and cars in an urban setting. He used the same techniques as Monty Roberts to rebuild the confidence and to release Lass in the green pastures near Vancouver, Canada. There she found her true calling as a sheep dog.

On the human side of the story, psychologist Flip Flippen has taught public school teachers for years a similar model of transformation that can capture a kid's heart—the EXCEL program. As a result, thousands of children have found a liberating confidence because of the deliberate involvement of teachers who care about them.

A technique so pervasively effective in altering human behavior should have precedence somewhere in Scripture or imbedded in the principles that flow from its teaching. We find it in the way Jesus approached the woman at the well (John 4). This Samaritan woman had much going against her. She was a minority person in her sexual identity, her cultural setting, her religious surroundings, and she was damaged from many failed relationships with men. She was like Lass—chained by her circumstances—or like one of the beaten horses who found a new lease on life at the liberating hands of Monty Roberts. She was changed because Jesus took the time to focus on her, speak kindly to her, and see potential in her.

The steps taken by Jesus, Roberts, Keller, and Flippen boil down to five phases that allow a dramatic connection to take place. This builds

Confidence doesn't just happen.

a new foundation for confidence and a new creation operating out of a new core of understanding.

The Engage Phase

Monty Roberts gets the horse in the ring and lets him know he wants to have a relationship. He calls this *joining up*. It's the same as when Phillip Keller unchained Lass and put her in the back seat of his car for a trip to the country. It's also Jesus speaking to a Samaritan woman (something Jews never did) and saying to her, "Will you give me a drink?" (John 4:7). In all of these occasions, an intentional connection was made where the initiator was making the statement, "I want to be a part of your life."

That is the starting point in building confidence in children. We take the time to stoop or kneel to get on their eye level. We let them know we have no other agenda than to connect, to engage in such a way that the child will think that no one else or no other thing at this moment matters.

The Explore/Story Phase

Once we have their full attention and they know they have ours, we ask questions that will help open their world.

After the *joining up* phase, Monty Roberts will rub his hands over the horse's body to find where the muscles vibrate or where the horse tries to back away, lift his head, or avoid contact. Monty calls this finding the story—the place that the horse has been kicked, whipped, or abused. He then removes the leash and encourages the horse to run—to be free—to see that he is not being chased or attempting to be dominated. Phillip Keller did the same thing with Lass. He knew her story of confinement and knew that she had to be released to run away from the ranch house, with the possibility that she might never return. Jesus explained the life-story of the Samaritan woman in John 4:16. He said, "Go call your husband and come back." Being the God of the Universe, Jesus knew that this woman currently had a man living with her who was not her husband and that she had been married many times. At that point, Jesus wanted to explore with her the conditions of her life, but also to give her a chance to run if she was now overly uncomfortable.

No child is emotionally healthy if he or she has to live with the reality that no one cares enough to ask penetrating questions in an atmosphere of love. The Samaritan woman formed an immediate connection of trust with Jesus that allowed her to open up and start talking rapid-fire about issues that were important to her. Monty

> No child is emotionally healthy if he or she has to live with the reality that no one cares enough to ask penetrating questions in an atmosphere of love.

Roberts' horses don't run long before they come back to the center of the ring to reconnect. Lass was gone for several weeks but would appear around the perimeter of the ranch from time to time until she eventually came from behind Phillip Keller to nudge him with her wet nose as if to say, "I'm ready to talk."

Not every conversation with a child will be deep and profound, but all conversations will be meaningful. And when you want to hear their stories, they will grow up wanting to hear yours.

The Communication Phase

After the "Engage" and "Explore" phases, real communication is possible. Jesus can talk about worshiping God in spirit and truth with a person who is ready to listen. Lass can be trained both verbally and with hand signals on how to be an obedient sheep dog and a partner with her master. The child doesn't see instruction as another nagging session, but as a time to learn and to grow.

The Empower Phase

When we deeply touch another person, we empower that person to do things they never imagined.

When Jesus revealed to the woman at the well that He was the Messiah, everything in her life changed. Monty's horses take a saddle on their backs—highly unusual because a horse sees anything on its back as a predator. That's one of the places a mountain lion would target, a vulnerable spot in the life and death encounter. And Lass returned to the liberation of once again following her true nature, to be a sheep dog.

The point of empowerment is different for every child, but it is the point at which he or she sees the world differently. The old fears fall away and new possibilities become excitingly clear. We are ready for the fifth phase.

> "Come, see a man who told me everything I ever did. Could this be the Christ?"
> *John 4:29*

The Launch Phase

With the saddle on its back, the horse now takes the rider and is ready to run. The sheep dog, Lass, works in tandem with her master to move sheep, chase wandering sheep, protect sheep, scold sheep, and stay with and guard sheep. The woman of John 4 runs home and says, "Come, see a man who told me everything I ever did. Could this be the Christ?" (John 4:29) In a matter of minutes, the Samaritan's nature changed from a woman without morals or focus to an evangelist.

Every child, once empowered, is launched like an arrow toward a target, usually in the direction that reveals his or her created nature.

Children may experiment with their gifts and talents but always with their parents' affirmation.

In addition to the five phases of building confidence in a child, four areas need special attention within the home. These are like adding protein powder or complex carbohydrates to a health drink.

Confidence from Predictable Parents

It's nearly impossible for a child to develop confidence if his or her parents are unpredictable in how they act or react regarding punishment for rules that are violated. Clearly communicating that constant responses to unwanted behavior can be counted on, creates remorse but not confusion. The same is true for hard work. Predictably rewarding or praising a job well-done also boosts the confidence. This applies in many areas. No parent is perfect, and we all will fail at being consistent. When we return to the predictable patterns, we reinforce not only what we are trying to teach but also the confidence level of our children.

Our predictable response cycle should also include humor.

Jim is a good father. After scolding or reprimanding his kids, he doesn't follow with a barrage of insults like, "Suck it up, kid, and stop crying like a girl." Jim knows the importance of connecting on another level after he has been stern, maybe even harsh. He knows the importance of laughter through the tears. He may say something funny or witty; he may playfully wrestle his child to the floor and tickle him; he may even act silly. But he knows the important role humor plays in reestablishing the kids' identity and confidence, and he is a master of the well-timed transformation from serious discipline to light-heartedness. His kids are well-adjusted and have few problems with their confidence levels.

Confidence in Boy/Girl Relationships

Every boy and girl wonders, even frets, over how to handle dating. Hallway talk at school can make it appear that some students are old pros and conquering kings and queens of the dating realm. But dating isn't easy for the majority of students. So Mom and Dad can help build confidence in this area by taking an adolescent on a "practice date."

Roger did that with his daughter, Kathy. They went to a nice restaurant. Roger opened the door of the car for her and politely sat her at the table—he showed her how a young lady should be treated. He helped her with ideas from the menu, carried on a light conversation with the waiter, and used his best manners, but always with an eye on how he could make Kathy feel comfortable while enjoying the meal

> No parent is perfect, and we all will fail at being consistent.

and the ambiance of this special evening. Roger opened the subject of what to look for when she was on a date with her special someone. The topic was a little awkward because he had to reveal the more prurient side of a boy's thoughts and intentions. Having this "practice date" not only taught Kathy what to expect from a decent young man but also to know the warning signals that come from off-color remarks or other comments that make it obvious that it is time to go.

Boys need that special time of sharing with their mothers as well, and both sexes need to understand that dating boundaries established by their parents are for their protection and should be more welcomed than challenged.

Confidence comes from knowing what to expect but also in having respect for themselves and others. This respect is not only taught, it is reinforced over and over again for years. Respect for their peers, respect for the opposite sex, respect for adults, and learning how to address someone with focus and manners take time and practice.

Confidence to Become Independent

A teenage girl was attending a summer youth camp high in the Colorado mountains and feeling uncomfortable with all of the "God talk" from the evening services. She grabbed a counselor and blurted out, "I don't believe in God!" The counselor didn't bat an eye or act alarmed. He calmly responded, "Tell me about the God you don't believe in. Maybe I don't believe in Him either." All of the steam was taken out of her shocking statement. She had no one to argue with, especially one who should have reacted with alarm.

Confidence comes when one finds himself or herself in what family therapist Dr. Rod Cooper calls an "Open System." He divides family living styles into either open or closed systems. Here is the basic description of each.

Closed System

In this situation, those who are in authority (the parents) are very authoritarian. They require their children to be rigidly obedient to rules, expectations, and values. This high demand of obedience, however, is more for the sake of the parent than the children. Mom and Dad are more worried about how they appear, their status and reputation, than the development and emotional inner strength of their children.

The atmosphere in a closed family system is usually tense, tight, defensive, and negative. You don't see a lot of laughter or fun. In fact, the kids tend to stay outside a lot and don't feel comfortable inviting

> The atmosphere in a closed family system is usually tense, tight, defensive, and negative.

their friends over to the home. They are taught what to think, how to conform, and how to maintain the family reputation.

Open System

Parents who take the open approach still have rules and boundaries for behavior. Their emphasis, however, is more on *why* than *what*. In trying to create a warm, trusting environment, the parents' caring and good-natured approach are attempts to help children to internalize the values that hopefully are being caught, not just taught. These parents listen a lot, laugh a lot, communicate a lot, ask lots of questions, discipline their children when necessary, and build a foundation of confidence that what the parents hold dear is worthy for the children as well.

With this environment, the parents are confidant that their sons and daughters are on their way to a healthy independence and with an internal compass to make solid decisions in life.

As in our stories of Monty Roberts' horses or with Lass the border collie, each animal eventually returned to his trainer because it could do so freely and without compulsion. The story of the Prodigal Son in Luke 15:11–32 is an example on the human scale of what happens when a wayward child knew he had the freedom to return home to a father with out-stretched arms as well as the freedom to run away and fail. If that son had grown up under a closed system, he may never have returned.

> A parent who applauds his children's skills is a confidence builder.

Confidence in Career Choices

A parent who applauds his children's skills is a confidence builder. Each child has areas of competence—the key is to find these and to provide every opportunity to see them developed. That takes experimentation and much patience. It also takes testing for abilities that motivate the child. The sad child is the one who has no adult to help him find himself, find his interests and passions, find what school is best suited for him, find a menu of jobs that would be a "fit."

With all that is said in this chapter about confidence, you can usually see it reflected in one place—the eyes. The confident child's eyes are bright, they twinkle, they are enthusiastic, they are hopeful, they are a little mischievous, and they make you want to look inside and say, "I don't know where you are going, but it will be fun to watch you get there!"

After spending three years with Jesus, His disciples had that look in their eyes. They were transformed by the love and openness He showed them, knowing they had the freedom to encounter anyone at any time with His life-changing message. And if they failed, they always had another day. Those who follow Jesus' example would provide their children with the same opportunity.

Daily Reflection Questions

Day One

1 What role does confidence play in the development of a happy child?

2 What factors helped you become a confident child?

3 How confident are your children?

Why?

Day Two

1 Why is "engagement" the starting point in building confidence in children?

2 What does it take to discover a child's "story"?

3 How do the "Engage" and "Explore" phases make real communication possible?

Day Three

1 How does having predictable parents help a child develop confidence?

2 What can parents do to help children gain confidence in relationships with the opposite sex?

3 How do children learn respect?

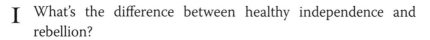

Day Four

1 What's the difference between healthy independence and rebellion?

2 Why do some parents insist on a "closed system"?

3 What "closed system" families have you observed?

What are the children like?

Day Five

1 Would you describe your home as "closed" or "open"?

Why?

2   What can you do to develop a more "open system" in your home?

3   In what ways has your relationship with Christ helped you gain confidence?

CHAPTER TWENTY-SEVEN

THE IMPORTANCE OF SMALL GROUPS

It seemed like everyone was talking about First Church. Jim, Pete, and John were pastors at this amazing church. Even though it was a congregation that met in an old building in the heart of the city, it was vibrant and alive. Almost overnight First Church had experienced exponential growth.

Most credit the influx of converts to controversial remarks Pete had given in an open-air rally not far from the church building. The former commercial fisherman turned associate pastor had made a case for the right to refer to Jesus as being the only way to God. He had challenged those who were offended by the bottom line of Christianity to evaluate the source of their objections. The reaction had been unexpected. Scores of people had begun falling to their knees confessing their sins and asking how to become followers of Jesus.

Sunday services were filled to capacity. Word spread throughout the community. Visitors showed up to see what was going on. Former members who had not attended regularly in years began coming back. Old folks and young folks sat side by side in celebrative worship. The music wasn't fancy. The lyrics were quite simple. Many of them came straight out of the Bible. Like many other churches, the high point of the service were practical messages from God's Word. The pastors who took turns speaking were heavy on application.

It soon became obvious to the staff that a church of five thousand couldn't meet the individual needs of its members without breaking the huge congregation down into smaller settings. The most obvious way of doing this seemed to be the creation of home groups. In these small groups the big family "did church" between Sundays. They took turns hosting fellowship dinners in each other's homes. Following dessert they enjoyed long conversations about the pastors' sermons from the previous Sunday. It wasn't uncommon for them to also celebrate the Lord's Supper before having a time of extended prayer.

These small group gatherings allowed First Church members to connect with each other on a vulnerable level. Individuals shared personal needs such as health concerns and financial challenges. They admitted to issues in their marriages or ethical dilemmas at work. Men of the group began to meet together to hold each other accountable. Women did the same. Members didn't let their informal small group involvement take the place of their more formal public worship. They

> Almost overnight First Church had experienced exponential growth.

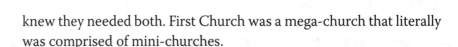

knew they needed both. First Church was a mega-church that literally was comprised of mini-churches.

The Rest of the Story

Would it surprise you that the church just described is not one that was started in the past ten years? Actually, it is one mentioned in the New Testament. In Acts 2:42–47, we read,

> They devoted themselves to the apostles' teaching and to the fellowship, to the breaking of bread and to prayer. Everyone was filled with awe, and many wonders and miraculous signs were done by the apostles. All the believers were together and had everything in common. Selling their possessions and goods, they gave to anyone as he had need. Every day they continued to meet together in the temple courts. They broke bread in their homes and ate together with glad and sincere hearts, praising God and enjoying the favor of all the people. And the Lord added to their number daily those who were being saved.

From the very beginning of Christianity, small groups have been essential to healthy growth of the church. Large public gatherings were common, but small private groups were even more prevalent. The temple continued to be a place where followers of Jesus remained true to their Jewish roots, but homes were where Christians remained true to each other and themselves through accountability, encouragement, and fellowship. It was in the context of caring community where people tossed by the storms of life were sheltered and prevented from being washed out to sea.

The Importance of Lifeboats

Perhaps you saw that blockbuster movie James Cameron produced several years ago about the Titanic. Although a fictionalized account, that film was based on factual research. That ship was amazing. Three football fields long, eleven stories tall, and ninety-two feet wide, it tipped the scales at 46,000 tons. It took 14,000 ship builders three years to complete construction. No wonder the price tag attached to the Titanic was $7.5 million (a hefty sum in 1912 currency).

The ship, whose captain said not even God could sink it, was equipped with swimming pools, restaurants, Turkish baths, a Persian sidewalk café (complete with strolling musicians), squash courts, and sixteen watertight compartments below sea level. But it did sink.

> "They broke bread in their homes . . . praising God and enjoying the favor of all the people."
>
> *Acts 2:46–47*

Just after midnight on April 15, 1912, the luxury liner split in half after colliding with an iceberg in the North Atlantic. Although 706 of those on the Titanic's maiden voyage were rescued, more than 1,500 passengers and crew perished.

As tragic as that unprecedented loss of life was, what is even more tragic was the reality that the people who perished could easily have been saved. Really! Amazingly for a ship that carried in excess of two thousand people, the Titanic had only been equipped with twenty-one lifeboats. It should have had twice that many.

What is even more tragic is how the available lifeboats were utilized. Initially only women and children were allowed to board the small crafts. But in the panic of the moment, others, fearing for their lives, forced themselves on as the lifeboats were being lowered. Only a few of the twenty-one boats were filled to capacity. Many were only half full. Some had but a handful of passengers in them. When the ship eventually capsized, hundreds of people wearing life jackets were floating in the frigid water calling for help to those in the lifeboats not far away. Of the twenty-one boats, only one came back to offer help. The rest closed their ears to the cries that pierced the frosted air and huddled in their boat grateful they were saved, but apathetic to those who eventually died due to hypothermia.

We All Need a Lifeboat

Given the frequency with which the waves of calamity crash in on us as well as the tendency for our dreams to capsize, we are at risk when not in relationship with other Jesus followers. We were not created to survive on our own. And given the fact that we are in over our heads much of the time, we all need a lifeboat of those who will keep us afloat.

> "Two are better than one, because they have a good return for their work." Ecclesiastes 4:9

In his candid evaluation of the human experience, King Solomon celebrated the life-saving nature of community. He wrote, "Two are better than one, because they have a good return for their work: If one falls down, his friend can help him up. But pity the man who falls and has no one to help him up! Also, if two lie down together, they will keep warm. But how can one keep warm alone? Though one may be overpowered, two can defend themselves. A cord of three strands is not quickly broken" (Ecclesiastes 4:9–12).

What a graphic portrait of our common need for other believers. God never intended that we attempt the Christian life solo. When He first created Adam, He said it wasn't good for the man to be alone. We were created for community. Reaching our God-given potential depends on interaction and introspection with others. Having a small group of people regularly inquiring about our personal well-being and progress can keep us from desperate, or even diabolical, behavior.

A Case Study in Isolation

The lack of meaningful interaction played out tragically for one young man. His mother was a dominating woman who had been married three times. His father, who was the third husband, died before he was born. The home had no love or discipline. When this young man was a teenager, girls would have nothing to do with him, and he continually fought with his male classmates. In spite of a high IQ, he dropped out of high school. After enlisting in the Marine Corps, he was dishonorably discharged. Friendless and shipwrecked, he moved to a foreign country but was rejected there as well. In an attempt to latch on to love, he married a beautiful girl in that foreign place, but soon she wanted nothing to do with him. He couldn't please her. After one fight in particular, she locked him in the bathroom of their home. Later he tried to make it on his own, but failed. He proceeded to crawl back to his wife who only ridiculed his series of failures. If that wasn't bad enough, she made fun of his sexual impotency in front of her friends. As you might guess, he felt utterly isolated and extremely lonely. He was drowning in despair.

Would it surprise you to learn that the person just described was Lee Harvey Oswald? Lacking a cadre of individuals to extend unconditional love, acceptance, and forgiveness, he focused his hunger for belonging through the telescopic lens of an automatic rifle. Not finding a lifeboat for his sinking soul, he not only perished but a popular American president did as well.

> Lacking a cadre of individuals to extend unconditional love, acceptance, and forgiveness, he focused his hunger for belonging through the telescopic lens of an automatic rifle.

The Benefits of Belonging

Do any of these descriptions sound like you?

� The pressures of mid-life are making it nearly impossible for you to tread water. You're becoming more realistic about your chances grasping those rungs of the corporate ladder you had always assumed were within reach. Your strength isn't what it once was, and you're aware of your own mortality like never before. You're concerned about your aging parents who live several states away. At the same time you are stressed out about keeping current on your kids' college tuition payments.

✖ You're on the verge of drowning after your Love Boat capsized. You never would have thought your honeymoon cruise would run aground and end in divorce. But there you are struggling to hang on to whatever piece of hope that keeps you afloat.

✖ A devastating diagnosis from your family doctor has thrown you overboard. You're scared. Your faith floated away. You find it easier to imagine a worst-case scenario than the possibilities of a successful outcome.

✖ You are the parent of a teenager who has jumped ship "spiritually speaking." He or she dived off the deep end into the murky waters of a rebellious lifestyle. Rejecting the values of your home, he or she has stated unequivocally they want nothing to do with you or your God. Your heart is broken. You fear for your child's safety.

✖ You're a new Christian. You don't know Genesis from Jeremiah. Or maybe when you keep hearing your minister refer to John and Paul, you wonder why he keeps leaving out George and Ringo. Your understanding of the degree to which the Creator has gone to have a relationship with you in this life and the next blows you away. But you have so many questions. And you have so many family members and work colleagues who make fun of what you are so serious about these days.

If you identify with any of the above scenarios, you need a lifeboat. In a small group you will find a place to unload your deepest worries and fears while finding encouragement as you verbalize your heartfelt hopes and dreams. Your broken heart will be bandaged. You will feel the warmth of those who blanket you with understanding and prayer.

No wonder the person who wrote the epistle to the Hebrews cautioned those who read his correspondence to not neglect hanging with each other in home groups. He knew that in a godless culture like his (and ours) we can't afford to drift away from a discipline as simple as involvement in a small group. He wrote, "Let us not give up meeting together, as some are in the habit of doing, but let us encourage one another—and all the more as you see the Day approaching" (Hebrews 10:25).

> "Let us not give up meeting together, as some are in the habit of doing, but let us encourage one another."
>
> *Hebrews 10:25*

Daily Reflection Questions

Day One

I Do you consider yourself to be a "people person"?

Explain.

2 What keeps people isolated from each other?

3 Do you agree with the statement, "God made people for relationship"?

Why or why not?

Day Two

1 When have you felt lost in a crowd?

2 When do you most feel the need for a close friend or group of friends?

3   In what ways might a small group meet this need?

Day Three

1   In what ways are small groups like lifeboats?

2   How can small groups help a church grow?

3   Why do you think some churches don't employ small groups?

Day Four

1   Why do you think Christians should have a regular small group experience?

2   What kind of person would benefit most from a small group?

3 What keeps people from getting involved in small groups?

Day Five

1 When were you in an effective small group?

2 What made it good—why did it work?

3 What keeps you from being in a small group (if you aren't in one)?

4 What could you tell someone to convince him or her to join a small group?

CHAPTER TWENTY-EIGHT

SMALL GROUPS: FROM ISOLATION TO RELATIONSHIPS

Do you remember Randy Fogle, Thomas Foy, Harry B. Mayhugh, John Unger, John Phillippe, Ronald Hileman, Dennis Hall, Robert Pugh, and Mark Popernack? No, they aren't NASA's astronauts-in-waiting. They are the miners from Somerset County, Pennsylvania, who won our hearts in the summer of 2002.

On the afternoon of Wednesday, July 24, 2002, eighteen miners entered the Quecreek Mine, as was their routine. Seven hours later, the men were digging in the mine when a wall separating their tunnel from an abandoned, flooded mine gave way. Millions of gallons of cold water spewed into the cavern where the eighteen were working 240 feet below ground.

Nine of the miners managed to struggle to safety. But nine others were trapped by the rapidly rising water that climbed to their necks. For three days Americans watched live televised coverage of round-the-clock rescue efforts. We rode an emotional roller coaster as conflicting reports of the likelihood of survival surfaced. We prayed as we watched and hoped for the best while bracing ourselves for the worst.

After seventy-seven hours the governor of Pennsylvania announced that all the miners were alive. One by one each man was transported in a bright yellow rescue capsule to the surface. As each stepped out to freedom, he was greeted with the cheers of a hero's welcome.

Later, in a series of news conferences, the nine rescued miners told their story. Despite the cold and darkness, they determined they would not give up. Finding a ledge that gave them breathing room, they huddled together in a cramped space. They fended off their hunger by sharing a corned beef sandwich and a can of soda they found in a lunch bucket.

Thomas Foy, one of the nine said, "We just covered each other up, hugged each other, whatever it took just to keep each other warm. Some guys would shake more than the others."

When asked how they passed the time, Foy said they talked about "anything and everything." He added, "We can't tell you everything we talked about, but we talked about everything. We done a lot of praying—that was number one. We done a lot of praying."

The nine in the mine were not your typical small group, but what took place 240 feet underground is a remarkable picture of how we

> "We done a lot of praying—that was number one. We done a lot of praying."

survive as Christians. What was true of those rescued miners is true of those who have experienced the life-giving power of a small group.

The miners were forced into a small group experience, but most men and women will only go there if they realize that it is critical for their spiritual health, maybe even survival.

We live on a crowded planet, but even if we have a residence on the fourteenth floor of a high-rise building, it can be the loneliest place on earth. There are reasons why men and women avoid a small group experience. Maybe it is because they don't want to risk opening up or being vulnerable about sharing the personal side of life. Some have tried it and later regretted it because what they thought was shared in confidence was told in public. Some don't want to admit that they have weaknesses or struggles in their life that seemingly don't have a solution.

Boys and girls who have played sports know that a typical response of a coach when they get hurt is to yell, "Just suck it up, tape it up, and keep going." They assume that is the way to handle all problems—don't let them see you sweat, keep your pain to yourself, and keep going. There is also an accepted superficiality in most adult conversations. We aren't used to talking about things that really matter. Most men talk about sports, money, sex, politics, or the latest dirty jokes—not necessarily in that order.

We also don't have role models that help us see why small groups are important. If you ask a man or woman how their parents handled life, they would say they just kept most things to themselves. That pattern of life is handed down from one generation to the next. The kids, to a large extent, are turning out just like their parents.

Competition also has a way of keeping us from opening up. In nearly every aspect of life, we feel we must win, especially in the corporate world. Any negative thing that is discovered can be used against you. That's why the loneliest people on earth are politicians or the presidents and CEOs of large corporations.

There are three critical words for creating personal wholeness and they are, "I need help." What happens when a person realizes this need but has no one to turn to? They go to the self-help section of a bookstore hoping they can find the answer without having to share their dilemma with another human being.

There are **four characteristics** of people that lead to the characteristics of a culture when people live in isolation.

1. Anemic Living

Anemia is a lack of vital red blood cells that transport oxygen. The result is weakness, exhaustion, shortness of breath, in other words, not reaching our physical potential.

> There are three critical words for creating personal wholeness and they are, "I need help."

Anemic people are not able to drink deeply from what life offers, they take shallow sips. That is a metaphor of most people's existence. They are living shallow, unfulfilled lives because there is a lack of vital relationships which invigorate their existence.

2. Addiction

Very few people who have addictions want them. They realize that something is dying within and they hate it. They hold secrets for years, maybe a lifetime, not knowing that sharing their struggles with a small group of trusted friends could be the key to their liberation.

3. Guilt

Most psychologists or psychiatrists will tell you that a certain amount of guilt or bad feelings about bad behavior is a sign of health. But if that guilt is unresolved, it can lead to a psychosis and eventually hospitalization. Psychologist Karl Menninger says that 60–65 percent of people in mental institutions could be released if they were free from their guilt. A small group can provide the catalyst to separate healthy from unhealthy guilt, to hear appropriate confessions, and to release the old dead baggage that people are carrying around on their backs.

4. Emptiness

To have a booming gross national product, a consumptive lifestyle, a bank balance with lots of zeros and commas is not the indication of individual or cultural happiness. Try using the "smile indicator" in determining which groups of people are the happiest and which ones are the most empty. Go to the Dominican Republic, rent a car or take a taxi to one of the poorest barrios. Walk down the street lined by lean-to houses and watch the parents and children as they interact with one another. They are talking, giggling—big smiles are on their faces. How can that be? They don't have two pesos to rub together. Then compare them with a statement from Lee Iacocca, former CEO of Chrysler Corporation: "Here I am in the twilight years of my life wondering what it is all about. I can tell you this, fame and fortune is for the birds."

> When any man or woman belongs only to themselves, they will suffer.

On February 13, 1933, an Italian immigrant, Guiseppe Zangara, attempted to assassinate President Franklin Roosevelt after being unable to find a job during the Depression. An interviewer was reported to have asked him if he belonged to a church. His reply was, "No, I belong to myself and I suffer."

When any man or woman belongs only to themselves, they will suffer. Swiss psychologist Paul Tournier was counseling a man one day and said, "I am very much afraid when you have been molded for several decades of life by the great machine of society, you will probably have neither the inclination nor the ability to return to the essential realities of life." In other words, if you don't develop the patterns for small groups, learning to share and care in that kind of environment, it will only become harder to do so as you get older.

How Do You Move Out of Isolation?

You start by realizing Christ never meant for you to go through life alone. One writer says there are fifty-five "one another" verses in Scripture, where it says to serve one another or love one another. The importance of being there for another person is paramount to how we are to function as a part of Christ's Body.

You must see that God has a plan for your life. The psalmist David said, "May he give you the desire of your heart and make all your plans succeed" (Psalm 20:4).

God's plan involves a relationship with a small band of like-minded brothers or sisters who share our journey. Paul said, "But I think it is necessary to send back to you Epaphroditus, my brother, fellow worker and fellow soldier . . . whom you sent to take care of my needs" (Philippians 2:25). Paul needed a fellow brother as well as a fellow worker and so do we. That is the way we survive the difficulties of life and celebrate the victories.

> "May he give you the desire of your heart and make all your plans succeed."
>
> *Psalm 20:4*

The Requirement of a Dynamic Small Group

There must be a commitment to one another as firm as your commitment to Christ. You didn't seriously follow Christ until you became intentional about it. The same is true for the relationships developed within a small group. You intentionally commit to the well-being of the brothers or sisters within your group.

True fellowship consists of honesty to the point of vulnerability. The discussions move beyond superficiality to candidly dealing with the messy side of life. At this point, they deal with "what if" questions: "What if I lose my job?" or "What if my wife moves out?" That's when conversation enters a new level and brotherhood/sisterhood takes effect.

True fellowship involves accountability to one another. Every week you need to "report in" and tell how Christ is working in your life, or how you struggled with staying on track. Each person in the group can be both an encouragement and a challenge to the others to be the best they can be.

True fellowship means expressing our dreams and aspirations. The collective wisdom of the group plus their contacts might be just what is needed to send that dream toward fulfillment.

So How Do You Get Started?

1. Start by praying for a few good friends to join you.

2. Take the initiative and ask them to meet together for eight weeks.

3. Model unity and watch how others observe what is going on and long for the same experience.

4. Use the following schedule during your time together and watch your small group grow into a **supportive team.**

✖ *Share the Scripture.* Each person should talk about what they've learned on their own in private study. More is caught in this environment than listening to seminars.

✖ *Share your schedule.* What will you be doing over the next couple of weeks? Will the Four Priorities be reflected in that schedule?

✖ *Share your relationships.* Who will you be spending time with? Where will it be? What do you expect to happen?

✖ *Share where you are now.* Are you excited? Let's hear about it! Are you struggling? Let your team share the load.

5. Wrap up in prayer and cover the things that have just been shared and then watch God work through everyone's life over the next few weeks. Jesus said, "A new command I give you: Love one another. As I have loved you, so you must love one another. By this all men will know you are my disciples, if you love one another" (John 13:34–35).

> "A new command I give you: Love one another. As I have loved you, so you must love one another."
>
> *John 13:35*

One Person's Experience

Psychologist Henry Cloud discovered that truth firsthand. He had aspired to be a professional golfer. But when a hand injury derailed those dreams, he began tumbling down the emotional stairs into the basement of depression. As a young Christian, Henry was disillusioned with God, wondering why God didn't instantaneously make him better. But through the context of a meaningful relationship with a Christian couple and involvement with a small group of fellow strugglers, Henry experienced release from depression. He realized that God's primary way for bringing about His purposes for our lives is through the people in our lives.

As the old Swedish proverb says, "A shared joy is a doubled joy and a shared sorrow is half a sorrow." You can discover that truth for yourself if you get into a small group.

Daily Reflection Questions

Day One

1   When you heard about the mine disaster on the news, how did you imagine the miners' experience?

2   What would be most difficult about that experience for you?

3   When has life felt that way for you?

Day Two

1   What factors built the miners' relationships with each other *before* the disaster?

With whom do you have close relationships like theirs?

2   When have you seen a "life threatening dilemma" draw a group together?

3   When have you been in that kind of support group?

Day Three

I   Why do people avoid a small group experience?

What has kept you from getting involved in a small group?

2   With which of the "four characteristics" could you most identify?

Why?

3 How have you dealt with those feelings?

Day Four

I In what ways does a person who "belongs to himself or herself" suffer?

2 What can a person do to "move out of isolation"?

3 In what ways have you been isolated?

What steps have you taken to move out of isolation?

Day Five

1 In what kind of small group would you like to be involved?

2 According to 1 Peter 4:10–11, how are people God's primary means of doing His work?

What gifts would you bring to a small group?

3 What do you need that a small group could provide?

What will you do to plug into an effective small group?

CHAPTER TWENTY-NINE

THE UNIVERSAL CHURCH

Of those who religiously watch the summer Olympics on TV every four years, what do you think most people would say they enjoy the most? Track and field? Swimming? Diving? Gymnastics? We all have our favorite venue, and some would say they like watching the opening ceremony best of all.

The reasons are many. There is an unmistakable excitement that we can vicariously experience in our family rooms thousands of miles removed from Olympic stadium. The anticipation of months and years has been building through media coverage and time trials. The Olympic torch has been carried over a stretch of countless miles across borders and even oceans. As the final torchbearers enter the stadium, circle the track and eventually light the giant flame, we can't help but feel the fulfillment of an ancient tradition being maintained.

But the highlight of the opening ceremonies is without a doubt the parade of the nations. As athletes from hundreds of countries wearing their national uniform walk around the track, they wave enthusiastically to spectators in the grandstands. Some carry flags. Some hold video cameras or digital cameras as they capture the magic of the moment. We can't help but smile as we witness the genuine joy on the faces of these athletes who have earned the right to represent their countries.

Here before our eyes is a microcosm of the world. Six billion human beings, boasting a common residency on planet earth, are represented by a few thousand Olympians. Competitors with different skin colors who speak different languages and who embrace a diversity of governmental structures have this in common—they are members of the Olympic family.

The Contenders for the Faith on Parade

Have you ever thought of the Church that way? No, not the congregation where you hang your spiritual hat—that's just a small expression of a much larger whole. The worldwide body of believers has more in common with the parade of nations at the opening Olympic ceremony than you might initially think.

In every country of the world, Christians gather Sunday after Sunday. While some make their way to a suburban multi-purpose auditorium to sing songs projected on a wall, others assemble in gothic stone cathedrals dwarfed by stained glass windows and the

> The world-wide body of believers has more in common with the parade of nations at the opening Olympic ceremony than you might initially think.

majestic music of a pipe organ. Some believers step on broken glass in the gutter just before stepping inside storefront buildings with cardboard-covered windows and then sing to the accompaniment of a Hammond organ. Some sit on split-log pews under thatched grass roofs on a sub-Sahara plateau. Others huddle in single-family houses. Fearing persecution or interrogation, they congregate under the cover of darkness. Still others who have come to faith in Christ while serving life sentences in prison find creative ways to "do church" behind bars.

Or imagine this. The Israeli government is mistreating some Christians in Palestinian refugee camps. Even though the Bible encourages us to pray for the peace of Jerusalem, and even though it reminds us that Israel and the Jews are to be honored as God's treasured, the worldwide church includes Arabs who worship wearing head coverings that resemble those worn by political extremists in the Middle East.

In all these settings and more, the church of Jesus Christ parades its allegiance as believers sing worshipful songs, publicly confess their faith, attend to the reading of Scripture, listen to someone expound the meaning of a particular text, gather around the communion table, and minister to each other through prayer, encouragement, and fellowship.

Every Christmas Eve followers of Christ gather to celebrate the Savior's birth in their own unique ways. On Palm Sunday they remember Jesus' triumphal entry into Jerusalem. Each Good Friday, Christians on every continent recall the bloody cross on which our Lord was crucified. Then on Easter, praise songs in every imaginable language provide a vocabulary of worship in which God's power over death is celebrated. Don't forget about Pentecost Sunday or World Communion Sunday. On each of these holy days God's people around the globe are united by a common task and a common joy.

Pause for a moment and think about it. Broaden your horizons. Redefine your working definition of those who are your brothers and sisters in the faith. Can you fathom it? Those who claim Christ as Savior and Lord and who welcome His rule in their lives ring the earth. Like the Olympic athletes, they are brimming with enthusiasm as well as boasting a diversity of cultural expressions of their faith.

> Those who claim Christ as Savior and Lord and who welcome His rule in their lives ring the earth.

The Universal Church Portrayed in Scripture

The Scriptures picture this family portrait of all God's children in the last book of the Bible. Revelation allows us to look at a page of heaven's family album. Even though it's a snapshot of the future, what we see corresponds to the reality of a multi-ethnic inter-continental Church here and now.

The Apostle John describes the scene: "After this I looked and there before me was a great multitude that no one could count, from every nation, tribe, people and language, standing before the throne and in front of the Lamb" (Revelation 7:9).

The Apostle Peter used his palate of words when he painted a similar portrait. In the first letter that he wrote to Christians in the first century, he identified where they were. We need a Rand McNally map to get a feel for the many places he has in mind. "To God's elect, strangers in the world, scattered throughout Pontus, Galatia, Cappadocia, Asia and Bithynia" (1 Peter 1:1).

Even in the Old Testament, the prophets predicted how the people of God would be found in every imaginable nation: "Arise, shine, for your light has come, and the glory of the Lord rises upon you. See, darkness covers the earth and thick darkness is over the peoples, but the Lord rises upon you and his glory appears over you. Nations will come to your light, and kings to the brightness of your dawn" (Isaiah 60:2–3).

According to David Aikman, in his book *Jesus in Beijing*, the Church (under persecution and with great difficulty) has grown to an estimated 80 million people. David is not given to exaggeration. He is the former senior foreign correspondent for *Time Magazine* and bureau chief in Beijing.

According to the 1949 statistics, only 4 million were Christians. Aikman says that within three decades "Christians will constitute 20 to 30 percent of China's population." This will have a profound impact on the universal Church and on the ethnic makeup of that Church in the years to come. Chinese Christians believe they are called to evangelize the nations between China and Israel. Aikman said such numbers and intensity of mission could change the global balance of power. Isaiah was right—"Nations will come to your light."

In Light of That, This

But recognizing the reality of the church's global dimension can't just be a mind-stretching exercise. When we understand that we have brothers and sisters who are outside of the comfortable community in which we worship, our awareness demands that we become involved.

For example, more Christians are being persecuted for their faith right now than at any other time in history. Pastors in Pakistan are being gunned down in their pulpits. Husbands are being carted off to prison, separated from their wives and children. Women are being tortured in an attempt to get them to renounce their faith. And these are members of our eternal family. We can't just sit back and complain

"There before me was a great multitude that no one could count, from every nation, tribe, people and language."

Revelation 7:9

about the fact that we're singing off-the-wall songs in our state of the art sanctuaries. We must pray for them.

In light of this unprecedented persecution, we must find ways to be tangibly involved with those forced to worship in secret. Ministries like Voice of the Martyrs (VOM) connect Christians and churches in North America with the challenge facing believers in countries where Christianity is denounced. The statistics provided by VOM are staggering. There have been more martyrs for Christ during the twentieth century than during the previous nineteen centuries combined, and the number of martyrs exceeds all battlefield deaths of all wars during the twentieth century. By reading up on what is going down in places the media neglects, we have the means to make a difference. Through organizations such as VOM, contributions can be channeled to provide tangible encouragement and support to those in the underground church.

Missions Redefined

But our financial involvement should not be limited to family members at risk. Those to whom we are related by virtue of our common faith in Christ are attempting to evangelize within their country. Years ago, North Americans congregations took the lead in sending out missionaries. We would learn the language of those we were trying to reach. We would translate the Bible. We would try to convince them that Jesus had died for them. We would start churches. We would even spend a lifetime giving leadership to those churches. And all the while we would get friends and family to give money to support us.

As more and more churches became established in previously unevangelized countries, it became obvious that Christians in those nations made the best missionaries. They knew the language and the culture and were more easily accepted by their peers. But in most cases these Christians live in parts of the world where the per capita income is a fraction of ours. Giving to missions through World Vision, World Concern, Wycliffe Bible Translators as well as the denominational mission agencies is a way we can "be" the worldwide church.

Mission Possible

Even though the old paradigm of hands-on career missions has given way to behind-the-scenes facilitation, there is still the need for North Americans to cross cultural borders and serve. A short-term mission trip is an awesome way to get a handle on what in the world is going on. It is also a way to personally experience the breadth, depth, and diversity of Christ's global family. Chances are your local church has

There have been more martyrs for Christ during the twentieth century than during the previous nineteen centuries combined, and the number of martyrs exceeds all battlefield deaths of all wars during the twentieth century.

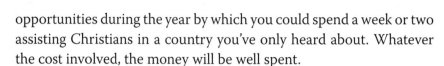

opportunities during the year by which you could spend a week or two assisting Christians in a country you've only heard about. Whatever the cost involved, the money will be well spent.

An example of this is Mission Emanuel, a ministry of The Gathering/USA in the Dominican Republic. Over the past two decades, teams of men, women, and children have entered in to the two villages of Nazaret and Cielo. They have built schools, sponsored children to get an education in these schools, built clinics, churches, baseball fields, a youth center and now have plans for a vocational school.

A spiritual awakening has taken place in these villages; many have come to Christ and the churches are at capacity. The impact comes from dedicated people who make these trips with a national passport **and** the passport to life—the Scriptures lived out in love in the presence of the Dominicans.

Daily Reflection Questions

Day One

1 In what ways is the Olympic parade of nations like the universal Church?

2 What variety of peoples do you see in your local congregation?

3 When have you been most aware of the universal Church?

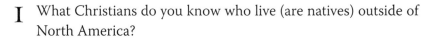

Day Two

I   What Christians do you know who live (are natives) outside of North America?

2   In what ways is their worship experience and expression of faith similar to yours?

In what ways is it different?

3   What challenges to their faith do they experience?

Day Three

I   What do you have in common with believers in other nations?

What differences might you find?

2 In heaven, which will be more important—the commonalities or the differences?

Why?

3 Read Revelation 7:9 and put yourself in that crowd. What are you doing?

What are you feeling?

Day Four

1 Why should Christians be involved with believers in other nations?

2 How can they be involved?

3 What can you do for the persecuted Church?

Day Five

I When you were young, what was your idea of "missionaries"?

In what ways has that changed?

2 God considers you to be a missionary. In what ways has that been true for you?

3 What can you do to become more involved in missionary endeavors?

CHAPTER THIRTY

CHURCH: THE LOCAL BODY OF BELIEVERS

Author Greg Asimakoupoulos has a humorous poem that describes the inevitable difficulties that mark extended family gatherings at the holidays. He writes:

The day the family gathers for our yearly Christmas feast,
I pray for Heaven's mercies, lest I turn into a beast.
My sister tells a story that demeans a certain race;
while cousin Ken consistently puts fat folks in their place.
My grandfather is snoring in a rocking chair that creaks.
My brother Joe just doesn't know how much his BO reeks.
My dear Aunt Kate arrives too late to help out in the kitchen;
and based upon her husband's breath, you know what he's been
*   nippin'.*
The nephews are a nuisance. The nieces can't sit still.
And Grandma gripes about the noise while choking on her
*   pills.*
They say this day's for families. I know that in my head.
But when it comes to joining them, I'd rather stay in bed.

No doubt you can relate to the way relatives undermine special occasions. But because they are family, we tend to make allowances for them. After all, we all have our issues. We are imperfect people who live in an imperfect world. Unfortunately, we don't always apply the same rules to our local church family.

> We are imperfect people who live in an imperfect world. Unfortunately, we don't always apply the same rules to our local church family.

The Dysfunctional Church Family

Suzie Walker discovered that fact the hard way. Her life growing up in an alcoholic home had been anything but easy. Her parents had been abusive to each other and to the kids. They were not successful in keeping their marriage together. Neither were they successful in providing a positive role model for how to make life work. Suzie and her sisters were not raised in the church and were not raised with a definable set of values. They learned by trial and error the pluses and minuses of embracing life as a continuous party. Drinking, despite their parents' abuse of alcohol, was not viewed as a taboo. Neither were relationships with boys. They had no limits. As a result, lust was often mistaken for love. Still their commitment to being family compensated for the deficits. They made allowances for each other.

The one thing Suzie had going for her was her music. Being blessed with a great voice, she often would be asked to perform at parties and in bars. The affirmation she received when she sang compensated for the lack of recognition she got at home growing up. It was no surprise when Suzie fell in love and married a man twenty years older. She was looking for a father figure to take the place of the hungover dad who never said, "I love you."

When Suzie and her husband Barry had a baby, they wanted to provide their little girl with a place where her values would be shaped and she'd be exposed to the love of God. In the process of bringing Bethany to church, Suzie discovered for the first time in her life what Christ had done for her on the cross. Although Barry attended worship only occasionally, Suzie and Beth were there every Sunday. Suzie had found the healthy family she had been denied. Or so she thought.

With her bluesy voice Suzie began to sing in church. She loved being able to praise her newfound Friend with her music. But since her style was unlike the other members of the worship team, some folks in the congregation began to make negative comments behind Suzie's back: "What kind of a church are we becoming?" and "She sounds more like a lounge singer than a praise leader."

When Suzie got wind of what was being said, she was devastated. Since her faith was fragile and her understanding limited, the comments bruised her tender spirit. Within a month or two, she and Bethany left the church, never to return. What is even more tragic is that they didn't find a new place to get involved. Sadly, they simply quit going to church.

The Kind of Church Family God Intends

Suzie's story presents a true-life scenario that points to the need for someone new to Christianity to find a place of belonging in Christ's family. It also points to the need for those within the local congregation to reach out to those who are new in the faith. We can't afford to leave the church because fellowship is not an option—it's *essential*. God intends for us to have dynamic fellowship with other Christians with whom we worship, serve, and sort through the routines of daily life.

Normative Christianity assumes that the church operates as a family of imperfect-but-forgiven people who are committed to each other and involved in each other's lives. If a believer has no desire to make involvement in a local church a priority, something is out of whack. As someone once put it, "If your relationship with God

> We can't afford to leave the church because fellowship is not an option— it's *essential.*

doesn't overflow into caring relationships with other Christians, you aren't as close to God as you thought you were."

Consider again the passage in Acts chapter 2 that we considered in our examination of small groups. Obviously the first century church was an organism more than it was an organization. They "devoted themselves" to each other. Even though there was activity going on at the temple and in homes, "being the Church" was based in relationships, not programs.

Calling the building where coffee and cookies are served following the sermon every Sunday "Fellowship Hall" doesn't insure that authentic fellowship takes place there. The Greek word for our word "fellowship" means sharing something in common. And that implies more than sharing from the same pot of coffee or the same plate of cookies. Rather, it has to do with the sharing of lives that flows out of having a common experience of God's love.

No Lone Ranger Christianity

In too many churches, some individuals who have discovered the First Priority and embraced the reality of a relationship with Christ have stopped there. Like Suzie they have seen their relationship with the Lord as a private matter that doesn't require them to participate with others. If something goes wrong, they just pack up their personal Jesus and leave. Their union with God made possible by the Savior has not resulted in communion (a common union) with the others who attest to being First Priority people.

That kind of privatized piety smacks of American individualism and not Biblical Christianity. It's what you might call "Lone Ranger" Christianity. You've probably seen it. People show up at church all alone. Oh sure, they smile and perhaps offer a superficial greeting. Perhaps they comment about the weather or a sports score, but no in-depth conversation occurs. And like the Lone Ranger, they wear a "mask" that protects them from letting people at church know who they really are.

Professing faith in Christ without being dynamically involved in the lives of other believers is like going through the wedding ceremony without investing yourself in a marriage. If you have union without communion you're in need of a tune-up. The service engine light is illuminated on your spiritual dashboard, and you may not even know it.

Acts 4 reveals how this sharing life in common was fleshed out in the first century:

> All the believers were one in heart and mind. No one claimed that any of his possessions was his own, but they shared

> Professing faith in Christ without being dynamically involved in the lives of other believers is like going through the wedding ceremony without investing yourself in a marriage.

everything they had. With great power the apostles continued to testify to the resurrection of the Lord Jesus, and much grace was upon them all. There were no needy persons among them. For from time to time those who owned lands or houses sold them, brought the money from the sales and put it at the apostles' feet, and it was distributed to anyone as he had need. (Acts 4:32–35)

If only Suzie had found that kind of commitment—if only she had experienced a reflection of God's unconditional love and acceptance, perhaps she would still be in the church reaching out to former Mary Magdalenes like she had been. But then again, why didn't Suzie peel off her mask and admit how the comments of insensitive fellow Christians had hurt her? If only she had been willing to be vulnerable.

The Telltale Signs of Fellowship

The willingness to commit to the local Body in dynamic fellowship has three observable results. First and foremost, when our union with the Father spills over into communion with His other children, that kind of fellowship results in *unparalleled joy*. If you've tasted that flavor of authentic inner fulfillment, you know all about it. Being committed to others and sharing the highs and lows of life with them exposes you to a joy factor you didn't even know existed.

The Apostle John wrote a postcard length letter to some early believers. He was convinced of the fact that authentic union with the Lord naturally results in communion with His people. John was also aware of the direct correlation between the amount of joy a believer experiences and that believer's level of intimacy with fellow Christians.

In the first chapter of 1 John, he wrote: "We proclaim to you what we have seen and heard, so that you also may have fellowship with us. And our fellowship is with the Father and with his Son, Jesus Christ. We write this to make our joy complete" (1 John 1:3–4).

In addition to experiencing the kind of joy God intends for us, dynamic fellowship with other believers also results in a sense of unity with them. We will not be guilty of turning wounded souls like Suzie away if we are consciously seeking to get to know people and celebrate what makes them unique. Had someone at Suzie's church taken the time to wander into the painful corridors of her past, they would have likely been less judgmental of her singing style.

And, finally, dynamic fellowship is a means by which we capture the attention of those who look at the church and scratch their heads in amazement. In other words, when we are sharing a level of life that

> "We proclaim to you what we have seen and heard, so that you also may have fellowship with us."
> *1 John 1:3*

is transparent, intimate, and engaging, the source of our common life is seen as extremely attractive. Jesus said, "By this all men will know that you are my disciples, if you love one another" (John 13:35).

> "By this all men will know that you are my disciples, if you love one another."
> *John 13:35*

Daily Reflection Questions

Day One

I When you were young (living with your parents), what church did you attend?

What was it like?

2 How did your church experience help or hinder your relationship with God?

3 How did you react to your early church experiences?

Day Two

I Why can some local churches be compared accurately to a dysfunctional family?

2 Who do you know that has been driven away from church by a bad experience?

What happened?

3 Where are they now in relation to church?

What would it take for them to get involved in a local church?

Day Three

1 Contrast that experience with what church should be. How should that person(s) have been treated?

2 Why do churches have problems?

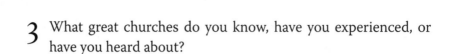

3   What great churches do you know, have you experienced, or have you heard about?

What makes them great?

Day Four

1   Why should Christians be involved in a local church, especially since so many seem to be mixed up?

2   When have you seen a church and church people reach out to someone in need?

3   Why is the experience of Acts 4 so rare these days?

Day Five

1 Why should you be involved in a local church?

2 In what ways does church meet your need for worship?

Instruction?

Fellowship?

3 What are you doing to meet the needs of others through your church?

What more should you be doing?

PRIORITY

FOUR

OVERVIEW OF PRIORITY FOUR:

A Personal, Progressive Commitment to the World

It is impossible to have a heart for God and not have a heart for the world. Jesus said, "Go and make disciples of all nations" (Matthew 28:19). John tells us, "God so loved the world that he gave his one and only Son" (John 3:16). The opening line in Rick Warren's *Purpose Driven Life* states, "It's not about you," and that's true. So our focus needs to be outward, toward God and others.

As a Christian you have a new identity according to 1 Peter 1:9. This includes being a part of a new group of people called a "holy nation," which is made up of believers from all over the world. With this new identity comes a new perspective, the way you view the world. You no longer see your neighbor down the street as just another stranger, but as a person who needs Christ, someone with whom you can build a relationship. You no longer examine your lifestyle based on your desires but on how it impacts those around you. You no longer see social problems as someone else's responsibility, but from the desire to bring a godly solution. When you see suffering, it brings you pain. When you see the earth, you see a wonderful creation that needs protection. You now see everything through God's eyes.

This doesn't mean you can right every wrong or solve every problem. But as you live out **Priority Four**, you will seek to find God's call on your life so you know where to focus your attention and energy. As a believer you will be intentional about touching the world by touching *your* world. To do less will fall short of both your potential and God's expectations.

CHAPTER THIRTY-ONE

CALLING

Tom is a uniquely gifted craftsman. He is a homebuilder who seldom has the chance to exhibit his skills because the amount of hours he can put into herring-bone patterns of walnut on the dining room floor or the multi-paneled columns built from scratch are beyond the budget of most purchasers.

He decided, however, to build his own house, to showcase what the hands of a master can produce. He ordered hundreds of feet of walnut, pine, cherry, and Brazilian hardwood and set up shop in the garage of his uncompleted home. When he returned home from a hard day's work on other people's homes, he would eat dinner and then head to the garage. The sound of the saw and other power tools could be heard late into the night. He would take a plank of unshaved wood, cut it, plane it, router it, groove it, and often reduce it to a stack of pieces no bigger than 6 or 8 inches long.

Then Tom would begin assembling. The pieces became flooring, columns, ceilings, walls, railings, and crown moldings. He built desks, cabinets, hutches, bookshelves, mantels, and much more.

If you asked Tom if he were called to be a carpenter, he would look at you and think, *"What kind of question is that?"* He might mutter something about ministers being "called" by God to the work of the church but that he was just a blue-collar laborer, a simple carpenter.

The word "called" often causes confusion because people believe it means going into full-time Christian work. Sadly, many have felt like second-class citizens in God's kingdom because they have never received such a call. Os Guinness has written a compelling work on the subject. In his book *The Call*, he writes, "Calling is the truth that God calls us to Himself so decisively that everything we are, everything we do, and everything we have is invested with a special devotion, dynamism, and direction lived out in a response to His summons and service."

Bottom line—everyone has a *primary* call from the Lord: to follow the Lord. Then we all have a *secondary* call: what we do as we follow the Lord. This we refer to as a career. So how do we know what career to follow—knowing that if God has called us, whether we wash dishes or preach the Word, we have a sacred calling?

The challenge often comes when a person suddenly realizes, "I really don't like this job. It isn't me, and I can't continue to do it." This can be very disconcerting, but it can also be a positive moment if

> Bottom line—everyone has a *primary* call from the Lord: to follow the Lord.

we learn or process three aspects of the calling equation: passion, giftedness, and role preference.

Passion

We make finding our calling more difficult than it has to be. The starting point is to ask about one's interests and concerns. For example, when you receive the daily newspaper, what sections do you read first (not including the comics)? When you go to a bookstore, what topics do you check out? When you sit in front of the television, which of the 500 channels on cable or satellite do you tune in?

If you have passion for a topic, you can spend hours reading about it and find you still have an appetite for more. Hints of this passion show up in early childhood. The child who spends hours in his or her room working with Legos or other building toys has a God-given desire to build. It's the way that person is wired, and an attentive parent would recognize this and buy even more toys that can expand the child's abilities.

Another indication of one's passion is daydreams. So when you are alone, what consumes your thoughts? And whom do you envy because they are doing what you would like to do?

Nearly everyone needs a job to provide money. So often we will take a less-than-ideal job out of necessity. As long as we see this as a temporary solution and are praying for God to open the door to a job we love, we can survive.

It was obvious that Labri didn't belong in the administrative assistant role. She had many of the necessary skills, especially being proficient on the computer and with PowerPoint and the ability to interact with clients. She did a good job. But sitting at a desk most of the day felt to her like sitting at a traffic light that stayed perpetually red. Her green light was in the musical arts and working with children. That's what she dreamed about, talked about, and prayed about.

She was like Nehemiah. Nehemiah had a great job as the cupbearer to King Artaxerxes in Babylon, but it was not his passion. Instead, he was consumed with concern for Jerusalem because he had received word that the walls of the city were in great disrepair (Nehemiah 1:1–11). The king recognized that Nehemiah was deeply disturbed and would continue to function as his cupbearer out of a sense of duty but without much enthusiasm. Therefore, the king gave Nehemiah a leave of absence to follow his dream.

In one sense, three-quarters of the battle is won when a person knows what he or she is passionate about. The person then knows how to pray with focus. He or she understands what it would take to bring enjoyment on the job. Eventually Labri was hired by a church

> In one sense, three-quarters of the battle is won when a person knows what he or she is passionate about.

to use her skills in children's worship. Her light had turned from red to green.

If you are not sure about your passion, ask others to observe you. What do they hear you talking about? Your friends may see things that are not obvious to you and make suggestions that can help you discover what is apparent to everyone but you.

Giftedness

Dick Hagstrom (Hagstrom Consulting, Inc.) says we learn more about our passions and gifts from our positive experiences than we do from our failures. Everyone who comes to Dick for career counseling receives instruction on how to list positive experiences. Dick tells the person to divide his or her life into two time frames. If the person is 30 years old, he or she should list experiences for the first 15 years on the left side of the page and years 15–30 on the right side.

These experiences don't have to be earth shattering but meaningful events and accomplishments that the person enjoyed doing, was good at it, and was acknowledged by others. These positive experiences are revealing. We enjoyed doing them in part because we were good at them. Of course, not every skill is a true indicator for a career path. For example, not everyone with cooking skills should become a chef. But whom God calls, God equips. Some might ask, well, what about Moses? He was called by God to oppose Pharaoh and lead Israel out of Egypt, but he had a speaking problem. Doesn't Paul say to the Corinthians, "But [God] said to me, 'My grace is sufficient for you, for my power is made perfect in weakness.' Therefore I will boast all the more gladly about my weakness, so that Christ's power may restore me"? (2 Corinthians 12:9).

> "My grace is sufficient for you, for my power is made perfect in weakness."
> *2 Corinthians 12:9*

Both Moses and Paul were talented men. Both had the gift of leadership powered by a strong realization of their personal spiritual inadequacy. Moses' past failures were the biggest barriers to his assuming God's mantel of leadership, and he used his lack of speaking ability as an excuse. Both of these men had keen minds; both had natural courage and were not intimidated by any rank of leader.

No matter what skill you possess, you need God's grace and strength because any true calling faces opposition and you soon realize victories cannot be won without His presence and His power.

Role Preference

Many people are in the right career but the wrong role. They are passionate about their career choice but are quickly burning out at the job.

Richard provides a good example of this. A gifted architect and enthusiastic about his craft, Richard's reputation spread so he had more work than he could handle. With expanded opportunities came employees, increased overhead, and greater headaches. Instead of spending the majority of his workday at the drafting table, he was dealing with banks, personnel problems, and government regulations. He was no longer happy; he questioned whether he should be an architect. Richard was in the right job, but he had assumed a wrong role.

Bobb Biehl knows something about the roles people play within organizations. He has spoken to thousands of people and introduced them to his Team Profile, formerly called the Role Preference Inventory. He starts with the assumption that no role is better than another, much like on a football team. The roles are complementary, and the team does not succeed without each role being filled by a talented player. Some roles, however, are more glamorous, get more attention, and garner higher pay. People are tempted to seek those roles, but usually it doesn't work out. In order to find your role, you have to understand the five-step process through which an idea develops in your company, your organization, or your church. You can contact Bobb at Master Planning Group International (800-443-1976) and ask for a copy of the Team Profile, which explains in-depth each of these five stages.

> The general idea is that every idea goes through a design phase, a development phase, and a management phase.

The general idea is that every idea goes through a design phase, a development phase, and a management phase. Whether it's a telecommunications company, a restaurant, a real estate company, or a church, everything starts with someone filling the role of designer. Someone has to have the gifts and the responsibility to create something from scratch. Richard started his architecture company from scratch—he was the designer. His gift was designing and drawing master plans for complex building projects. As the company grew, he gradually assumed more of a developer's role and then a manager's role. It was killing him. He hated being a manager.

The solution was not to leave architecture, but to sell his business and become a one-man operation, never to hire another employee again (except for an administrative assistant). He is back in his element. Gone are some of the perks that go with being an owner of a large business, but the satisfaction of being in the right role is the greatest perk he can achieve.

Daily Reflection Questions

Day One

I   When you hear the word "calling," what usually comes to mind?

2   Why do we tend to restrict "calling" to full-time Christian work?

3   When have you felt like a second-class citizen in God's kingdom?

Day Two

I   What did you think when you read, "Bottom line—everyone has a *primary* call from the Lord: to follow the Lord"?

2   What have you done to determine your "secondary call"?

3   How did you choose your career? What were the criteria?

Day Three

1   In what ways do we make finding our call difficult?

2   What's your passion?

How do you know?

3   In what ways does your occupation match with your passion?

Day Four

1   What do you think might be some "red light" areas for you?

2   What areas might be "green lights" for you?

3   What percentage of your work, church, and volunteer life involves your "greens"?

What could you do to raise the percentage?

Day Five

1   When have you experienced burnout?

2   How might a role change on your job help you experience more of your green lights?

3   What steps will you take to begin to live in your passion?

CHAPTER THIRTY-TWO

A WORLDVIEW

Can you hear Alex Trebek's voice? "The answer is: The perspective you have from your Space Shuttle window while traveling in space looking back at the blue planet called earth." One of the Jeopardy contestants rings the buzzer and speaks. "What is a worldview?"

That would likely be considered a correct response in a game show, but in terms of a definition to help us explain the decisions we make, it is sorely inadequate.

What Is a Worldview?

A worldview is the sum total of our values, beliefs, preference, and prejudices that cause us to look at life in a certain way. In other words, a worldview is the contact lens we wear that determines what we focus on, what we ignore and what we are indifferent to. In short, it's the way we "view" the "world."

Whether they are aware of it or not, everybody has a worldview. It is the personal filtering perspective used in making choices or prioritizing how a person spends time. According to George Barna, an astute observer of North American culture, **"Your worldview is the product of all the information, ideas, and experiences you absorb to form the values, morals, and beliefs that you possess."** He contends it largely defines who you are and how you behave.

With that as a foundation, consider the worldview of someone who does not believe in the existence of God. That person does not approach his or her personal behavior with any sense of ultimate judgment or reward. If someone believes in a higher power but does not subscribe to the concept of life after death, that person will likely operate on the notion that whatever he or she does has no eternal consequences. Because the worldview limits that person from looking for ultimate retribution when injustice is done, he or she must either live with the fallout of an unfair world or take matters into his or her own hands.

A person who does not believe in absolute truth has a view of the world that results in gut-reactions and flying by the seat of the pants. Everything is relative for that individual. Depending on who stands to benefit, or what others might think, or what currently is considered politically correct, the person's view of what is right or true will change from one set of circumstances to another.

Conversely, a person who acknowledges the existence of God and

> "Your worldview is the product of all the information, ideas, and experiences you absorb to form the values, morals, and beliefs that you possess."

believes the Bible to be the composite of God's revealed knowledge will come at life differently. Unlike those who view themselves as the ultimate authority of what they do or say, people of faith measure popular opinion or what may be deemed to be expedient or polite against principles that may not make sense at the moment.

We would likely assume that those who view themselves as Christ-followers have a different worldview than those who are not motivated by personal faith. But this assumption is not necessarily true.

A Biblical Worldview
Out of Focus: A Case Study

Sherm Douglas was raised in Oklahoma and educated in Texas. In terms of the Bible belt, his notch in life was near the buckle. His dad was a well-to-do hardware store owner in a suburb of Tulsa. His mom had no need to work but was quite involved in volunteer groups around town.

He was reared in a Sunday-go-to-meeting Baptist family. They never missed church. The family Bible was prominently displayed on the coffee table in the living room. Though rarely read, Sherm's mother dusted the Bible weekly without fail.

Sherm grew up believing in God. "After all, doesn't everybody?" he would ask when questioned about his belief in a higher power. He knew, by heart, old-time hymns like "Amazing Grace" and "How Great Thou Art." Often the family would gather around the piano in the den on a Sunday afternoon to sing church songs in four-part harmony. If the pastor and his wife were guests for Sunday dinner (a common occurrence), the hymn-sing was a given. The Douglas family was also big on singing the "Doxology" before every dinner. A plaque of the Lord's Prayer hung in the entryway of their large colonial home.

Although church attendance was a guarded core value, the choices of Douglas family members were not necessarily consistent with sermons they heard their pastor preach. For example, Sherm's dad failed to report on his income tax return the income he received in cash payments. The family liquor cabinet was stocked with whiskey, vodka, brandy, and wine, and it was not unusual for Mr. Douglas to have a hangover on Saturday mornings. Sherm's sister got pregnant in junior high school and had an abortion. (Her daddy drove her to the clinic and paid the doctor bill.) And Sherm's two brothers both chose not to marry but to live with their girlfriends after graduating from college.

Sherm graduated with honors from Baylor University and proceeded to get his MBA at the University of Texas. It was during

> Although church attendance was a guarded core value, the choices of Douglas family members were not necessarily consistent with sermons they heard their pastor preach.

graduate school that he exchanged his nominal churchianity for a deeply personal Christianity after a campus ministry leader succeeded in getting Sherm to attend a weekly Bible study with sharp, intelligent grad students who loved the Lord. In this small group of CEOs in training, Sherm realized that Jesus was more than a cultural mascot.

Unlike the superficial religion to which his parents and siblings had subscribed, Sherm embraced the Word of God as his guide for life. Because he viewed the Scriptures as absolute truth inspired by the Creator, the lifestyle principles he discovered framed his views on compassion, interpersonal conflict, the use of alcohol, the stewardship of the environment, as well as the kind of commitment marital vows imply. No longer did Sherm march to the cadence of what culture deemed appropriate. Instead, he asked two questions: "What does the Bible say about this issue?" and "What would Jesus do?"

After getting his masters, Sherm returned to Oklahoma where he went to work for an oil company. He married the attractive daughter of the company's president, and within ten years he was vice president. Ten years later he replaced his father-in-law as top man with a salary that he was embarrassed to mention at MBA class reunions. He wasn't embarrassed, however, to talk about Jesus. Sherm was an outspoken Christian who kept a dog-eared copy of his Bible on his desk. It wasn't for image sake. He read it everyday and referred to it in his weekly staff meetings.

At the age of 62, Sherm was blindsided with devastating news— diagnosed with an inoperable brain tumor. The team of surgeons who reviewed his case gave him nine months to live. When Sherm shared his news with his small group at church, they rallied around him and prayed, asking God to heal him. They also prayed (if God's will was not to remove the tumor) that the malignancy's growth would be slowed. One of Sherm's best friends in the group attempted to comfort him with verses that referred to the brevity of life and the confidence we have as Christians that death is not to be feared but welcomed.

Sherm could give mental assent to the fact that Christians are not to run away from death but to accept it when all medical efforts failed. It was difficult to embrace that reality in his heart. He and his wife began to fly to Mexico and Europe seeking alternative treatments. Sherm finally died eleven months after he was first informed of his tumor. He did everything he could to find a cure but in the end, it was not to be.

> Unlike the superficial religion to which his parents and siblings had subscribed, Sherm embraced the Word of God as his guide for life.

A Conflict of Worldviews

That story illustrates how many Christians struggle to apply their worldview in all of life's circumstances. Sherm's choices in life following grad school were consistent with the Christian faith. When it came to accepting death as transition that promotes Christians to the next level of existence, Sherm wanted to have a faith like Paul when he said: "I am torn between the two: I desire to depart and be with Christ, which is better by far; but it is more necessary for you that I remain in the body" (Philippians 1:23–24). Letting go of this life is not easy.

Society exerts enormous pressure for us to take our cues from what the media suggests is appropriate behavior or what the current prophets of tolerance in our culture consider acceptable. According to George Barna's research, the high percentage of Bible-believing Christians who view the world as non-Christians is astounding. From his vantage point, he sees several popular perspectives that account for this belief-action disconnect.

Barna contends, for example, that among born-again adults, only six out of ten follow a set of specific principles or standards that serve as behavioral guidelines. Two out of ten committed believers do whatever feels right or comfortable in a given situation. One out of ten of those we would call born-again Christians do whatever they believe will make the most people happy or will create the least amount of conflict with others.

Barna goes on to say that a lesser numbers of believers—about one out of ten—make their moral choices on the basis of whatever they think will produce the most personally beneficial outcome, whatever they believe their family or friends would expect them to do, or whatever they think other people would do in the same situation.

In his book *Think Like Jesus*, Barna writes: "Among those who say they rely on Biblical standards and principles as their compass for moral decision-making, only half believe that all moral truth is absolute. The rest either believe that moral decisions must be made on the basis of the individual's perceptions and the specific situation, or they haven't really thought about whether truth is relative or absolute.

"That means the bottom line is that only 14 percent of born-again adults—in other words, about one out of every seven born-again adults—rely on the Bible as their moral compass and believe that moral truth is absolute. While these perspectives are not, in themselves, the totality of a Bible-based worldview, they form the foundation on which such a life lens is based. Very few born-again Christians have the foundation in place.

"If you are more inclined to digest statistics, consider this: 91 percent of all born-again adults do not have a Biblical worldview; 98 percent of all born-again teenagers do not have a Biblical worldview. As of 2003, the United States has about 210 million adults. About 175 million of them claim to be Christian. About 80 million are born-again Christians. Roughly 7 million have a Biblical worldview. That is less

> "I am torn between the two: I desire to depart and be with Christ, which is better by far; but it is more necessary for you that I remain in the body."
> *Philippians 1:23–24*

than one out of every 30 adults in this nation."

Based on that data, is it any wonder that the divorce rate among Christians and non-Christians is a statistical tie? It stands to reason why Christian teens are not much more inclined to abstain from premarital sex than non-Christian ones. Given what you now know, are you surprised that living together before marriage is increasingly an option for young people raised in the church? If the basic assumptions most church-going adults and teens have aren't radically different from those held by the majority of society, their behavior won't be that different either.

Piecing Together a Mosaic Worldview

You no doubt know that Moses was the author of the first five books of the Old Testament. But did you also know that he wrote a psalm? According to Bible scholars, Psalm 90 was written by the same person who brought down the two tablets of Ten Commandments from atop Mt. Sinai.

In addition to being a sobering reflection on the brevity of life, Psalm 90 offers a candid picture of the realities of living in an imperfect world in which pain, suffering, and consequences of sin take a toll. Moses writes, "We are consumed by your anger and terrified by your indignation. You have set our iniquities before you, our secret sins in the light of your presence. All our days pass away under your wrath; we finish our years with a moan. The length of our days is seventy years—or eighty, if we have the strength; yet their span is but trouble and sorrow, for they quickly pass, and we fly away" (Psalm 90:7–10).

But Moses' perspective was not limited to what he saw around him. While his peers became jaded and let the injustices and hardships of life derail their hopes and dreams, Moses remained steadfast in his outlook.

He wrote, "Satisfy us in the morning with your unfailing love, that we may sing for joy and be glad all our days. Make us glad for as many days as you have afflicted us, for as many years as we have seen trouble. May your deeds be shown to your servants, your splendor to their children. May the favor of the Lord our God rest upon us; establish the work of our hands for us—yes, establish the work of our hands" (Psalm 90:14–17).

Moses does not strike us as one overwhelmed by world. He hasn't given up even though it appears people or circumstances have let him down. His words drip with hope in what God will yet do. The reason? He has a worldview that is larger than the box into which his difficult years have deposited him. Look at the first two verses of Psalm 90: "Lord, you have been our dwelling place throughout all generations.

> "Satisfy us in the morning with your unfailing love, that we may sing for joy and be glad all our days."
>
> *Psalm 90:14*

Before the mountains were born or you brought forth the earth and the world, from everlasting to everlasting you are God."

Despite what goes on in the world, Moses was convinced that God was sovereign and all-powerful and that God had a plan into which his life would conform. Seeing the Almighty as Creator and Lord is the lens through which the prophet looked at the world. For him it was a life-defining perspective that impacted behavior. That is why Moses drew a correlation between the way he viewed life and the need to behave in an informed manner. No wonder he wrote: "Teach us to number our days aright, that we may gain a heart of wisdom" (Psalm 90:12).

That's what a Biblical worldview calls us to as well. Knowing what we know is true of God, we must seek His guidance so that we make wise choices and act appropriately in accordance with that knowledge.

> "Before the mountains were born or you brought forth the earth and the world, from everlasting to everlasting you are God."
> *Psalm 90:2*

Basic Assumptions

So what are your assumptions about the world? That it is round and not flat? That people are inherently selfish? That there is no direct correlation between integrity and success? Hey, don't be too daring! But given the fact that you are reading this book, you probably also have some assumptions about the world based on what you've heard at your church or read in your Bible. Is it safe to say that your basic assumptions about include the following?

- ✳ God is the all-knowing, all-powerful Creator of the universe who still rules the universe today.

- ✳ When Jesus Christ was on earth, He lived a sinless life.

- ✳ Satan is not just a symbol of evil but is a real, living entity.

- ✳ A person cannot earn eternal salvation by being good or doing good things for other people; salvation is the free gift of God.

- ✳ Every person who believes in Jesus Christ has a personal responsibility to share his or her faith in Him with people who believe differently.

- ✳ The Bible is totally accurate in all that it teaches.

Practicing What We Preach

But believing the truth and actually incorporating those beliefs into the grid that guides our behavior are two different matters. That has been the case for more than two millennia. Back in the first century, a church leader by the name of James wrote a letter to a group of Christians whose "orthopraxy" (practice) did not reflect their orthodoxy (beliefs). Here's what he said: "Do not merely listen to the word, and so deceive yourselves. Do what it says. Anyone who listens to the word but does not do what it says is like a man who looks at his face in a mirror and, after looking at himself, goes away and immediately forgets what he looks like. But the man who looks intently into the perfect law that gives freedom, and continues to do this, not forgetting what he has heard, but doing it—he will be blessed in what he does" (James 1:22–25).

> "The man who looks intently into the perfect law that gives freedom . . . will be blessed in what he does."
> *James 1:25*

Daily Reflection Questions

Day One

1 What factors help determine a person's outlook on life?

Which of those factors influenced you the most?

2 How does a person's belief or non-belief in God affect his or her worldview?

3 When you came to faith in Christ, how did your perspective change?

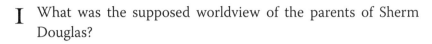

Day Two

1 What was the supposed worldview of the parents of Sherm Douglas?

2 In what ways were his parents inconsistent or hypocritical?

How did that affect Sherm?

3 What caused Sherm to struggle with the tension of hanging on to life and going to be with the Lord?

What do you think you would have done in his situation?

Day Three

1 Why do some Christians struggle so much with living out what they profess to believe?

When has that been a struggle for you?

2 Barna found that many Christians have the same worldview as non-Christians. Why do you think that is the case?

3 How should a Christian's worldview differ from that of a typical non-Christian?

Why?

Day Four

1 Why do so few Christians rely on the Bible for truth and morals?

What has been the result?

2 In what ways have you seen this demonstrated in your church?

3 When have you struggled with this?

Day Five

1 What caused Moses to stay strong in his outlook?

2 In what ways does your worldview need to change to line up with God's?

3 What will it take to make that happen?

What "basic assumptions" need to change?

CHAPTER THIRTY-THREE

Kingdom Mandate

The Lord of the Rings trilogy grossed nearly $3 billion from worldwide theaters and sales distribution. This classic story takes us on a journey through a fantasy world where there is global conflict between good and evil, light and darkness, with both sides struggling to claim victory over human hearts or geographical territory.

The screen is filled with one battle after another, as opposing armies lock in mortal combat to secure a position from which they can launch their next offensive action. Each side represents a mentality—their "kingdom" mentality. They are loyal to their kingdom, will fight for their kingdom, and are willing to die for their kingdom.

Hidden, but much more real, are spiritual kingdoms. In teaching His disciples to pray, Jesus said, "Your kingdom come, your will be done on earth as it is in heaven" (Matthew 6:10), making it clear that God has a kingdom. We can deduce, therefore, that God's kingdom stands in stark contrast to another kingdom. Paul made this clear when he said, "For he has rescued us from the dominion (kingdom) of darkness and brought us into the kingdom of the Son he loves, in whom we have redemption, the forgiveness of sins" (Colossians 1:13–14).

The kingdom of darkness is Satan's kingdom. It's made up of those who are opposed to everything Jesus stands for. Jesus predicted that all hell would try to destroy this kingdom, but it would be a futile battle (Matthew 16:18–19).

This war would be waged on two fronts: in individual lives and in earth's institutions. This is called spiritual warfare, and, as we discussed in Chapter 3, after establishing a beachhead in our lives, Christ moves in us and through us to advance the kingdom of God into enemy-held territory.

> "Your kingdom come, your will be done on earth as it is in heaven."
>
> *Matthew 6:10*

Personal Advancement

The ultimate goal of the Christian life is to keep advancing, keep growing, never quit. This is never easy because Satan knows you will be a weapon in God's kingdom, and he will do whatever possible to stop your progress. One of the surest ways to keep going is by **transforming your mind** (Romans 12:2). So when you have battled greed for days upon end and finally feel you are gaining ground against its vicious grip, you continue steadfast in God's Word, arming yourself with Scriptures that will continue to turn your mind in a positive direction and protect you from the Enemy of your soul. About the time greed is under control, old man lust appears and a new battle starts afresh.

A preacher once said, "Any believer who is living the Christian life has the smell of gun powder on him." He's been in battle. He gets off a few rounds, but then he is dodging Satan's RPGs and traversing precariously through enemy mine fields.

Personal advancement means sharing your faith with those who are held captive by the other side. Every army has commissioned officers; God's kingdom is no different. God's commission is to "go and make disciples of all nations" (Matthew 28:19).

When you make a disciple, you have liberated a captive from the other side. The person may not realize that he or she was a captive, but after experiencing Christ's love, he or she understands.

In the mid 60s, an American couple was living in the Ras Beirut section near the Cornish and beautiful coastline of Lebanon. They lived on the third floor of the Emir Faisal Ben Turkey Building, which had a young Palestinian from Nablus, Jordan, as its concierge. Hussein was a jovial and conscientious young man who loved to interact with the Americans in light-hearted banter, but occasionally turning to serious subjects as well.

One day, Hussein was missing. The Americans became concerned and, in their clumsy attempt to speak a combination of Arabic and English, tried to find out what had happened. They were informed that the Lebanese police had arrested him for not having the proper work permit and that he was in prison, but no one knew for sure which one.

The American husband talked to everyone he could and even went to the Jordanian Embassy to see if Hussein could be located. After going down numerous dead end streets, he finally was informed of the name and location of the prison. One Saturday, his wife fixed a lunch for Hussein in case he was undernourished, and the husband spent the day trying to jump through all the hoops necessary to get in and make contact. Finally, he sat in a room as different inmates filed by, but Hussein was not one of them. Oh, he was at the right prison, but the guards refused to let the two of them make contact.

It was a discouraging situation, a day wasted in the American's mind. Thirty days later, however, Hussein was released and returned to the apartment building. Upon the joyous reunion, he informed the Americans that in the prison he heard his name called but couldn't answer. Then he made a profound statement: "There are 99 names for God in Islam, but I have not yet found one that describes the kind of love you tried to show me. Would you tell me about the God of love?" Hussein was both a physical and spiritual captive, but he found the

> "Go and make disciples of all nations."
> *Matthew 28:19*

freedom than only comes through Christ.

Personal advancement includes doing what you can to find the wounds, sores, or irritations of society and do what you can as one person to be a voice of hope or to organize an effort to reverse the casualty rate. You may not have as earth-shaping of an impact as William Wilberforce who spent a lifetime at the British Parliament trying to stop the slave trade, but you can touch one life at a time and over time, that effort will be meaningful. The needs are all around us. There's the homeless dilemma, low-income housing, breakdown of the family unit, teenage pregnancy, drug and alcohol addiction, the jobless crisis that many face, and the problems go on and on.

Personal advancement must include a view from an eternal perspective, especially your eternal home. Randy Alcorn hit a nerve with his book, *Heaven*. Most Christians have, at best, a foggy view of what awaits them after death, let alone what crowns or rewards mean and whether they represent a lure for being faithful. Paul says it has something to do with reigning with Christ (2 Timothy 2:12) and participating in His future rulership (Revelation 3:21). It's also about receiving an inheritance (1 Peter 1:4) that has been specifically reserved for us.

Roger kept teasing his grown daughter and son-in-law. Every time he wanted them to do something he would say, "Remember the **i** word"—in other words, remember your future *inheritance*. The Apostle Paul also said remember the "i" word. "Whatever you do, work at it with all your heart, as working for the Lord, not for men, since you know that you will receive an inheritance from the Lord as a reward" (Colossians 3:23–24).

We still need clarity as to what that inheritance might include. Is it playing a harp in the clouds all day? No, that has no appeal. As Alcorn writes, "Jesus says that those who have properly stewarded God's assets on earth will be granted ownership of assets in heaven."

Those assets have to do with the same kinds of things that motivate us on earth. Abraham was considered wealthy because he owned land, had great flocks, and was responsible for many people. The assets of heaven will be the inheritance of land and the right to experience power over the universe as a co-heir with Christ (Romans 8:16–17). In other words, we will be busy. With the effects of sin lifted in our eternal home, we will think clearly, work productively, and joyfully reap the benefits of the talents and assets God has given to us. That is a great incentive to keep growing, keep faithful, and keep advancing in our personal journey.

> "Jesus says that those who have properly stewarded God's assets on earth will be granted ownership of assets in heaven."

We Are God's Weapons

In the conflict between kingdoms, the one with the most powerful weapons wins. Like it or not, for good or for bad, we are the weapons in God's kingdom. That's why Paul said that we should put on the whole armor of God (Ephesians 6:11). We need a defensive and offensive strategy. Defensively, we need to be shielded from the weapons of the Enemy, and offensively we need the Spirit's work empowering God's Word as we "pray in the spirit on all occasions" (Ephesians 6:18). Prayer is not just a nice activity, it's the difference between victory and defeat. Anyone who has been in the military knows that certain armaments have no destructive power unless they have been armed. A believer becomes an "armed" weapon when he prays.

Another thing that determines our effectiveness as an offensive weapon is whether we are salt and light to those around us (Matthew 5:13–16). We didn't say being a *lump* of salt or a saltshaker, but those scattered granules that bring flavor to life or preserve and protect against decay.

Jim is a real estate attorney who sits on the Board of Governors for the Florida Bar Association. He's known as a clear-headed thinker, a man of integrity, and a winsome addition to any meeting. On one occasion, an associate made a derogatory comment about Christians: "Those fundamentalist Christians think that God speaks to them through their car radio."

"Wait a minute . . ." Jim responded. "That's a ludicrous statement. I'm a Christian and if God wanted to speak to me through the radio, He could, but He hasn't, and you can't make such a categorical statement."

The other attorney quickly backpedaled and apologized. Jim accepted his apology graciously, and the conversation continued. In that moment in time, Jim was a granule of salt, both adding flavor and preserving the reputation of Christianity in that conversation.

That is just an example of what Jesus meant in the Sermon on the Mount. Jim was also a light, giving perspective and clarity to a situation that was void of understanding.

Being salt and light also means tearing down walls that prevent non-believers from seeing or tasting the real thing. It means obliterating some of the negative stereotypes generated by well-intentioned but thoughtless Christians, such as:

> "Pray in the spirit on all occasions."
> *Ephesians 6:18*

Christian Jargon

Using words that non-Christians don't understand or clichés that are only understood by the church crowd.

Pre-set Formulas

Canned speeches that don't take into consideration the real questions the hearer wants explained.

Heartless Connections

Real communication takes place when there is empathy, and the listener feels the communicator really cares about him or her.

Credibility Gap

Nothing nullifies a message more than a discrepancy between what the communicator says and does.

The Ultimate Confusion

Just because a person belongs to a church, doesn't mean he or she is living according to God's kingdom. Many attend church for the wrong reasons and never realize the gap between churchianity and Christianity. In fact, their *churchianity* is the very thing that prevents others from coming inside to "kick the tires," to see what the church has to offer. The following comparison will help show the difference.

Kingdom People	Church People
�֍ Kingdom people seek first the kingdom of God and His justice.	✖ Church people often put church work above concern for justice, mercy and truth.
✖ Kingdom people think about how to get the Body of Christ distributed into the world.	✖ Church people think about how to get people into church.
✖ Kingdom people work to see the Body of Christ change the world.	✖ Church people worry that the world might change the church.

At some point in your journey of faith, you will need to decide where you cast your lot. Is it really the kingdom you're about, or is it the shadow kingdom of earth that appears to be the real thing but quickly disappears against the light of what Scripture teaches?

Daily Reflection Questions

Day One

1 How do you know that "hidden, but much more real, are spiritual kingdoms"?

2 What do you know about "spiritual warfare"?

3 Of what "enemy-held territory" are you aware?

Day Two

1 Why do we say that those who don't know Christ are "held captive by the other side"?

2 Which of the "personal advancement" actions have you done recently?

Describe.

3 Which one of those actions do you need to work on most?

Why is that one important to you now?

Day Three

1 In what ways are believers "weapons" in the conflict between kingdoms?

2 What will be your "defensive" strategy?

3 What will be your "offensive" strategy?

Day Four

1 In what ways have you contributed to the negative stereotypes of Christianity in the world?

2 What have you done, or are you doing, to obliterate some of those negative stereotypes?

3 In general, what's the difference between "churchianity" and Christianity?

Day Five

1 What can you do to "seek first His kingdom and His righteousness"?

2 What can you do to help "get the Body of Christ distributed into the world"?

3   What can you do to see the Body of Christ change the world?

CHAPTER THIRTY-FOUR

THE NEED FOR EVANGELISM

On a beautiful Saturday afternoon, Larry was enjoying a family picnic on Casper Mountain with his parents and siblings. As any normal 12-year-old boy, he loved to explore the rocks and crevices. So weaving in and out of the tall Rocky Mountain pines, he hoped to find an abandoned miner's cabin or even a mine. He forgot to keep track of two important survival prerequisites during his afternoon exploration: knowing the time of day and knowing his way back to the picnic site.

Around 4 p.m. Larry realized that he had better head back to camp, but which way was it? He ran down the most recent ridge he had climbed and into a familiar looking meadow. As he glanced at the sky and noticed the sun beginning to set beyond the horizon of pine trees, he swallowed his first gulp of fear. He was lost—at least, he didn't know which way to turn next. "All right, don't panic" he told himself. "Just think calmly and try to backtrack the path that got you here." But no matter which direction he went, he couldn't find familiar terrain. With the encroaching darkness and the evening chill adding to his sense of desperation, he thought he heard a voice in the distance. He strained every nerve to see if his mind was playing games or if he really heard what he thought he heard. It was a woman's voice, and now he could make out the name she was calling: "Laaarrrrryyyyy!" Immediately he recognized his mother's voice. He yelled back, but he didn't think she could hear him, so he kept walking through the dark woods, trying to head in the direction of the voice. Soon two voices were calling—his mother and his father. Before long he knew he was no longer lost. His parents, upon seeing him, treated him like a prodigal son. As a 12-year-old is known to do, he acted as though it was no big deal and wondered why they made such a fuss. Deep down, however, Larry was turning somersaults of joy and had never been so happy to hear the voices and feel the embrace of his parents.

> We live on a wonderful planet. It is breathtakingly beautiful, but it is also a place where not all is right.

Why People Feel Lost

We live on a wonderful planet. It is breathtakingly beautiful, but it is also a place where not all is right. In this world a person can live in a multi-story apartment in downtown Chicago and be totally lost. Why? What is it about our world that looks so good and often tastes so good, but before long, leaves gravel in our mouths? There are many reasons, and here are a few.

The world is dark.

One person said it was "like men with sore eyes, they find the light painful while the darkness which permits them to see nothing, is restful and agreeable." When people become accustomed to the dark, it takes over and they forget what sunlight looks like.

Not only do they forget the light, but they will forever be lost unless light finds them. Like our opening story of Larry, lost on Casper Mountain, he would never have made it back to camp unless his mother and father had found him. This theme shows up repeatedly in Scripture. God is forever cupping His hands around His mouth and yelling: "Where are you?" or "I'm looking for you" or "Come home!"

The world is fallen.

God sovereignly designed the world to put Himself at risk, where people observing the pain and chaos of life would say either: "This doesn't look very good on Your resume, God" or "You aren't really in control."

God gets lots of bad press. We are the ones who provide the stories to be reported. We act like people with darkened minds—totally foolish—because we are fallen people living on a fallen planet. As a result, God gives us the privilege of messing up our lives and we follow through gloriously.

When addressing the Romans, Paul said that God has revealed Himself to man through His creative acts, but humankind's "thinking became futile and their foolish hearts were darkened" (Romans 1:21).

> "You were dead in your transgressions and sins, in which you used to live when you followed the ways of this world."
>
> *Ephesians 2:1–2*

The reason a person can't look at a sunset over a beautiful mountain range and stand to sing the *Hallelujah* chorus is because he or she is spiritually dead. Paul says, "You were dead in your transgressions and sins, in which you used to live when you followed the ways of this world" (Ephesians 2:1–2). A dead person can't respond. A doctor can shine a halogen light directly on the dead person's pupil and he or she will see nothing.

John and Ruth Anne Tolson gave birth to a beautiful little girl, Adrienne. Unfortunately, within the first five days in the hospital she picked up a germ and she never recovered. Every procedure used by physicians on her tiny, lifeless body would not work—she was gone.

Paul describes spiritually dead people as "darkened in their understanding and separated from the life of God because of the ignorance that is in them due to the hardening of their hearts" (Ephesians 4:18). These are not the kindest words you can say about a person, but a spiritual physician must be truthful. People who are lost without Christ have three characteristics; they are **dead, blind,** and **ignorant.** And because they have no ability to respond, to get themselves out of their darkness, they need faith to come from an outside source and to be planted in their hearts. Paul calls this a "gift" (Ephesians 2:8).

The world is relativistic.

Dr. Francis Schaeffer was a small man with a great intellect and a heart as big as the world. He and his wife, Edith, moved from St. Louis, where he was a seminary professor to L'Abri, Switzerland, where they would host lost and seeking souls crisscrossing Europe in search of the truth. The 60s and 70s were decades where college students were searching deeply for the meaning of life and any guru who could shed light on their paths.

As people found their way to L'Abri, they would sit and listen for hours to Dr. Schaeffer give lectures on the direction of western civilization as it was reflected in philosophy, art, architecture, the cinema, and other art forms. One of his classic statements was that "in our present day of relativism, there is no true truth." In other words, people do not believe in absolutes; truth is relative. This is not the place for a thorough debunking of this thought process, only to acknowledge that according to Dr. Alan Bloom, author of *The Closing of the American Mind*, "There is one thing a professor can be absolutely certain of . . . every student entering the university believes that truth is relative."

A relativistic world is a world in chaos and one only has to look around and read the newspapers to know this fact is not relative.

> Suffering is class blind, race blind, gender blind, denominationally blind, and age blind.

The world is hurting.

Every person, Christian or not, experiences pain. Suffering is class blind, race blind, gender blind, denominationally blind, and age blind. Pain comes in a variety of options, whether it is psychological, emotional, physical, or relational.

In December 2004, the conductor for the Crystal Cathedral in Garden Grove, California shot himself in his office prior to the first performance of the Christmas concert. This man had been depressed for most of his 30 years as an employee of that great church. Psychiatrists say that people commit suicide when the pain of living is no longer tolerable. The Genesis account of creation explains that sin entered the world when Adam sinned, and the planet fell with him. One of the tragic results is that from then on, all living creatures experience pain and yearn for the coming of a new earth.

God's Plan for the Lost

There's a story told that after Jesus finished His thirty-three years of ministry, went to the cross, was resurrected, and ascended into heaven, He was met by a great host of saints who had gone before. They asked

Him about the wonderful plan laid out before time and how His death and sacrifice would result in salvation for all who would respond to His invitation of new and eternal life. Then one of the angels asked, "But if people don't respond, what is your plan?" Jesus responded, "There is no other plan. If my disciples don't share the good news with others, they will remain lost."

Jesus told His disciples, "I am the way and the truth and the life. No one comes to the Father except through me" (John 14:6). No one else is qualified to save humankind. Jesus lived a perfect life. He alone can forgive sins. He alone meets the deepest needs of the human heart. He alone meets the need for significance. He alone can wipe away all guilt. He alone is the One who can find us in the dark and lead us to safety.

> "I am the way and the truth and the life. No one comes to the Father except through me."
> *John 14:6*

Johnny Cash and June Carter starred in the TV special, *Is There A Family In The House?* It was a multi-hour telethon to help raise finds for Youth for Christ. During one section of the production, Johnny told the story of a little girl from Kansas who one day was missing. Her distraught parents looked frantically around the house and farm for her but to no avail.

Soon friends and neighbors from that part of the state showed up to help in the search. The state troopers were involved and helicopters hovered over cornfields, but there was no sign of the missing girl. Then someone suggested that everyone hold hands and form a human chain that would stretch from one end of the farm to the other. Step by step they moved forward, eyes straining for any hopeful signs. Finally, they came upon her lifeless body. Out of the agony and heartbreak of the situation, one person asked, "Why didn't we join hands sooner?"

That is the ultimate question for evangelism. Why don't we join hands to find those who are lost, who desperately want to be found, but they don't know the way home? If you ever wonder if there is a need for evangelism, you have to first ask if people are really lost and then the follow-up question is **do you really care?**

Daily Reflection Questions

Day One

I   In the story about lost Larry, what helped Larry find his way back to camp?

2 When have you had a similar experience?

3 In what ways does the story parallel "lost and found" people in the world?

Day Two

1 What evidence do you have that the world is "dark"?

2 Why is the gospel like "light"?

3 Who do you know that provides a good example of being lost in darkness and then seeing God's light?

Day Three

1   What evidence have you seen in the news today that the world is "fallen"?

2   How about in your relationships and in yourself?

Why is the world in such bad shape?

3   Why does the Bible describe people without Christ as "dead, blind, and ignorant"?

Day Four

1   What examples have you seen recently in the world of relativism?

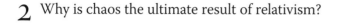

2 Why is chaos the ultimate result of relativism?

3 How do you know that "the world is hurting"? (Give specific examples.)

Day Five

1 What is God's plan for reaching the lost?

2 In what ways are you part of His plan?

3 What can you do to join hands with other Christians to find and reach the lost?

CHAPTER THIRTY-FIVE

Methods of Evangelism

Once upon a time, a man from a far off country purchased an apple orchard and hired hundreds of workers. Each worker was given a tent by the owner and instructed to pick the apples around his own tent, in return for which he would receive free lodging.

In the early years, everyone was faithful in picking the apples from those trees for which he was responsible, and there were very few apples that fell to the ground and rotted. Eventually the owner had to return to his own country, and so he left a detailed book of instructions and asked a few people to act as supervisors. For several of these men, the job was large enough for them to devote their full time to picking and guiding others in picking. The other workers, who earned income from outside jobs, contributed to their support.

As time passed, some of the workers started saying about their supervisors, "He's such a good apple-picker. He gets paid to pick apples. I'll have him come pick my apples."

It was only a matter of time until it was just the paid apple-picker who picked any apples. On occasion there would be a few volunteers to assist in the picking, but everyone knew that it was the supervisor's job.

Once or twice a week, special apple picking services would be held. All the people of the orchard would come and sit and watch as the supervisor climbed up his stepladder to begin picking apples. But he was SO slow. Apples from the whole orchard kept falling to the ground and rotting. Many people didn't notice, however, and those who *were* concerned only wanted the supervisor to come over and pick apples in *their* section of the orchard.

The people built a special hall and heard wonderful lectures about picking apples, and discussions about the best techniques to use in picking them. In order to encourage those who had lost their vision for seeing apples picked, musical groups were brought in to sing good old apple picking songs. Everyone loved to sing about picking apples. Every once in a while, guest apple pickers from other orchards would be engaged, in hopes that they would pick a few extra apples that the supervisor could not reach.

Building and maintenance of the lecture hall, bringing in great apple pickers and purchasing special apple picking machinery all cost money. *A lot of money.* Many special meetings were held to discuss all the money being spent to pick apples. Wasn't there some *less expensive* way to pick apples?

> Once upon a time, a man from a far off country purchased an apple orchard and hired hundreds of workers.

Careful count was kept of every apple that was picked and of the attendance at apple picking ceremonies. All the people were pleased if attendance at apple picking meetings was up, particularly if expenses were kept to a minimum and more apples were picked this year than last.

And yet . . . and yet . . . there were those that had a disquieting concern about all those rotten apples. No count was ever taken of those that rotted, however. But there were *millions* of them. In front of almost every tent; all throughout the orchard. Why . . . as you walked out the front door of the lecture hall, you couldn't help tripping over them! Everyone's life was complicated by all those rotten apples. Rotten apples in the school building, rotten apples in the Town Hall, rotten apples in the neighbor's tent. Some people even had rotten apples in their own tents! You would think if the supervisor couldn't handle the job, at least the owner of the orchard would do something . . . maybe even send a new supervisor.

Then an amazing thing happened! One day, two men discovered some pages from the apple-picker's guide that must have fallen out of the book years before. They were old and wrinkled and lodged inside the hollow trunk of an ancient apple tree. They immediately brought the pages to the supervisor (since everyone believed that only the supervisor could interpret the apple-picker's guide). He read these words: "The job of the supervisor is to exhort the people to do their work of picking apples. Everyone has special gifts to pick the apples from the trees around his own tent. Only in this way can all the apples be picked."

Some of the people were angry. "It *can't* say that! Everyone knows it's the supervisor's job to pick the apples."

Others were excited. "Why, that makes sense!" they said. "If we each just pick the apples around our own tents, almost all the apples could be picked, and very few would fall to the ground and rot. The supervisor would still have enough to keep himself busy, as he helps *us* and guides us as *we* pick the apples."

And so the people did as the apple-picking guide suggested. As a result, they harvested more apples than they ever thought possible! When the owner in the far off country heard of it, he was very pleased! (A fairy tale written by Ron Peri)

Surveys show that 98 percent of Christians never pick apples, never lead another person to Christ, even though the apple-picker's guide gave specific instructions to all people by the owner of the orchard to "go and make disciples of all nations" (Matthew 28:19).

Acts 8 contains a life-changing encounter and an effective pattern for communicating your faith. If you want to be faithful, if you love

> Surveys show that 98 percent of Christians never pick apples.

people and you want them to know about Christ, yet you are reluctant because you lack confidence, this chapter contains **six keys** to sharing your faith that proved to be effective in Philip's life.

6 Keys to Sharing Your Faith

Key 1—Sensitivity to the Lord's Leading (Acts 8:26–27)

Philip was in a high state of being tuned in to God. Believers in Jerusalem were beginning to feel the fire of persecution. Stephen became the first martyr for the faith, and many fled to places like Samaria. While in Samaria a spiritual awakening took place and many were coming to Christ due to the influx of the Jerusalem believers. Philip was a part of this spiritual activity and had no intentions of leaving. God, however, had other plans. The text says an angel of the Lord instructed Philip to go to the desert on the way to Gaza.

Being instructed by an angel was not totally foreign to Philip; he knew that was the primary means by which God guided the faithful in the Old Testament. However, he could have chosen to refuse this leading. The old TV show, *Mission Impossible*, always began with a self-destructing tape giving the next assignment to two agents with the caveat, "This is your mission if you choose to accept it."

Philip chose to accept his assignment—he doesn't argue with God—but being a devout follower, he is very sensitive to God's wishes. Sensitive people are available people. This kind of sensitivity develops over time as people walk close to the Lord. He is like the person referred to in Psalm 1:1–2: "Blessed is the man who does not walk in the counsel of the wicked or stand in the way of sinners or sit in the seat of mockers. But his delight is in the law of the Lord, and on his law he meditates day and night."

> "His delight is in the law of the Lord, and on his law he meditates day and night."
> *Psalm 1:2*

Key 2—Availability to Move (Acts 8:27–29)

Philip is available because he is prepared. God is going to use him to help an Ethiopian official in high office and of great importance because the man is reading a portion of Scripture that he doesn't understand. The Ethiopian is a Gentile who was exposed to the conversations in Jerusalem, heard about Jesus the Messiah, and heard about a possible link to a prophetic passage in Isaiah.

God needed someone who knew the Scripture, who was sensitive to this man's position and questions, and didn't need to excuse himself while he tried to figure out the meaning of that specific passage. When young Henry Kissinger was the Secretary of State, he talked about the political and intellectual preparation needed to serve the President of the United States. If he was summoned to the White House and asked his opinion on a conflict in a remote part of the globe, he couldn't respond by saying, "Let me go get my map and see if I can find where that is and I'll get back to you." The President needed cabinet members who had already done their homework and had the intellectual capital necessary to be a good advisor. Philip had that kind of capital and was available to move.

Key 3—Initiative (Acts 8:30)

Philip ran up to the chariot and heard the Ethiopian reading from Isaiah. In one verse, we learn a lot about this extraordinary man. He uses a combination of skills to engage him in a way that will lead the Ethiopian to the most important discovery of his life. He combined patience with zeal and intelligence. He was bold but not brash. He knew how to explore the man's soul with a penetrating question: "Do you understand what you are reading?"

> It's one thing to take the initiative; it's another to do it effectively.

It's one thing to take the initiative; it's another to do it effectively. Philip is on a mission, and he didn't have to determine whether it is the right mission. God has opened the doors, and Philip showed up. That is half the battle—just showing up.

Whether it is selling a product or building a relationship with a potential believer, it will not happen without being there. Business studies show that most deals are consummated after the fifth visit. Philip needed to show up only once because the heart of the Ethiopian had been prepared in advance. Undoubtedly he would have returned as many times as necessary to see this man come to Christ.

Key 4—Tactfulness (Acts 8:31)

Philip joined the Ethiopian in his chariot but not before he was invited. He listened as the man confessed his ignorance. Philip didn't make him feel foolish but rather showed genuine concern. He was courteous and helped to hold up the dignity of this seeker.

Too often a person moves from an attempted witness for Christ to an argument. No one is argued into God's kingdom. When a person genuinely is seeking the truth, when his or her heart has been prepared by God's spirit, any messenger who can tactfully and inoffensively declare the content of the good news can be used to lead them to Christ.

Key 5—Precision (Acts 8:34–35)

After the Ethiopian read the passage from Isaiah 53, Philip honed in like a laser on how Jesus was the One being spoken about as the suffering servant. There was no theological mumbo-jumbo. He didn't take him down a side road but focused on what it meant to follow Jesus.

Philip explained the need to let go of whatever concept he had of God and trust Christ to catch him and provide him with the answers that had escaped him up to this point. Like a trapeze artist, that's exactly what the Ethiopian did. He let go of one bar and grabbed another. He was now a part of the family of faith and ready to be obedient in the next step.

Key 6–Decisiveness (Acts 8:36–39)

How did the Ethiopian know about baptism? Perhaps Philip had told him, or maybe he had heard it being discussed among the believers in Jerusalem. Notice that it wasn't Philip trying to convince the Ethiopian of his obligation to follow up his decision with baptism. The man didn't tiptoe lightly into his new faith, he ran boldly and decisively and, most important, obediently.

In Chapter 3, we looked at the big picture of the Christian life and used Lane Adams' analogy of the beachhead to illustrate how Christ establishes a foothold in a person's life and then progressively conquers more territory that is held by the Enemy for the rest of that person's journey.

Now we want to use the same illustration as a model for sharing your faith with someone in a private conversation. This involves a four-step process. We will write as if we are speaking to a non-believer as we lay out the plan for inviting Christ into his or her life.

1. Go back to the beginning.

When God created the universe, He also created humans to be in fellowship with Him. The world was perfect when God and His creation enjoyed harmony, until the humans decided to violate the ground rules. In one act of disobedience, man and woman found themselves cut off from God and, as a result, cut off from their own sense of well-being and fulfillment, and also cut off from the rest of humanity. That act of disobedience was called SIN.

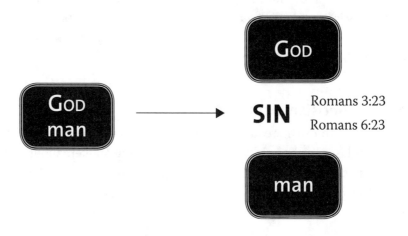

2. People try to get to God on their own.

Knowing that things are not right, humans yearn to have a relationship once again with their Creator. They know they have messed up and that they have done things that make them ashamed, so they attempt to reconnect by going to church, doing good deeds for others, giving money to charity. Some people (under the domination of scary religious teaching) even cut or beat themselves in order to gain God's favor. But Scripture teaches that no one can earn his or her way into God's favor; it can only be received as an act of God's grace according to Ephesians 2:8–9.

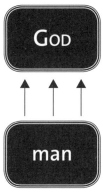

3. Christ establishes a beachhead.

During World War II, the Allies banded together to reclaim a chain of islands in the South Pacific. Aircraft carriers moved in and planes were sent for aerial reconnaissance to find the strengths and the weaknesses of the enemy. Other aircraft were then sent in to bomb and strafe the island in a softening up process so the Allied forces could establish a beachhead. Just as this invasion was critical to the outcome of the war, so, too, an individual needs to be invaded by Christ.

> "Yet to all who received him, to those who believed in his name, he gave the right to become children of God."
>
> *John 1:12*

The Invasion   John 1:12: "Yet to all who received him, to those who believed in his name, he gave the right to become children of God."

John 3:36: "Whoever believes in the Son has eternal life, but whoever rejects the Son will not see life, for God's wrath remains on him."

The Position   1 Corinthians 1:8–9: "He will keep you strong to the end, so that you will be blameless on the day of our Lord Jesus Christ. God, who has called you into fellowship with his Son Jesus Christ our Lord, is faithful."

1 John 5:12–13: "He who has the Son has life; he who does not have the son of God does not have life. I write these things to you who believe in the name of the Son of God so that you may know that you have eternal life."

The Condition Hebrews 10:14: "because by one sacrifice he has made perfect forever those who are being made holy."

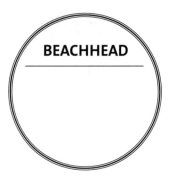

Christ invading a person's life does not end the conflict. The enemy was not completely eradicated in the believer, but he was relocated. Enemy-held territory remains. Once a person becomes a Christian, he or she still has areas of life that create problems: lust, greed, anger, selfishness, pride, etc.

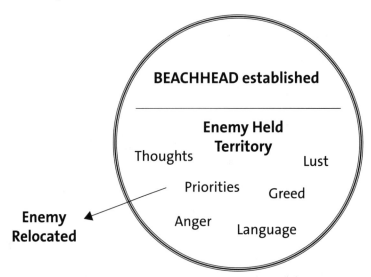

4. The Invasion comes by personal invitation.

I need to tell you my story. There was a time I was lost and confused. I saw that I was in serious trouble. I had sinned and I tried every trick I could find to get to God, but it didn't work. Then someone showed me this illustration, and I did what it says in John 1:12. I received Christ into my life. As a result, Christ took up His position in my life.

I am by no means perfect. I still struggle, but I know Christ is there. Why? Because He said so. That's the beauty of John 1:12. Now when I fail and disappoint both God and myself, I do two things: I confess and I obey. I confess my sin and ask for forgiveness. First John 1:9 states, "If we confess our sins, he is faithful and just and will forgive us our sins and purify us from all unrighteousness." I then turn my back on the thing that tripped me up and go the other way. I obey God and His Word. John 14:15 says, "If you love me, you will obey what I command."

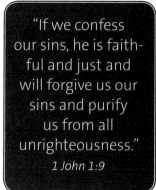

> "If we confess our sins, he is faithful and just and will forgive us our sins and purify us from all unrighteousness."
>
> *1 John 1:9*

I know Christ's position in my life is permanent (1 John 5:12–13), but by the power of the Holy Spirit, He forgives those temporary failures where I do what I don't want to do (Romans 7:15). He continues to claim more territory in my life, and He will do the same for you.

If you would like for Christ to invade your life, do what Jesus asks in Revelation 3:20. He said, "Here I am! I stand at the door and knock. If anyone hears my voice and opens the door, I will come in and eat with him, and he with me." Having Christ enter your life is as close as your willingness to ask Him in. He doesn't beat the door down. He doesn't try to manipulate you to open the door. He simply knocks. The question is, **WILL YOU INVITE HIM IN?**

Daily Reflection Questions

Day One

I   At what point during the "fairy tale," did you realize it was about evangelism?

2   Where do you see yourself in the story?

3   Why do you suppose 98 percent of all Christians never lead another person to Christ?

Day Two

1   When have you sensed that God was leading you to talk with someone about Christ?

2   What can a person do to be more sensitive to the Lord's leading?

3   Philip was available because he was prepared. What can someone do to be prepared to follow God's leading?

Day Three

1   What opportunities have you had recently to discuss your faith with someone who doesn't believe?

How did you respond? Did you take the initiative? What could you have done differently?

2 When did your attempt to tell someone about Christ turn into an argument?

What could you have done differently to avoid arguing?

3 Why can it be difficult to be tactful?

Day Four

1 If someone asked you how to become a Christian, what precise answer would you give?

2 How was Philip decisive in his presentation of the Gospel to the Ethiopian official?

3 In what ways was the Ethiopian official decisive in his response?

Day Five

I Which steps in the sharing the faith process are most familiar to you?

Which ones aren't that familiar?

2 What would it take for you to be comfortable enough with this process that you could use it to share the Gospel with a friend?

3 With whom would you like to share the Gospel if you had the opportunity?

CHAPTER THIRTY-SIX

CHRISTIAN LIFESTYLE

A couple decades ago Robin Leach hosted a popular television program called *Lifestyles of the Rich and Famous*. Although each episode featured a different celebrity and even though their mansions were unique, all of the programs were much the same. The rich and famous had expensive tastes and embraced opulent excesses. In all honesty, if you'd seen one you'd seen them all.

When it comes to the lifestyles of Jesus' followers, it's a house of a different color. Literally. You can find wealthy Christians as well as those on welfare. Some enjoy an after-dinner cigar, while some believe all use of tobacco a sin. Certain believers spend part of their Sunday at the office, catching up on what they didn't get done the previous week. Others are very conscientious when it comes to keeping the Sabbath day holy. Christians have differing views on alcohol, entertainment, and war. They also approach the doctrine of grace from different perspectives. Some see it as an invitation to live by the *spirit* of the law at all times, while some believe it merely cancels past transgressions but doesn't negate our obligation to strive for holiness.

As we seek to understand the diversity (as well as the difficulty) in views of the Christian life, consider the following scenario of two men who came at life and faith quite differently.

Although you probably would be hard-pressed to explain why, Paul and Pete were good friends.

A Tale of Two Brothers

Although you probably would be hard-pressed to explain why, Paul and Pete were good friends. They were poles apart in their approach to life. Paul had been reared by intellectual parents in a large city in the Northeast. Pete had been born into a blue-collar family in a rural community. Paul prided himself in his academic achievement. Peter boasted about his ability as a commercial fisherman. One was accustomed to the finer things of life; the other quite happy with a hot meal and a warm bed.

Pete came to faith in Christ first. After a dismal fishing season, the symptoms of a mid-life crisis were quite evident, and he was battling self-esteem issues. What he had spent his life pursuing was failing to offer the fulfillment it once had. When confronted with the claims of Christianity, he took the bait. His conversion was quite noticeable. With the confidence of a prizefighter, Pete started taking swings at unethical practices in his community. He made friendly jabs at longtime acquaintances and family members who balked at his

newfound faith. They began calling him Rocky. That only seemed to fuel Pete's passion. He became as conscientious in his commitment to Christ as he had been devoted to his profession. Some thought he bordered on being fanatic. He was very strict with his observance of Sunday and decided that as far as he was concerned, drinking any form of alcohol was wrong.

Meanwhile, Paul graduated with honors from a prestigious university. In the process of pursuing his degree, he had become quite intolerant of anything Christian. Truth be told, the arrogant academic had even been involved in some word wars that had disintegrated into fistfights. He joined an activist group who shared his concern that Christianity was casting too long a shadow on the landscape of the country. But while Paul was traveling out of state on behalf of his group, something happened that knocked him off his self-sufficient high horse. Momentarily blinded by a ray of direct sunlight, he lost control of his vehicle and was thrown from his car. In the midst of his eventual recovery, Paul claims to have encountered Christ and, in the process, confessed his need of a Savior.

> Sometime later, Pete and Paul met through mutual friends, and, ironically, they hit it off.

Sometime later, Pete and Paul met through mutual friends, and, ironically, they hit it off. They learned from each other. Paul challenged some of Pete's legalistic views on the faith, while Pete's winsome personality challenged some of Paul's presuppositions about those who had never been to college. In a rather amazing series of events, the once-agnostic academic activist became an itinerant Christian speaker, while the uneducated former fisherman assumed the pastorate of a mega-church in a major city.

On one occasion the bonds of friendship between Paul and Pete were seriously tested. While attending a conference together, Pete observed Paul drinking a glass of wine with some Christians who had traveled to attend the convention. Initially he thought nothing of it. Frequently he and Paul had sipped Chablis together during dinner with Christian friends. But when a delegation from Pete's church, who believed drinking alcohol to be a sin, began making comments about the "liberal" lifestyle of those attending this "Christian conference," Pete began to side with them. They were large contributors to the church, and he didn't want to risk offending them. In order to assuage their concern, he affirmed their legalistic attitude about drinking.

When Paul discovered what Pete was doing, he wasted no time in calling him on the carpet. Pete's face turned as red as the Persian rug on which they were standing in the hotel lobby. As far as Paul was concerned, Pete was acting disgracefully. He was sacrificing the priceless doctrine of grace on the altar of pleasing people.

The Rest of the Story

If this unlikely friendship sounds familiar, it's because you've read it before, in the Bible. It's a modern-day retelling of the lives of Peter the fisherman-turned-disciple and Paul the persecutor-of-Christians-turned-apostle. Galatians 2 tells how sparks flew when these two good Christian friends crossed wires.

"When Peter came to Antioch, I opposed him to his face, because he was clearly in the wrong. Before certain men came from James, he used to eat with the Gentiles. But when they arrived, he began to draw back and separate himself from the Gentiles because he was afraid of those who belonged to the circumcision group. The other Jews joined him in his hypocrisy … When I saw that they were not acting in line with the truth of the gospel, I said to Peter in front of them all, 'You are a Jew, yet you live like a Gentile and not like a Jew. How is it, then, that you force Gentiles to follow Jewish customs?'" (Galatians 2:11–14).

From the earliest of days of Christianity, issues of lifestyle have threatened the delicate balance of unity and fellowship. Those who came to Christ from a strict Jewish background assumed that their viewpoints and values would be maintained in their new religious practice. Seeing Jesus as the long-awaited Messiah shouldn't change that—at least that's what many thought. The circumcision knife would continue to be sharpened, but it wouldn't be used to slice bacon.

Those embracing Jesus as Lord who came from pagan perspectives, however, had no appreciation for foreskin rituals or kosher-only menus. They had no reason to value such odd practices. And according to what Christian leaders like Paul were preaching, they weren't required to become "Jewish" in order to become a follower of Jesus.

Paul had good cause to be furious. Peter was backpedaling on the one overarching principle that Jesus had died to make possible. Apart from faith in God's promised forgiveness made possible by the cross, being welcomed into Christ's forever family had no condition. And Peter had discovered that firsthand.

Once while Peter was staying with a friend in Joppa, God gave him a vision. In his midday dream Peter saw a piece of fabric the size of a tent descending from the sky. It held all kinds of non-kosher animals. The shocked disciple heard a voice instructing him to kill and eat. Although Peter resisted, the voice challenged his reservation by saying that he had no right to call unclean what God had declared to be clean.

As we read through that section of the book of Acts, we learn that Peter's episode wasn't just about Jewish Christians' freedom to eat all kinds of previously forbidden food. It had to do with God's

> Paul had good cause to be furious. Peter was backpedaling on the one overarching principle that Jesus had died to make possible.

unconditional love that is available to everyone. While Peter was recovering from his troubling daydream, God sent a group of Gentiles to him who wanted to know about Jesus. Realizing that legalism has no place in the Christian's life, Peter swallowed his longstanding prejudice and accompanied them back to a man named Cornelius. With Paul's help he started eating pork chops—and liking them. But for Peter, old ways died hard. And thus the confrontation described in Galatians chapter 2.

An Age-Old Tug of War

Paul is often called the apostle of grace. That's because, after becoming a Christian, he spent most of his time helping Gentiles and Jews see that neither of them had God in their corner. Rather, by offering a relationship with Himself based on a free gift instead of good works, God had them in *His* corner. Because of grace, two culturally different groups of people now had something very significant in common. He helped them to see that the ground is level at the base of the cross. In response to the free gift that God had given them, both groups were called to forget their past preferences and make choices they believed would honor Him.

All the same, throughout the initial decades of Christianity, Gentile Christians would, from time to time, slip back into self-destructive patterns of their pre-Christ days when they lived for themselves. Jewish believers also had a tendency to fall back into a comfortable pattern of "performance" righteousness, where they attempted to obligate God to accept them. Even though debates between Jewish and Gentile practices are no longer the norm, Christians continue to disagree over lifestyle issues. Is it appropriate for Christians to drink alcohol? Should Christians go to R-rated movies?

> Grace is the dominant theme of the New Testament.

It's All Grace

Grace is the dominant theme of the New Testament. The prolific letter-writer Paul leaves no doubt in the minds of his readers that all actions are permissible for him. But he quickly adds, not everything is expedient. Although we do not earn God's love by acting certain ways, we have a responsibility as those graced and accepted into His family to behave in ways that prefer other ways and honor Him. Paul provided the Christians in Rome a context for understanding grace. He cautioned those who celebrated their freedom in Christ by eating and drinking without concern for cultural taboos, to be concerned for fellow believers who hadn't yet reached that point of spiritual maturity.

To the Christians in Galatia, Paul trumpeted the grace notes of freedom. They are notes that signaled a departure from a performance-based religion. But lest they see God's unmerited favor in terms of eternal salvation as a license for permissive living, he added, "You, my brothers, were called to be free. But do not use your freedom to indulge the sinful nature; rather, serve one another in love" (Galatians 5:13).

> "Do not use your freedom to indulge the sinful nature; rather, serve one another in love."
> *Galatians 5:13*

Guidelines for Tightrope Walking

By definition, freedom in Christ allows His followers to work out their understanding of faith as they perceive it. No cookie-cutter Christianity is intended. A grace-based lifestyle means that we are no longer chained to a weight of demands that impact our eternal destiny. For the sake of minimizing regrets, maximizing our earthly life (and health), as well as being sensitive to others; however, there is a place for self-discipline and self-denial. Walking the Christian lifestyle tightrope requires balance.

When it comes to issues that are not forbidden by the Bible, Christians are invited to make responsible choices. Moderate drinking and smoking are not prohibited, but a history of lung cancer or alcoholism in your family would suggest not pushing the envelope. Gambling is a hot button over which Christians divide. The Bible warns about get-rich quick schemes, greed, and the "lust of the eye," but some Christians are able to enjoy games of chance as an inexpensive form of entertainment. When it comes to gambling (as with dancing, theater-going, and nightclubs), the bigger question we should ask is the impact the atmosphere will have on our ability to enjoy the presence of God. In other words, would we be comfortable inviting Jesus to join us?

Lack of exercise and overeating is not at first blush a moral issue. The Scriptures do not explicitly refer to this prevalence of our culture. But the Apostle Paul does leave little room for doubt that our bodies are the temples of the Holy Spirit (1 Corinthians 6:19). He also says that we are to present our bodies as "living sacrifices" (Romans 12:1). Such comments would imply that we have a responsibility to be disciplined in the way we care for our bodies. God won't love a person with a toned physique who doesn't tote around excess pounds any more than an overweight couch potato, but that person might qualify to be used more effectively this side of heaven.

Some issues remain black and white. Being under grace does not mean we are free to violate the moral laws God gave His people in the Ten Commandments. It is never right to murder, commit adultery, or worship idols. Incest, abortion, and euthanasia are not debatable

acts. Neither is turning a deaf ear to a person in need with whom you have a relationship. Such insensitivity is never warranted. Gossip is specifically addressed as wrong. So is sexual promiscuity.

Lastly, there is the consideration of how our lifestyle issues impact others. If we are in the presence of someone who strongly believes that Sunday should not be treated like every other day of the week, it is not loving to open your briefcase or power-up your laptop and get a head start on your week. If you enjoy a glass of Chardonnay with your chicken Caesar salad, cheers! But if you are dining with a new Christian who has just completed a residency recovery program, celebrating your freedom to drink could be a stumbling block. It's not so much a matter of being held hostage by other people's opinions (which could be entirely unbiblical), it's a matter of being sensitive to the situation and the inner voice of the Holy Spirit and acting accordingly.

> ... it's a matter of being sensitive to the situation and the inner voice of the Holy Spirit and acting accordingly.

Daily Reflection Questions

Day One

1 What dramatic differences have you seen in lifestyles of people at your church?

2 How does an emphasis on "law" impact how a believer lives?

What about an emphasis on grace?

3 On which side, law or grace, do you tend to live?

How did you get to that point?

Day Two

1 When have you seen lifestyle issues divide Christians?

2 Why do you think this has been an ongoing problem for the church through the centuries?

3 If you were to have a vision similar to the one Peter had on Joppa, what do you think would be on the sheet?

Why?

Day Three

1   What is grace?

How should grace affect this issue of lifestyle?

2   When it comes to how we live, what's the difference between what is "permissible" and what is "excellent"?

3   In what ways might your "freedom in Christ" harm a weaker or younger believer?

Day Four

1   How might someone use "freedom in Christ" as an excuse?

2   In what ways is living the Christian life similar to walking a tightrope?

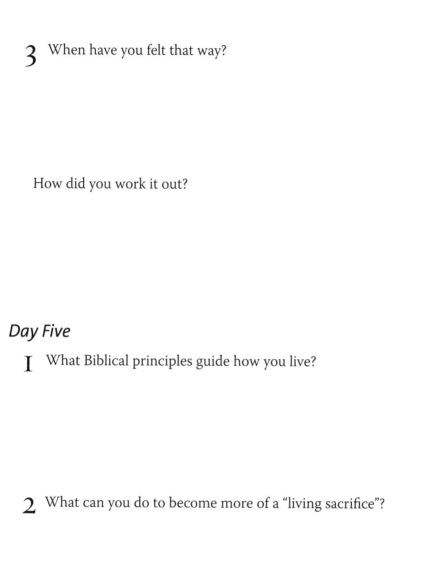

3   When have you felt that way?

How did you work it out?

Day Five

1   What Biblical principles guide how you live?

2   What can you do to become more of a "living sacrifice"?

3   As a result of reading this chapter and the conviction of the Holy Spirit, what changes will you make in your lifestyle?

CHAPTER THIRTY-SEVEN

CULTURAL STRATEGY

Evangelical Christians are in the news a lot these days. These outspoken followers of Jesus embrace family values and lobby for moral decency and traditional marriage. They were credited by the media as being a major force in George Bush's re-election in 2004.

By definition an evangelical is someone who contends that the Creator came to earth in the form of a sinless human being who died for the sin of the world and then was raised from death as proof that He accomplished His purpose. They believe the Bible to be an infallible revelation of God that transcends time and culture and is applicable to life. Furthermore, they admit to a life-changing encounter with Christ and believe that such an encounter is required for others to be reconciled to God and experience eternal life in His presence. As such they are motivated to share their faith and intentional about ways of doing that.

What's in a Name?

If you look at the word evangelical, you can see another word embedded in it. Do you see it? That's right. Angel is at the heart of what it means to be an evangelical. Not a bright celestial being with wings on the shoulders, holding a harp. Rather, the Greek word *angelos* simply means "a messenger." In terms of the word evangelical, it means messengers of good news: those who are committed to spreading a life-changing message about Jesus.

Sadly, if you were to ask most non-believers what an evangelical is, nothing related to angels or angelic or even good messengers would enter their minds. On second thought, they just might define an evangelical as someone who is constantly "harping" about prayer in school or posting the Ten Commandments in a courthouse lobby. Evangelicals are viewed as right wing extremists who are continually complaining about one thing or another. They are branded by society as combative and disengaged.

What's interesting is the fact that our culture's impression of evangelical Christians is not lockstep with their view of Christ. Conduct your own research. Go to a shopping mall and take a survey. Ask passersby what they think of Jesus, and chances are good that the majority will identify Him as a moral leader, a loving prophet, and a winsome teacher. But when you ask those same shoppers what they think of evangelicals you will likely hear words like intolerant, judgmental, and arrogant.

> What's interesting is the fact that our culture's impression of evangelical Christians is not lockstep with their view of Christ.

Ironically, people don't have trouble with Jesus. It's His wife. The bride of Christ (as the church is called in Scripture) is the culprit. She struggles to know her place in society. She has difficulty remembering that her primary responsibility is to be a messenger of good news. Too often she fails to take her cues from her Husband who won the hearts of His hearers through love not legislation.

Lest we are too hard on ourselves, walking the tightrope of "being in the world but not of the world" isn't easy. Finding a balance as we seek to engage culture while remaining true to values the Bible voices is an ongoing challenge. Throughout history several approaches have been tried.

A Rejection Strategy

The Amish have historically viewed themselves as a movement within society whose members are called to eschew the contamination of culture. Unwilling to compromise with a secular mind-set that would dull the edge of their fundamentalist faith, they have closed themselves off as a cloistered group.

In an Amish community you will see no power lines connected to the homes. Electricity is not permitted. They drive horse-drawn buggies, not cars. They do not take advantage of computerized farm implements. A John Deere won't do, but a manual tiller will. They wear dark clothing without accessories. And as you'd probably guess, lipstick is not their shtick. The motion picture *Witness* portrays the Amish culture fairly accurately.

Not only do the Amish resist modern conveniences, they refrain from willingly engaging in the lives of non-Amish. They take the Apostle Paul's admonition to the first century Corinthians quite literally. "Come out from them and be separate" (2 Corinthians 6:17). For them, living out their faith in the world does not include infiltrating society or attempting to influence it by active participation.

While those who are part of the Amish community are a vanishing minority, millions of others embrace a similar mind-set. These include Christians who believe it is all right to drive cars, light their homes with electricity, and own televisions, but then they homeschool their children or enroll them in private Christian schools. Rather than running for a position on the local school board, participating in the PTA, or giving leadership to the band booster club, they have opted out of the system. They are either unconvinced their voice will be heard, or they fear their children will be contaminated by those who do not share their worldview.

When it comes to friends, these Christians tend to socialize with those who share their perspectives on life and faith. Mark and Cindy Hanson are a case in point.

> For them, living out their faith in the world does not include infiltrating society or attempting to influence it by active participation.

They are far from Amish in the way they live. They are both fashion plates, wearing only the latest trends. Their $600,000 palatial home is smartly furnished and boasts Mark's success as a print salesman. The Hansons both drive late model SUVs. They are active members in a church that prides itself on believing right doctrine and not accepting into membership those who don't agree with every article of belief. Their son and their daughter have been in parochial schools since they were preschoolers.

Although neighbors routinely invited Mark and Cindy over for barbecues when the Hansons first moved in, they don't anymore. After being turned down over and over, the neighbors got the message. Once Mark told his prayer group the reason he didn't feel he should fraternize with his non-believing neighbors was a matter of witness. The neighbors served beer with their burgers and since he and Cindy didn't drink alcohol, he felt by showing up he would be endorsing a lifestyle he didn't approve. As a result Mark and Cindy only have a superficial relationship with those in their neighborhood. They only go out to dinner with people from their church and only entertain Christians in their home.

Mark and Cindy are deeply troubled by the moral decay they observe in society. They realize that people all around them need the Lord, and they hope their neighbors and business associates will see their lifestyle and want to be like them. They ask God regularly to keep them unstained from the world around them.

> They ask God regularly to keep them unstained from the world around them.

Accommodation Strategy

Another way of responding to a culture that is disinterested or opposed to Christianity is to tacitly go along with it. In this strategy, you don't expect the world to believe what you do, but since you recognize this is the harbor in which you've been anchored, you do your best to float without making waves.

Heidi and Grant Barth illustrate this particular approach to interacting with society. The Barths received Christ through a campus outreach at the university at which they met in the Midwest. Neither had grown up in a church-going family and were quite thrilled to discover assurance of salvation and the freedom from past regrets. When Grant took a job in New York City following graduate school, he and Heidi moved to a high-rise apartment uptown. As best as they could tell they were the only Christians in a building comprised mostly of Jewish, Muslim, East Indian, and Korean families.

The Barths read their Bibles and prayed regularly but rarely went to church. Because they relied on public transportation to get around and the nearest evangelical church was five miles away, faithful attendance on Sundays was a challenge. In time, lack of regular fellowship with other believers began to take its toll. Heidi and Grant spent most of their time with non-practicing Jewish professionals who partied hard and drank plenty. Early vows to abstain from alcohol were forgotten. Longing for friendship, the young couple compromised their code of conduct. Soon they found themselves going along with their friends' viewpoints on abortion, same-sex marriages, and other issues.

If you were to ask Heidi and Grant today if they were committed followers of Christ, they would assure you they are. In the same breath, however, they would tell you they do not feel obligated to foist their beliefs on others. Christianity is their *personal* choice when it comes to religion, and since we live in a nation that celebrates diversity and tolerance, Jesus' words about being salt and light don't apply today (at least not in America).

The trouble with simply accommodating culture is that you are quite apt to be branded by it. We see that played out again and again in the Old Testament. The children of Israel were instructed not to marry those who worshiped other gods. But disregarding the Lord's advice, they did so anyway. Before long those who claimed to worship the one true God were sacrificing to pagan deities. Instead of determining to live by the commandments Moses had given them, the Israelites began to give in to peer pressure and simply went along with the majority.

Perhaps you've heard the old fable about the man who caught a frog and tried to boil his catch for dinner. At first he brought the kettle of water to a boil and dropped the frog in. To his amazement the frog jumped right back out and hopped away. Then the man evaluated the situation and devised a new strategy. Placing the frog in a pan of tepid water, he watched the green reptile rest on his haunches. Then he proceeded to gradually turn up the heat on the stove. Ever so slowly the water reached the boiling point. Because the temperature was changing very gradually, the frog was not aware of his predicament. By simply accepting his surroundings, he failed to realize how life-threatening it was.

One high profile Protestant denomination spent big bucks on a Christmas ad campaign some time back. Using the title of the popular Christmas carol "O Come All Ye Faithful" as their catch phrase, church leaders made a case for the fact that their brand of Christianity did not bar any religious viewpoint from joining them. All were welcome. And the word "all" meant exactly that.

The Barths would not feel comfortable in a denomination that is as open-minded as the one just described. But that denomination

> Perhaps you've heard the old fable about the man who caught a frog and tried to boil his catch for dinner.

hasn't always been that open-minded. At one time it held to Biblical orthodoxy and articulated the unique message of Christianity that identified Jesus as the only means of salvation.

Reformation Strategy

Argentine-born evangelist Luis Palau has been preaching in American cities for more than four decades. In the early years, he called his preaching missions "crusades." He followed his cue from Billy Graham, whose example Palau studied and emulated. In recent years, however, he has jettisoned the term "crusade" in exchange for "festival." Given the less-than-Christ-like tactics of "the Crusaders" centuries ago, the word doesn't have a positive connotation. And it certainly isn't helpful in reaching those with Muslim backgrounds.

All that to say, Christians would do well to learn from the past. Those who view the task of evangelizing culture in the same way that they attempt to win a war may resort to strategies (consciously or unconsciously) that are as unethical and ineffective as the Crusaders. Boycotting certain corporations or engaging in smear campaigns against politicians deemed by some to be ungodly might be just as unethical as threatening bodily harm unless someone accepts Christ.

Still some evangelicals feel called to do their best to "Christianize" a country that was founded by those who sought a place to feely practice their Judeo-Christian beliefs. These Christ-followers believe that it is entirely appropriate (and possible) to influence decisions, laws, and norms in a country that is committed to majority rule and a government "of the people, for the people, and by the people." To that end they seek to elect individuals into office who will articulate, legislate, and propagate values and mores as depicted in the Scriptures. These Christians believe that society must be reformed not accommodated.

Jim Hobson is one such reformer. Because he takes Jesus' words to heart that Christians are the salt of the earth and the light of the world, he believes that the Church's primary agenda is to recreate culture in a way that it will eventually resemble the Church. Unlike Mark and Cindy Hanson, Jim is involved in the public school system. He ran (and was elected) to the school board. He views his position as an elected official as an avenue to challenge the purchase of textbooks that demean Biblical views. And he challenges budgetary allotments for the free distribution of condoms on high school campuses. Jim is involved with his political party and was elected to go to the national convention.

For Jim, Christians in the United States should not shy away from shaping government. He is grateful to live in a country where he is

> Christians would do well to learn from the past.

invited not only to be tolerant of opposing viewpoints but also to do his best to reverse laws that he believes affront the living God.

Although many Christian ministries have provided a structure by which those like Jim can attempt to redefine core values and reverse certain laws, there is a rub. As stated at the beginning of this lesson, the goal of reaching people for Christ can be lost amid the challenge of winning a certain campaign.

Creative Tension

There is still another approach to engaging culture—creative tension. Because of its more dynamic nature, this is the most difficult of all four to define. Unlike the other three, Christians who embrace this approach are unswervingly committed to loving people for Jesus' sake above any other goal. They recognize that it is not realistic to think that our nation will ever be truly a "Christian" nation, nor do they think that is necessary in order to experience God's blessing. Jeff and Sheryl Collins best illustrate this perspective.

They live in suburban Chicago with their three children. Jeff takes the train into The Loop each day to work while Sheryl stays at home, so she can care for their kids. Because they are convinced that the Great Commission ("Go and make disciples of all nations," Matthew 29:19) can only be accomplished by pursuing the Great Commandment ("Love the Lord your God with all your heart and with all your soul and with all your mind and with all your strength" and "Love your neighbor as yourself," Mark 12:30–31), the Collins are committed to being friends with those in their subdivision.

Jeff doesn't ordinarily drink beer, but he occasionally breaks open a Budweiser when he's watching the Bears game with the guys in the neighborhood on a Sunday afternoon. Similarly, Sheryl has been known to have a glass of wine at bunco parties next door. Neither one ever drinks to excess, but when asking about what Jesus would do, they can't find a chapter or verse in the Bible that would indicate that He was a teetotaler.

The Collins are active in the local public schools where their kids attend. Jeff volunteers with the local Fellowship of Christian Athletes group at the high school on weekends. Although he thinks it would be entirely appropriate for the football team (on which his son plays) to pray in the locker room before the game, he doesn't make an issue over it. According to Jeff, he'd rather maintain a good rapport with the coach and the principal so his life will be one they will want to emulate rather than avoid.

Sheryl has heard comments made at the bunco parties about Christians that cause her deep pain. But rather than defend those she

> "Love your neighbor as yourself."
> *Mark 12:31*

knows are being talked about, she chooses rather to take an interest in those who are down on these so-called Christians. She is more committed to finding ways to express Christ's love than finding ways to defend Christianity.

Daily Reflection Questions

Day One

I   What does the word "evangelical" mean to you?

What do your non-Christian neighbors and co-workers think it means?

2   How do you feel about being known as an "evangelical"?

3   In what ways are you a "messenger"?

Day Two

1 Why is there such a difference between the way people view Jesus and their view of the church?

2 What makes "being in the world but not of the world" so difficult?

3 What do you think about the Amish approach to living in the world?

4 When have you been tempted to withdraw from society?

Day Three

1 In what ways do some Christians withdraw from the world (besides the Amish)?

2 What do you think is wrong with the Hansons' approach?

3 What do you find positive about the Hansons and this attitude?

Day Four

1 What do you think of the "accommodation strategy"?

2 When have you seen this "strategy" in action?

What causes believers to act this way?

3 What's wrong with this approach?

Day Five

I What's good about the "reformation strategy"?

What are its weaknesses?

2 What does "living in creative tension" look like in your life?

3 What should you begin doing to make a difference in your world?

CHAPTER THIRTY-EIGHT

WORK

Several years ago, a man was driving his car at a snail's pace along a crowded freeway, only half listening to the music on the car radio. He was jolted into conscious thought by a song that didn't make sense. The tune was very familiar—"Whistle While You Work," sung by the famous seven dwarfs of Snow White fame. Only this time the lyrics were in Japanese.

The voice of the announcer came over the tune and said, "The Americans work to live; the Japanese live to work." He didn't remember much about the commercial after that, because he was trying to figure out whether that was a true statement; and if it were true, who had the right philosophy, the Americans or the Japanese?

Daily Work Is God's Idea

God is a worker. *He* loves work. In Genesis 1, we see God creating the heavens and the earth. The psalmist takes note of this creator God and declares, "I will extol the Lord with all my heart in the council of the upright and in the assembly. Great are the works of the Lord; they are pondered by all who delight in them. Glorious and majestic are his deeds, and his righteousness endures forever" (Psalm 111:1–3).

> God is a worker. *He* loves work.

After God created Adam and Eve, He placed them in the garden of Eden, not to lounge eternally in perpetual paradise, but to work it and take care of it. This kind of work is obviously good and has nothing to do with sin. Eventually, sin will make work backbreaking, painful, unproductive, and unfulfilling at times, but work itself was not a product of sin.

The Apostle Paul knew what it meant to work, and he expected other Christians to do the same. He set himself up as a model, "Surely you remember, brothers, our toil and hardship; we worked night and day in order not to be a burden to anyone while we preached the gospel of God to you" (1 Thessalonians 2:9). Then he told the Thessalonians "to lead a quiet life, to mind your own business and to work with your hands, just as we told you" (1 Thessalonians 4:11). If we read between the lines, we probably can hear Paul saying that no one is going to listen to anyone tell what God means to them if they aren't respected, and you can't be respected if you don't work.

Just in case some may want to play word games with Paul about what should be considered legitimate work, he gets quite specific and says that it should be honest work that is done well and that will provide enough to help others who are in need (Ephesians 4:28).

This daily work has a reward. It has very little to do with the size of the paycheck, although that is not discounted entirely. The reward is the God-given capacity to experience joy (Ecclesiastes 5:18–19).

Another reward comes when a Christian is in a place of responsibility in his or her company. The *Journal of Leadership Studies* (winter 1998, Baker College System, Center for Graduate Studies) addressed the topic of "The Leader and Religious Faith." Their conclusion after extensive research was that Christian CEOs were a reward to their corporation.

"Results support the premise that entrepreneurial Chief Executive Officers who 'always' consciously apply the teachings of their religion during the daily decision-making process, attain superior goal achievement results over those CEOs who never apply the teachings of their religion.

"CEOs of faith have more profitable companies and greater annual, personal net worth increases. They rank in the top quartile of questionnaire results that measure business acumen, leader performance and organizational goal achievement skills."

The bottom line is, the bottom line financial performance is a by-product of their faith-based production.

> Psychologists say that attitudes precipitate actions.

Attitudes Toward Employment

Howard Dayton is a very successful businessman who has committed all of his God-given talents and earthly resources to the Lord. Howard started Crown Ministries, a small group and financial-study organization. This was born out of a burden to see men and women grasp the Biblical mandates for handling their finances, to pursue the goal of getting completely out of debt, and to freely experience the joy of productive labor that comes from a sense of God's calling.

Here's what he says on the subject of work, in the introductory notes in his workbook. "Over a fifty-year span, the average person spends 100,000 hours working. Most of an adult's life is involved in work, but often with the job comes some degree of dissatisfaction. Perhaps no statistic demonstrates the discontentment of Americans more than their job-hopping tendencies. A recent survey found that the average man changes jobs every four and one-half years, the average woman, every three years."

Psychologists say that attitudes precipitate actions. A person can be dissatisfied with his or her work for many reasons. Often it is a result of not knowing what the Scriptures teach on the subject; not knowing his particular skills or gifts; not taking the time to figure out who is controlling his attitude; or failing to establish attainable goals for his life. Ultimately, we all have to take responsibility for our attitudes. If we are unhappy, we choose to be unhappy—or at least to remain unhappy once we identify the root cause.

God says the starting point in having a right attitude is in realizing for Whom you are really working. Colossians 3:23–24 says, "Whatever you do, work at it with all your heart, as working for the Lord, not for men, since you know that you will receive an inheritance from the Lord as a reward. It is the Lord Christ you are serving." You may receive your paycheck from your boss, but the Lord hands out the report card. This perspective is found in several passages dealing with having a positive attitude toward labor.

A Christian should be highly motivated and industrious. The believer should take his or her cue from the ants (Proverbs 6:6–8). Ants don't require a supervisor to force them to work, their activity results in provisions for now and in the future. (If they are Japanese ants, they save 17 percent of their income; if they are American ants, they save 4 percent.)

A negative attitude toward work is implicitly condemned: "Whatever your hand finds to do, do it with all your might, for in the grave, where you are going, there is neither working nor planning nor knowledge nor wisdom" (Ecclesiastes 9:10). Don't be halfhearted.

"Diligence is man's precious possession" (Proverbs 12:27, NKJV). Don't be a quitter.

"One who is slack in his work is brother to one who destroys" (Proverbs 18:9).

The Apostle Paul didn't cut any slack with those who were lazy. He told the Thessalonians, "If a man will not work, he shall not eat" (2 Thessalonians 3:10). So much for sugarcoated spiritual clichés! Paul's liberality didn't cover the slothful.

> "Whatever your hand finds to do, do it with all your might."
> *Ecclesiastes 9:10*

> "One who is slack in his work is brother to one who destroys."
> *Proverbs 18:9*

Historical Perspective

The concept of work has gone through various stages since the beginning of the Church. Whatever your attitude toward work today, you can look back in history and find its source and those who also held that view.

For instance, the early Church was greatly influenced by the thoughts of the Greeks and Romans. Work was, at best, a necessary evil and was only good when it was freely chosen. Otherwise, a person was a slave and lacked personal autonomy. These views spilled over into the teachings of the Church where Augustine felt that the contemplative life had a higher value than the active life. This resulted in the idea that the highest calling of God was to move into a monastery with ample time for contemplation.

Along came the Reformers and the Puritans who rejected this "withdrawal from the world" approach. They developed four basic attitudes toward work that became the foundation for thought among nations that were distinctly influenced by the Christian viewpoint.

Attitude 1: The Sanctity of All Honorable Work

Those who held this view rejected a division between secular and sacred work. Martin Luther said clergymen were not engaged in more holy work than housewives and shopkeepers. "Household tasks have no appearances of sanctity: and yet these very works in connection with the household are more desirable than all the works of monks and nuns."

William Tyndale, who was burned at the stake for making English translations of the Bible, said, "There is no work better than another to please God; to pour water, to wash dishes, to be a cobbler, or an apostle, all is one."

These individuals believed that work—all work—was to be performed as an act of worship. No one said it more clearly that John Calvin: "Paul teaches that there is no part of our life or conduct, however insignificant, which should not relate to the glory of God."

Attitude 2: God Calls Every Person to His or Her Vocation

Some believe that only those who are called into full-time Christian work are strategically placed by God. Stanley Tamm in his book, *God Owns My Business*, disagrees: "Although I believe in the application of good principles in business, I place far more confidence in the conviction that His purpose for me is in the business world. My business is my pulpit."

The practical result of this view is that it leads to contentment in our work. If a person really feels called to be a businessman, he no longer needs to feel like a second-class citizen in the kingdom. The Bible contains several principles regarding calling:

> *Principle 1:* God calls certain persons to religious vocations while others are free to select any work. We see an example of this in Acts 13:2 where Paul and Barnabas were set aside by the Lord for special services.

> *Principle 2:* God calls people to be Christians, but places of service depend on personal gifts and talents (1 Corinthians 12).

> *Principle 3:* God calls people to be Christians, gives gifts to many for special Christian work, and calls a few to specific tasks. In the Old Testament, you have the example of God calling Abraham to leave Ur of the Chaldeans, or Moses to lead the children of Israel

out of Egypt. In the New Testament, you have many examples of Christians being encouraged to use their talents and gifts as God gives opportunities (Romans 12:6–8; 1 Corinthians 12:4–10; Ephesians 4:11; 1 Peter 4:10–11).

Attitude 3: The Motivation and Goals of Work

If you were to ask the average businessperson in America what the primary goal of work is, he or she would probably answer, "To make money." This thought was set in concrete when Ben Franklin said, "Time is money," and "Early to bed, early to rise, makes a man healthy, wealthy, and wise." Although Ben may not have realized it, his thoughts downgraded the sanctity of the job itself, as well as volunteer work. This view seems to indicate that Bible study, family time, recreation, vacations, and other activities not affecting the bottom line of a financial statement are wasteful.

In the twentieth century, the technicalized world (which excludes very few nations) has carried Ben's thoughts even further. It concludes that economic survival is dependent not on just the simple premise that time has to be well invested in productive work, but also that survival will only be assured as nations move from the goal of economic necessity to economic freedom. In order to obtain this goal, we have to become relentlessly future-oriented. No company survives without an aggressive Research and Development department. This is all rightly justified in order to remain competitive in the marketplace. But there is a price to be paid—we are robbed of the daily joy of our labors.

As the Puritans looked at a pure motive for work, they concluded that it should meet six standards:

> **1. It should be useful to society.**
>
> **2. It should glorify God.**
>
> **3. It should be moral**
>
> **4. It should provide for the needs of the family.**
>
> **5. It should use God-given talents.**
>
> **6. It should provide a means to help the poor.**

Attitude 4: A Sense of Moderation in Work

Laziness is not the real problem in our society; it carries a stiffer social stigma than drunkenness, sexual immorality, and other taboos of past generations. Instead, workaholism is the addiction that is running at epidemic proportions. The Biblical view is found somewhere in

> Although Ben may not have realized it, his thoughts downgraded the sanctity of the job itself, as well as volunteer work.

between these two extremes. Martin Luther said, "God does not want me to sit at home, to loaf, to commit matters to God, and to wait 'til a fried chicken flies into my mouth. That would be tempting God."

So we work and we work hard, but we keep things in perspective. We also know that Jesus said, "But seek first his kingdom and his righteousness, and all these things will be given to you as well" (Matthew 6:33).

The Biblical approach is not to neglect the other priorities of life—our families, health, church, personal growth, and education. The Bible knows our frame, and it knows that if we have an inordinate lust for anything, then it will defile our spirit. The Lord gives a warning that should be heeded by all who bend toward a preoccupation with work: "In vain you rise early and stay up late, toiling for food to eat—for he grants sleep to those he loves" (Psalm 127:2).

> "But seek first his kingdom and his righteousness, and all these things will be given to you as well."
> *Matthew 6:33*

A Biblical Perspective

Men and women are created in God's image; and because God is seen as One who makes, forms, builds, and plants, He has touched all of labor with dignity. Nowhere is this more plainly seen than when God selected a man named Bezalel, of the tribe of Judah, to carry out the construction of the tabernacle in Exodus, chapters 35 and 36: "And he has filled him with the Spirit of God, with skill, ability and knowledge in all kinds of crafts—to make artistic designs for work in gold, silver and bronze, to cut and set stones, to work in wood and to engage in all kinds of artistic craftsmanship" (Exodus 35:31–33).

In spite of the fact that man sinned, he was to carry on this mandate even though there would be imperfect productivity, disappointment, and pain.

A Final Perspective

When Jesus was on earth, it wasn't an accident that He came as a blue-collar worker nor that His parables dealt with matters like sowing seed, vineyard laborers, harvesters, house building, and swine tending. He has no hierarchy of importance vocationally, only the wise use of the talents He dispenses. And according to the investment of these talents, we will be rewarded or judged.

Daily Reflection Questions

Day One

1 Do you "work to live" or "live to work"?

2 Why do we tend to have a negative view of work?

3 From the Bible, how do you know that work is good?

Day Two

1 What does the Bible say about how we should work?

2 What rewards does God promise for good work?

3 In what ways can a Christian be a reward to his or her company?

Day Three

1 Why do attitudes precipitate actions?

2 How can a bad attitude toward a job affect a person's performance on the job?

What about a good attitude?

3 What does Colossians 3:23 imply about a believer's attitude on the job?

What makes that difficult to do?

Day Four

1 Which of the "four basic attitudes" of the Reformers and Puritans spoke the most to you?

Why?

2 When have you tended to divide "secular" and "sacred" work?

What happened?

3 What will it take for you to see your vocation as a "call" from God?

Day Five

1 How can you find meaning in your work?

2 In what ways does your work bring glory to God?

3 On the job, how do you reflect God's image?

CHAPTER THIRTY-NINE

CARING FOR THOSE WHO HURT

Mother Teresa and Princess Diana were both cultural icons. Amazingly, both died the same week in the summer of 1997. These two women couldn't have been more different. One, dwarfed in stature and withered by age, preached grace. The other, tall and graceful was the epitome of youthful beauty. One died a pauper—the other a multi-millionaire. Her materialistic lifestyle was a message without need for words.

Still Teresa and Diana shared one thing in common. Each of them was moved with compassion to reach out to the poor, the maimed, the ostracized, and the homeless. Both of them responded in love and stooped to touch the untouchables of society. No wonder the world grieved their unanticipated deaths with unprecedented adulation. Both women distinguished themselves as heroines because of their unconditional love of humanity. But the call to care or to embody compassion is not limited to women.

A Storefront Merchant of Care

Taylor Field is about as manly as they come. His 6'4" athletic frame towers over most people he passes on the streets of New York City. Although his name sounds like an upscale department store, since 1986 Taylor has been the pastor of a storefront church on Manhattan's Lower East Side.

Although this native of Enid, Oklahoma, entered Wake Forest College as a pre-law major (hoping to follow in the footsteps of his lawyer father), he changed direction. After Taylor encountered Jesus in a profoundly personal way, he decided to follow the footsteps of a sandal-clad first century carpenter. At first, Taylor wasn't sure what that would mean. He received his divinity degree at Princeton Seminary and went on to get a PhD at Golden Gate Seminary in California.

His family and friends encouraged him to take a traditional pastorate in a comfortable suburb, but Taylor resisted. Deep in his heart he knew he wanted to minister among the homeless and disadvantaged where he could express Christ's love in tangible ways. He couldn't fully explain it, but he cared for the down and out.

That inner desire found expression as Taylor moved with his wife and two small boys to a neighborhood of abandoned buildings ruled by a drug lord. From a graffiti-covered storefront building this thirty-two year old inner-city missionary began to love the unlovables and

> He couldn't fully explain it, but he cared for the down and out.

touch the untouchables. Through literacy programs and soup kitchens, worship services and Bible studies—and friendship—prostitutes, drug addicts, alcoholics, single moms, and fatherless kids were introduced to the love of Jesus.

When the twin towers of the World Trade Center collapsed on September 11, 2001, Taylor watched in horror. His little church and outreach center stood only 5,000 feet from Ground Zero. In just a few hours, the dimension of his call to care for hurting people expanded exponentially. At last report, East 7th Street Baptist Church (known by most as Graffiti Church) has twenty-six ministries and about as many staff workers.

The Standard of Comparison

Not everyone who is moved with compassion toward the hurting and the hopeless is motivated by a desire to be like Jesus. But those who have invited the Savior to be their Lord can't easily dodge His agenda. Jesus lived with nonstop compassion toward people hurting physically, emotionally, relationally, or culturally.

From the very beginning of His earthly life Jesus identified with the plight of those with deep hurts. His earthly mother was a teenage girl who became pregnant out of wedlock. Mary was falsely accused and deprived of justice. Due to her helpless status and poverty, she had no choice but to give birth in a feeding trough for cattle. After Jesus was born, His parents were forced to take their newborn, flee their country, and live as refugees in Egypt. When it was safe for Joseph and his family to return to Israel, they sank roots in Nazareth, a town in backwoods Galilee that was often the brunt of cruel demeaning jokes. Jesus knew what it was like to grow up on the other side of the tracks.

When Jesus inaugurated His public ministry, He wasted no time in articulating why He had come to earth. One Sabbath shortly after His baptism by John and His period of temptation in the wilderness, Jesus went to the synagogue in Nazareth:

> The scroll of the prophet Isaiah was handed to [Jesus]. Unrolling it, he found the place where it is written: "The Spirit of the Lord is on me, because he has anointed me to preach good news to the poor. He has sent me to proclaim freedom for the prisoners and recovery of sight for the blind, to release the oppressed, to proclaim the year of the Lord's favor." Then he rolled up the scroll, gave it back to the attendant and sat down. The eyes of everyone in the synagogue were fastened on him, and he began by saying to them, "Today this scripture is fulfilled in your hearing." (Luke 4:17–21).

> "The Spirit of the Lord is on me, because he has anointed me to preach good news to the poor."
> *Luke 4:18-19*

By claiming the age-old prophecy in the scroll of Isaiah as pertaining to Him, Jesus not only identified Himself as Israel's long-awaited Messiah, He also announced the agenda of His earthly pilgrimage. Jesus' marching orders called Him to parade across the stage of history and serve the needs of those consistently overlooked by the masses. In Mark 10:45, Jesus reiterated His mission: "For even the Son of Man did not come to be served, but to serve, and to give his life as a ransom for many."

And we see that single-minded focus in the Gospels. Jesus befriended the Samaritan woman at Jacob's Well. He defended (and forgave) the adulterous woman about to be stoned. He was moved with compassion for the frantic leader of the synagogue whose little girl was dying. He raised Lazarus from the dead. He harnessed His last ounce of human strength to speak words of comfort to His mother as she watched Him die at the foot of His cross.

> "The Son of Man did not come to be served, but to serve, and to give his life as a ransom for many."
>
> *Mark 10:45*

WWJD?

Did you know that the word Christian simply means "little Christ?" In short, it means that by claiming His name we are asking the world to see Him in us. If that is true, isn't it fair to say that the passions that motivated Him should motivate us? When faced with real life situations where we see people trampled by injustice or bruised by neglect, we would do well to ask ourselves, "What would Jesus do in a situation like this?"

Jesus put the hurts and needs of others ahead of His own. We are called to do the same. We are His hands and feet and arms and heart while He is on temporary assignment in heaven. We are the means by which He reaches out to touch, carry, hold, help, comfort, and love.

If that isn't enough of a motivation, here's an even more powerful concept. Before leaving His earthly mission in the lap of less-than-perfect disciples, He told them that they were to see Him in the faces of those who are bleeding physically or emotionally. In Matthew 25 Jesus said, "Then the King will say to those on his right, 'Come, you who are blessed by my Father; take your inheritance, the kingdom prepared for you since the creation of the world. For I was hungry and you gave me something to eat, I was thirsty and you gave me something to drink, I was a stranger and you invited me in, I needed clothes and you clothed me, I was sick and you looked after me, I was in prison and you came to visit me.' Then the righteous will answer him, 'Lord, when did we see you hungry and feed you, or thirsty and give you something to drink? When did we see you a stranger and invite you in, or needing clothes and clothe you? When did we see you sick or in prison and go to visit you?' The King will reply, 'I tell you the truth, whatever you did for one of the least of these brothers of mine, you did for me'" (Matthew 25:34–40).

In other words, when we see those who are behind bars or imprisoned by poverty or physical disabilities, we should see an opportunity to care for Jesus Himself. Singing worship songs and being attentive to a sermon in a church service may be comfortable ways to express devotion to the Lord. But what He wants most of all is to see the mission He came to earth to accomplish being carried on by those who claim His name.

According to some beautiful prose written by the Apostle Paul in 1 Corinthians 13, our devotion to Jesus or other people can't be limited to careless routines or obligatory disciplines. Religious expression that doesn't include loving behavior and compassionate concern is empty and useless. The Apostle James offered similar advice when he suggested that faith without works is dead. And if ever the world needed faith that is fully alive, it is today.

The ABCs of Being a Caregiver

✖ **A**sk the Heavenly Father to give you Jesus' eyes that you can see the world around you as He does. Ask Him to break your heart with the things that break His. Begin each day by saying, "Lord, I'm available. Show me today who it is that I can best care for. Give me the courage to obey what You say."

✖ **B**e aware. Despite the temptation to close your eyes to the difficult people in your sphere of influence, try to look beyond the imperfect packaging that hides a broken heart or damaged emotions. Attempt to get your eyes off your own concerns (and often insignificant desires) in order to focus on people who are far worse off than you.

✖ **C**reate a list of practical responses to those who need help. Invite that colleague who is battling depression to have coffee with you at the local Starbucks. Suggest to your Sunday school class that you take on a nursing home as a place to give encouragement. Offer to provide a hot meal for a single mom who works and whose kids are in day care. Sign your family up to work at a soup kitchen on Thanksgiving morning or Christmas day.

✖ **D**on't be too hard on yourself when you blow it. Chances are you will rationalize reasons why someone doesn't really need your help or doesn't deserve it. You will likely give in to selfish inclinations despite your best intentions. But don't beat yourself up. Ask God for forgiveness and look for the next opportunity to serve Him by serving others.

✖ <u>E</u>xcuse those who don't seem to appreciate your overtures of friendship or compassion. No doubt some issues of pride will keep some who dearly want to be helped from publicly acknowledging their need. They may be embarrassed by what you do.

✖ <u>F</u>ind time each month to help a widow in your neighborhood or church. Chances are she has the need for small household repairs. Bring her groceries. Cook her a meal. Take her out for ice cream with your children. Talk to her about her deceased husband. Look at family photo albums and encourage her to talk about some of her happiest memories.

✖ <u>G</u>rieve with those the Lord prompts you to care for. Risk lowering your guard in order to enter into the plight of this one who feels overwhelmed or underappreciated. Remember the old Swedish proverb, "A shared joy is a doubled joy. A shared sorrow is half a sorrow."

✖ <u>H</u>ave a sense of your own well-being. In other words, know when to pull back and care for yourself. It is possible to be so preoccupied with helping others that your own mental health suffers. There is such a thing as *compassion fatigue*. Dietrich Bonhoeffer wrote in *Life Together*, his classic book on community, that there is a time to be with other people and there is a time when we need to pull back from them. Jesus Himself illustrated that spiritual reality in the first chapter of Mark's Gospel. Even though a seemingly unending line of people in Capernaum was coming to Him for healing, Jesus healed some but not all. Although the disciples assumed that Jesus would stay in the village to care for those with needs, He disappointed their expectations. He needed to get away by Himself.

Daily Reflection Questions

Day One

1 What examples of caring individuals, like Taylor Field, can you think of?

2 What causes or motivates people like that to give themselves to the poor?

3 In what ways did Jesus identify with the poor?

Day Two

1 How do you feel when you read that the world should be able to see Christ in Christians?

Why?

2 How can the world see Jesus Christ in you as you're going through struggles?

3 What about "the world" makes being Christ-like so difficult?

At times, how do Christians stand in the way of that happening?

Day Three

1 When you read Matthew 25:34–40, what words or phrases make you feel guilty?

Why?

2 When you can remember seeing Jesus in a needy person?

3 How did you respond? What did you do?

What do you wish you had done?

Day Four

1 What does it mean to you to see the world with "Jesus' eyes"?

How can you do that?

2 Why is it tempting to close our eyes to hurting people?

3 What can believers do to get their eyes off themselves and to focus on the needs of others?

Day Five

1   Who in your church and neighborhood has desperate needs?

2   What can you do to help them?

3   What else do you sense God telling you about caring for others?

CHAPTER FORTY

CARING FOR THE EARTH

We will not soon forget the tragic events of December 2004. The day after Christmas the western hemisphere awoke to news of a devastating chain of events in South Asia—a tidal wave followed by unprecedented flooding. A 9.2 earthquake underneath the Indian Ocean had set it all in motion. As a result, a silent night had given way to the deafening sound of 30-foot waves washing over entire villages. The initial news reports were bad enough. CNN reported that 7,000 had lost their lives in Indonesia, Sri Lanka, and Thailand. Once the final investigation of the tsunami disaster had been completed, the statistics were unfathomable. More than 150,000 people in nine countries had been killed by that monstrous tidal wave.

Ironically, just a few months before the tsunami hit, Hollywood released a blockbuster movie that pictured a series of natural disasters including a killer tidal wave. In "The Day After Tomorrow," Dennis Quaid plays a Washington-based climatologist whose warnings about global warming are ignored. As a result, a catastrophic shift in the world's climate leaves the planet on a collision course with Mother Nature. Tornados in California, ice fields in Scotland, blizzard-like conditions in India, and baseball-size hail in Japan buffet the planet.

Critics did not give the creators of "The Day After Tomorrow" a passing grade. The film did, however, pack a punch and peddle a message. In addition to the spectacular special effects, the movie called attention to the delicate balance in the environment—the disastrous possibilities that exist when we disregard the rhythms and resources of nature. Although no evidence links South Asia's massive quake and corresponding tsunami with any abuse of the environment, we have cause to be concerned. The possibility of shrinking icecaps, depleting the ozone layer, disappearing fossil fuels, and clear-cutting of rain forests have scientists worried. If precautions and correctives aren't taken, the actual scenario will be far worse than any screenwriter's imagination.

> Environmentalists have largely been stereotyped.

Political Activists or Biblical Disciples

Environmentalists have largely been stereotyped. They've been branded as graduates of Berkeley who are politically liberal and environmentally conservative. When it comes to saving spotted owls, they are wide-eyed fanatics who leave little doubt that they give a hoot about life. But when it comes to defending the rights of unborn humans, they are pro-choice. They are also members of the Sierra Club, hail John Muir as the thirteenth disciple, and boast Green Party decals on the back bumpers of their cars. They are not thought to be particularly religious. But if they did attend a church, it would most likely be a denomination that doesn't take the Bible seriously.

Such a branding is unwarranted and inaccurate. Take Roger Cousins in southern Oregon. He's a committed member of a congregation that is known in his community as the Born-Againers. They continually offer courses on "Why the Bible is Reliable," "How to Share Your Faith," and "Why Jesus is the Only Way to God." He readily admits to being born-again and is excitedly anticipating the second coming of Christ. Although Roger takes great delight in having a personal relationship with his heavenly Father, he is also unabashedly outspoken about his concern for Mother Earth. On the back of Roger's 1996 Honda Accord are three bumper stickers. One is a Christian fish. Another says "Jesus, Don't Leave Earth Without Him." The last one boldly contends for wildlife preservation: "Save the Whales!"

Why Should Christians Care about the Environment?

Because evangelical Christians view the Bible as authoritative for issues of faith as well as lifestyle, they can't help but be environmentalists. It doesn't take a seminary graduate to understand that the earth is important to God. Considering the first few pages of the Bible causes the most casual reader to land on that conclusion. When the Creator spoke the stars into existence and set the planets in motion, He seemed to be following a design consistent with His desire. When He created vegetation and the animal kingdom, He also created a system that would sustain life. What God had made had meaning to Him. He said that it is good. Even before creating the human race, God went on record attesting to the worth of our world.

The capstone of creation was men and women. Though resembling the animals, these delicate beings were different. They bore the Divine Image and were uniquely capable of reason, reflection, and worship. They also had the capacity to reflect the Creator's nature and serve as custodians of their world. As such, the Creator gave humanity a daunting privilege. We were given dominion over the plants and animals.

The next pages of Genesis reveal the details documenting the entry of sin into our world. Humanity's relationship with God was broken and the rhythm of the created order was undermined. Weeds began to overtake delicate crops. Rich soil lost its fertility. Natural

> Because evangelical Christians view the Bible as authoritative for issues of faith as well as lifestyle, they can't help but be environmentalists.

disasters destroyed animal and human life. Atmospheric changes and weather patterns proved unreliable and unfriendly. The first family's eviction from Eden was more than a humiliation for them personally. It included a curse that was placed upon the planet they called home.

But a cursed earth does not relieve humankind of the responsibility of doing our part to redeem it. This is still a world that bears God's fingerprints. The psalmist was aware of how valuable this cosmic blue marble was. He knew that it and all that dwelled on it was tagged with priceless worth. In Psalm 24:1 he declares, "The earth is the Lord's, and everything in it, the world, and all who live in it." If you read your Bible carefully, you can't help but reach the conclusion that the environment is not just earth, wind, and fire. It is part of God's creation, of which human beings are also a part. That's why we should care for all of God's creation.

But there are other reasons. For one thing, Christ died to reconcile all of creation to God (Colossians 1:20). All of creation belongs to Jesus (Psalm 24:1; Colossians 1:16). As one unidentified Christian once exclaimed, "It fulfills the Great Commandments to love God and love what God loves. . . . [Besides], it's hard to love a child with asthma when you're filling her lungs with pollution." Obeying Jesus' teaching to "love the poor" requires us to recognize how bad stewardship of the earth impacts those less fortunate. After all, pollution must hurt the poor the most.

If that doesn't convince you, try thinking of our responsibility to care for the earth from another angle. When Jesus was born into this sinful world, He graced our planet with His presence. An often overlooked aspect of the incarnation is that the Creator sanctified our world by walking on it. That which was originally created perfect only to be cursed by humankind's selfish choices has been hallowed again. In other words, since earth is the only cosmic orb God has ever visited, it has a special relationship to Him. As such, we cannot treat this planet as though it were disposable or expendable. Like the song we sometimes sing in church proclaims, "We *are* standing on holy ground."

When Giving a Damn Is Godly!

Dr. Tony Campolo is a Christian sociologist who has spent the past three decades traveling the globe challenging followers of Christ to take scriptural injunctions seriously. His lectures and books are often in-your-face and a tad edgy. His loud, prophetic, and raspy voice mocks Christians who quote the Bible but cave-in to culture when living the truth of the Gospel is unpopular. In his book *How to Rescue the Earth Without Worshipping Nature*, Campolo states that Christians must regard themselves as "caretakers of the environment and instruments

> "Praise the Lord from the earth, you great sea creatures and all ocean depths, lightning and hail, snow and clouds."
> *Psalm 148:7–8*

for the renewal of a polluted creation." According to Campolo, humans aren't the only ones who worship the Creator. He insists that nature does as well. He draws this conclusion from Psalm 148:

> *Praise the Lord from the heavens,*
> > *praise him in the heights above.*
> *Praise him, all his angels,*
> > *praise him, all his heavenly hosts.*
> *Praise him, sun and moon,*
> > *praise him, all you shining stars.*
> *Praise him, you highest heavens*
> > *and you waters above the skies.*
> *Let them praise the name of the Lord,*
> > *for he commanded and they were created.*
> *He set them in place for ever and ever;*
> > *he gave a decree that will never pass away.*
>
> *Praise the Lord from the earth,*
> > *you great sea creatures and all ocean depths,*
> > *lightning and hail, snow and clouds,*
> > *stormy winds that do his bidding,*
> *you mountains and all hills,*
> > *fruit trees and all cedars,*
> *wild animals and all cattle,*
> > *small creatures and flying birds,*
> *kings of the earth and all nations,*
> > *you princes and all rulers on earth,*
> *young men and maidens,*
> > *old men and children.*
>
> *Let them praise the name of the Lord,*
> > *for his name alone is exalted;*
> > *his splendor is above the earth and the heavens.*
> *He has raised up for his people a horn,*
> > *the praise of all his saints,*
> *of Israel, the people close to his heart.*
> *Praise the Lord.*

We all know how industrialization and affluence have negatively impacted our natural resources.

But the cumulative effects of sinful and selfish humans disregarding the ecosystem for thousands of years have inhibited the creation's ability to worship its Maker. We all know how industrialization and affluence have negatively impacted our natural resources.

According to cultural observer Richard "Doc" Rioux, "The industrialization that accompanied the march of civilization too often exploited and wasted much of the world's natural resources. In 200 years, the process of industrialization laid waste most of the earth's trees and is presently on its way to destroying the rain forests that have from the beginning of time replenished the planet's oxygen supply. We still dump trash into our oceans, turn major rivers into sewers, and transform lakes into huge pools of smelly chemicals that fish die in and birds avoid."

For Tony Campolo, such ecological destruction that interferes with and silences the worship of God is sin. He calls it blasphemy. As far as Campolo is concerned, not giving a damn about the delicate chain of life God created is far worse than slipping up and saying "damn" when you accidentally hit your thumb with a hammer. Blasphemy has been redefined.

Famous Christians Speak Up

Did you know that the man who started the Sierra Club was an avowed Christian? John Muir delighted in viewing the great outdoors as a grand cathedral in which to worship God and enjoy His creation. His writings were filled with references to the Almighty. Muir once said, "The forests of America, however slighted by man must have been a great delight to God, for they were the best he ever planted." Francis Schaeffer, the knickers-clad philosopher of the last century, put it this way in his book *Pollution and the Death of Man*: "If I am going to be in the right relationship with God, I should treat the things He has made in the same way He treats them."

One we ordinarily associate with evangelistic crusades appears to also have a crusader's heart for creation (as well as lost souls). Billy Graham once wrote, "I find myself becoming more and more an advocate of the true ecologists where their recommendations are realistic. Many of these people have done us an essential service in helping us preserve and protect our green zones and our cities, our water and our air" (*Approaching Hoofbeats*). And even John R. W. Stott, the esteemed emeritus rector of All Souls' Cathedral in London, can't keep quiet when it comes to the Biblical impetus for honoring creation. He writes in *Under the Bright Wings*, "Christian people should surely have been in the vanguard of the movement for environmental responsibility, because of our doctrines of creation and stewardship. Did God make the world? Does He sustain it? Has He committed its resources to our care? His personal concern for His own creation should be sufficient to inspire us to be equally concerned."

Did you know that the man who started the Sierra Club was an avowed Christian?

So What Should We Do?

Acknowledging we have a responsibility to care for God's earth is one thing. But acting on what we know to be true, is something else. Here are a few suggestions for getting started.

✖ Become acquainted with nature by spending time in the outdoors. Immerse yourself in the beauty that surrounds you by going for walks, taking hikes, taking photos of sunrises and sunsets and taking country roads instead of the interstate when time allows. Exposure to the wonderful world in which we live will give you more of a sense of the majesty and glory that needs to be celebrated and protected.

✖ Determine to recycle. If you don't do it already, separate your cans and paper goods from generic garbage. If your local waste management company does not provide separate pick-up for recyclables, locate some place that does. It may even provide your kids a source of income. And make sure you don't abuse landfills by consistently dumping toxic waste materials (motor oil, house paint, old batteries) in your curbside garbage.

✖ Resist the temptation to litter. With the exception of biodegradable apple cores or banana peels, don't succumb to throwing paper or cellophane from your car. Consider it dandruff on God's shoulders. Wouldn't you do what you could to make the Creator look His best? When you see a soda can or a candy wrapper, pick it up.

✖ Become informed about issues of the environment. Read news magazines. Watch CNN. Log on to websites like www.creationcare.org.

✖ Get involved. Why not get several copies of Tony Campolo's book and read it as a home fellowship group? Offer to teach a Sunday school class on "The Christian and the Environment." Caring for the environment is part of what it means to follow Christ. It's a stewardship issue.

Daily Reflection Questions

Day One

I   What do you usually think when you hear someone labeled as an "environmentalist"?

2   Why is the combination of evangelical and environmentalist seen as a strange mix?

3   Do you agree with the statement, "evangelical Christians . . . can't help but be environmentalists"?

Explain.

Day Two

I   Why is it said that concern for the environment begins in Genesis?

2 In what ways does the earth exhibit the curse of sin?

3 How does Christ's death relate to the responsibility of Christians to care for God's creation?

Day Three

1 What is the Biblical concept of "stewardship"?

2 Why is caring for the earth a part of Christian stewardship?

3 Why does Tony Campolo say that ecological destruction is sin?

Day Four

I Which of the statements/arguments by Christian leaders carries the most weight with you?

Why?

2 If you were to outline a Biblical argument for ecology, what would it be?

3 What is your church doing to highlight the importance of earth stewardship?

Day Five

I Which of the suggestions for action described at the end of this chapter do you feel you can carry out right away?

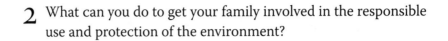

2 What can you do to get your family involved in the responsible use and protection of the environment?

How about your church?

3 Which of those suggested actions would you like to continue throughout the year?

THE GATHERING/USA, INC.

The Gathering/USA was formed in the 1980s as a ministry of evangelism and discipleship for the men of our country. It has spread to twenty communities, some groups led by volunteers and other groups led by full-time staff. The Gathering's main event is an annual or semi-annual outreach breakfast. Over the years, the attendance for these events has been from 300 to 3,000, and many men have found Christ by hearing some of the nation's most gifted communicators of the Gospel.

Each city has its own delivery system for discipling, including small group studies, large weekly Bible studies, mentoring and coaching programs, and individual counseling. In Orlando, Florida, the headquarters for The Gathering, there is a similar ministry for women.

The Gathering also has a mission emphasis in the Dominican Republic under the name of Mission Emanuel. Numerous teams of men, women, and children have gone to help build churches, schools, and medical clinics, and to sponsor the 500 children now receiving an education.

The Four Priorities is now the main strategy for connecting men and women with the Biblical model for the Christian life. This forty-chapter book is the first step in that strategy, while future steps are being developed and can be accessed on the website: www.the4priorities.com.

If you are interested in learning more about The Gathering, you can call our office at 877-422-9200, or look at our website: www.thegathering.org.